NAZI GERMANY'S NEW ARISTOCRACY

NAZI GERMANY'S NEW ARISTOCRACY

The SS Leadership, 1925–1939

HERBERT F. ZIEGLER

Princeton University Press

PRINCETON, NEW JERSEY

Copyright © 1989 by Princeton University Press
Published by Princeton University Press,
41 William Street, Princeton, New Jersey 08540
In the United Kingdom:
Princeton University Press, Oxford

Library of Congress Cataloging-in-Publication Data

Ziegler, Herbert F., 1949–
Nazi Germany's new aristocracy : the SS leadership, 1925–1939 /
Herbert F. Ziegler.
p.   cm.
Bibliography: p.
Includes index.
ISBN 0-691-05577-7
1. Nationalsozialistische Deutsche Arbeiter-Partei.
Schutzstaffel—Biography.   2. National socialists—Biography.
3. Germany—Politics and government—20th century.   I. Title.
DD253.6.Z53   1989
943.085'092'2—dc19   89-31401
CIP

This book has been composed in Electra

Clothbound editions of Princeton University Press books are printed on acid-free
paper, and binding materials are chosen for strength and durability. Paperbacks,
although satisfactory for personal collections, are not usually suitable
for library rebinding

Printed in the United States of America by Princeton University Press,
Princeton, New Jersey

To
Ursula Ziegler and her parents,
whose recollection of the SS,
like that of so many untold others,
is less distant and academic than my own

And to
Douglas A. Unfug,
mentor and friend

Contents

═══

Figures

Tables

Preface

═══

THIS IS A book about the SS and National Socialism. Many books have been written on the SS, and there will undoubtedly be many more. So far as those which have appeared in the past are concerned, they have one thing in common; they have for the most part dealt with the SS as an institution: its branches and formations, its ideology, its activities, or its crimes. The following pages are not meant to compete with such works, although many of their aspects will be touched upon. Rather, the focus here is on the individuals who constituted the leadership of Heinrich Himmler's Black Order; more specifically, this is an attempt to identify, with as much precision as possible, the social background of the men who joined the SS between 1925 and 1939 and were commissioned to the rank of SS-Führer during this time period.

But this study seeks more than simply to identify. Based on the assumption that the social composition of the SS-Führerkorps can serve as a fundamental indicator of the nature of the Nazi social and political system, it also explores the patterns of SS recruitment, prior socialization, changes in recruitment that occurred over time, and the role of social origins in advancement within the organization.

This is foremost a historical study. Yet the approach I use intrudes by necessity on many disciplines, such as sociological and political theory, but most notably statistics. Indeed, in the effort to uncover trends and regularities in SS recruitment, I have adopted an empirical approach. In the final analysis this work represents the collective biographies of hundreds of individuals. By taking such a large number of people into account I have sought to venture beyond the facile generalities and incidental anecdotes that surround the subject and, through the use of statistical methodology, to uncover recurrent patterns and regularities. I have attempted to indicate not only whether particular phenomena existed, but also to pinpoint matters of degree: how many, how much, how often, how long. It has thus been my goal to introduce a new level of precision into the debate on elite formation in Nazi Germany.

All this is not intended, however, to prepare the reader for a monotonous litany of tables, charts, and endless reiterations of blobs of arabic numerals, embellished as they usually are in this type of study with commas, periods, superscripts, and subscripts. On the contrary, an earnest effort has been made to integrate into the narrative as seamlessly as possible, without losing important information, the massive amounts of statistical data that this project has generated over the years.

Numerical information to be presented in the following pages has been chosen with an eye to parsimony and substantive significance. Statistics should, after all, enlighten rather than confound; they are not by themselves a panacea or substitute for informed and intelligent reflection. One outcome of this approach has been that tables and graphs that are presented as evidence have not been relegated apologetically to some obscure appendix, but instead form an integral and important part of the narrative.

When I first confronted the yield produced by years of data analysis and tried to integrate my findings into the historical literature of National Socialism, I convinced myself that the patterns I discovered meshed with those of other scholars. The leadership of the SS, it seemed, was recruited principally from those strata of society that in the past have been identified with the rise of fascism in general, namely the lower middle class. Furthermore, my evidence also seemed to buttress the contention that the working class did not serve as a vital base of recruitment for the leadership of the SS.

As it turned out, I did not trust my own evidence. Admittedly, different people are likely to interpret the same data in different ways, depending usually on their political, ethical, and ideological predilections. Still, I slowly began to realize that the evidence I culled from the personnel files of SS leaders did not really support the aforementioned sort of conclusions. What the data were really indicating was this: the social structure of Himmler's elite was characterized by heterogeneity rather than homogeneity; men from all walks of life and all classes of society donned the black uniform with silver runes. While lower middle class recruits accounted numerically for the largest contingent of SS leaders, their proportion matched precisely that found in the general population. Furthermore, almost one-third of Himmler's new knights came from the upper ranks of society, yet this proportion was very low compared to that found in traditional German elites. And finally, though underrepresented vis-à-vis the general population, working-class representation was surprisingly high. Between one-quarter and one-third of the Nazi elite, an elite that represented an antiproletarian regime, came from educational, parental, and occupational backgrounds that classified them as members of the working class.

Although the available information does not permit me to settle the question of precisely why these men joined the SS, my main interest is sufficiently close to this topic that I feel justified in pointing out evidence suggestive of their possible motives for joining Heinrich Himmler's new knighthood. One explanation that might account for the working class and lower middle class origins of SS leaders is that these people were attracted to an organization that tried to realize the Nazi ideal of a so-called people's community. In other words, the SS was for all intents and purposes an open elite with respect to entry requirements. Whatever the qualifications valued, the SS did not implement the same traditional barriers to elite access commonly found in other German elites. Social standing and formal education were never prerequisites for entry into the Black Order, nor were they an important factor in the quest for promotions. The SS might very well have appealed to such a variety of German men, especially young ones, because it provided a vehicle for social mobility as symbolized by the French Revolutionary dictum that "every soldier carried a marshal's baton in his knapsack."

The aims, scope, and limitations of the work are delineated in the first chapter. The subsequent chapter provides an overview of the development of the prewar SS. But rather than simply retelling the by now more or less familiar features of the evolution of Heinrich Himmler's organization, an attempt is made to define especially those factors that gave rise to SS elite pretensions, factors that might justify the designation of the SS as an elite. The social structure of the SS leadership is established through a descriptive analysis of social background variables, the results of which are presented in two chapters dealing respectively with ascriptive and achieved attributes of SS leaders. For the reader's use a comparative table of commissioned officers' ranks in the Waffen-SS and German and American armies is included in an appendix.

The rationale for dividing the social makeup of SS-Führer under the rubrics of achieved and ascribed characteristics requires a word of explanation. From a historical perspective two main principles of elite recruitment have contended with each other, and both pertain to the question of what constitutes merit. One principle is based on the presumed superiority of biological and social inheritance, that is, ascribed characteristics which differentiate individuals but which they are powerless to reproduce in themselves. The implicit question that is used to select an individual for a certain position or appointment is usually, "Who is that person?" The other axiom of elite recruitment stresses achievement and some sort of demonstrated merit, real or perceived. Here emphasis is placed on achieved characteristics, characteristics that may be attained by a person through his own efforts. Thus, instead of inquiring about somebody's inherited qualifications, those responsible for elite recruitment ask, "What has this person accomplished?" or better yet, "What can this person do?"

Accordingly, Chapter 3 will focus on the distributional characteristics of background variables, which measure ascribed attributes such as age, religious background, the region of birth, as well as the size of the community in which an individual was born and raised. In Chapter 4 the analysis is continued by concentrating on achieved attributes. In addition to information on previous military and paramilitary experience and organizational membership, particular emphasis is placed on key variables such as educational achievements and occupational pursuits of those who became members of the SS-Führerkorps. It is recognized, of course, that this neat organizational arrangement of ascribed and achieved characteristics does not exactly reflect realities for these variables are often interrelated and, in some cases, highly correlated with each other. A case in point is the prior educational achievement of an SS recruit. Even highly industrialized societies, and particularly Germany, were structured in such a way that advanced education was dependent to some degree on a person's social origin as determined by the income and social class of his parents. It is for this reason that an analysis of the variable measuring the father's social standing is examined in Chapter 4.

The fifth and final chapter takes the analysis of social-background variables beyond the presentation of distributional aspects. Using a multivariate approach, two questions will be addressed: (1) did SS recruitment needs vary with time as reflected in the social profile of its membership and (2) to what extent, if any, did social origins affect promotions and hence advancement within the SS-Führerkorps.

Acknowledgments

===

IT HAS BEEN more than twelve years since I first began research on this book. During those years I learned much. Most important, I realized that writing a book takes courage and, in the final analysis, is a most solitary endeavor. I alone collected and analyzed the data on which this work is based, and it was I who persuaded—and at times virtually begged—various mainframe and minicomputers into generating mountains of statistical tables, charts, and graphs and finally typed the manuscript in its entirety. For these reasons, the responsibility for any failings of the work is mine alone. Having said that, I nevertheless incurred many debts to both individuals and institutions. It gives me pleasure to acknowledge all of them.

Throughout my early research I benefited greatly from the encouragement and scholarly guidance of Douglas A. Unfug, my mentor. His acute reading of many rough drafts guided me around several pitfalls. I am also indebted to Rondo Cameron, not only for contributing his time to this work but, perhaps more importantly, for sending me off on the path of social science history. It was not always easy going, but I persisted and, with hindsight, the advice given to me back then has stood me in good stead ever since.

I am also appreciative of a number of scholars and friends who, over the years, have read all or parts of this book and generously offered me advice, insights, and criticisms, which improved both the style and substance of this work. In those instances where I ignored their counsel, I did so at my own peril. Although too numerous to mention, they must, I hope, know who they are and understand that they have my sincere and heartfelt gratitude.

This work also owes a great deal to the kind assistance provided by the staff of the Berlin Document Center. I wish, in particular, to express my gratitude to Egon Burchartz, Werner Pix, Heinz Kronenberg, and the late Richard Bauer. All of these individuals spent valuable time answering my queries and volunteered information and suggestions that considerably shortened my task. Similar sentiments are in order for the staffs of the Institut für Zeitgeschichte in Munich, the Library of the Hoover Institute, the University of Hawaii at Manoa Library, and the Bundesarchiv of the Federal Republic of Germany. I would not have been able to conduct my research if it had not been for the generous support of the Fulbright Commission and the University of Hawaii Research Council.

Finally, it is difficult for me to imagine how I could have brought this book to completion without the unfailing succor of Sally A. Hughes. I thank her especially for the erudition of the English language that she so unstintingly contributed, thereby saving me from numerous solecisms and easing the burdens of the reader.

NAZI GERMANY'S NEW ARISTOCRACY

1

By Way of Introduction

I swear to thee Adolf Hitler, as Führer and Chancellor of the German Reich, Loyalty and Bravery. I vow to thee and the superiors whom thou shalt appoint Obedience unto Death, so help me God

THIS WAS THE oath demanded of the men who from 1925 were collectively known as the Schutzstaffel of the National Socialist German Workers Party (NSDAP). The original purpose of the Schutzstaffel, abbreviated SS, was to guard Adolf Hitler's life with their own. In subsequent years, with its manpower growing, the SS assumed a multitude of additional duties and, as a result, developed by 1939 into "one of the largest and most powerful institutions of the Third Reich, and had become the dynamic core of the National Socialist State."[1] But it was the Second World War that became the *conditio sine qua non* for the further phylogeny of the SS. Under the cover of wartime exigencies the SS assumed the role of a catalyst and was responsible for the radicalization of National Socialist goals. Ultimately, it became nothing less than the fundamental instrument of Hitler's authority, the "Führer executive" that was "independent of the state administration and, as a matter of principle, subject to no official norms."[2]

[1] Charles W. Sydnor, Jr., *Soldiers of Destruction: The SS Death's Head Division, 1933–1945* (Princeton, 1977), xiii–xiv.
[2] Hans Buchheim, "The SS—Instrument of Domination," in Hans Buchheim, Martin Broszat, Hans-Adolf Jacobsen, and Helmut Krausnick, *Anatomy of the SS*

3

4 CHAPTER 1

In this capacity the SS carried out all those tasks that Adolf Hitler deemed most important, including the preservation of his own power, the persecution and destruction of the regime's opponents— whether real or imagined—and the execution of *Lebensraum* (living space) policies.[3] According to its leader, the Reichsführer-SS, Heinrich Himmler, the SS "hesitates not for a single instant, but executes unquestioningly any order coming from the Führer."[4] The SS never succeeded in becoming "a state within a state,"[5] for the nature of the National Socialist state was such that the SS, like any other agency of the Third Reich, predictably reached the limits of power when it was compelled to compete without the direct backing of the Führer. Nevertheless, the influence of the SS was both varied and extensive. Twenty years after its founding, the once minuscule bodyguard had grown into a multifaceted organization of almost one million men[6] and viewed itself as the praetorian guard of Hitler's New Order.

While some members of the SS were conducting ancestral and

State (New York, 1968), 139. Also of interest are W. Bihl, "Zur Rechtsstellung der Waffen-SS," *Wehrwissenschaftliche Rundschau* 16 (1966): 379–385 and Hans Buchheim, "Die SS in der Verfassung des Dritten Reiches," *Vierteljahrshefte für Zeitgeschichte* 3 (1955): 127–157.

[3] Buchheim, "Instrument of Domination," 139–140.

[4] Heinrich Himmler, *Die SS als antibolschewistische Kampforganisation* (Munich, 1937), 24.

[5] Gerald Reitlinger, *The Final Solution: The Attempt to Exterminate the Jews of Europe*, 2d ed. (London, 1961), 5.

[6] There still is no agreement on exactly how many men served in the Waffen-SS. Heinz Höhne, *The Order of the Death's Head: The Story of Hitler's SS* (New York, 1970), 2 cites 950,000 Waffen-SS men, including 310,000 racial Germans and 200,000 foreigners. Bernd Wegner, "The 'Aristocracy of National Socialism': The Role of the SS in National Socialist Germany," in H. W. Koch, ed., *Aspects of the Third Reich* (New York, 1985), 442 suggests that by 1944 the Waffen-SS amounted to over 900,000 men. Two pages later he says the SS by mid-1944 had grown to nearly 600,000 men. Wegner apparently is more comfortable with the lower of the two estimates. The reason for this is that by the end of 1944 large numbers of men had been drafted or transferred into the SS from the navy and air force. See also Bernd Wegner, *Hitlers politische Soldaten, Die Waffen-SS 1933–1945: Studien zu Leitbild, Struktur, und Funktion einer nationalsozialistischen Elite* (Paderborn, 1982), 210, table 8. George H. Stein, *The Waffen-SS: Hitler's Elite Guard at War, 1933–1945* (Ithaca and London, 1966), 286 cites a peak strength of 600,000.

archaeological research[7] or promoting the health and welfare of unwed mothers and their offspring,[8] untold others busied themselves with the management of some forty SS-owned enterprises whose products included building materials, mineral water, textiles, and porcelain.[9] Meanwhile, all along the German fronts hundreds of thousands of men in SS uniform were fighting in crack military formations, side by side with soldiers of the Wehrmacht, creating in the process the legendary military reputation of the Waffen-SS.[10] Still

[7] For this purpose the SS founded its own research society. See Michael Kater, *Das "Ahnenerbe" der SS, 1933–1945: Ein Beitrag zur Kulturpolitik des Dritten Reiches* (Stuttgart, 1974).

[8] This resulted in the creation of yet another institution, the so-called *Lebensborn*, or "well of life." The best treatment of this subject is provided by Larry V. Thompson, "*Lebensborn* and the Eugenics Policy of the Reichsführer-SS," *Central European History* 4 (1971): 54–77. Also of interest is Clarissa Henry and Marc Hillel, *Lebensborn e.V.: Im Name der Rasse* (Vienna and Hamburg, 1975). Less satisfactory is Richard Grünberger, "Lebensborn: Hitler's Selective Breeding Establishment," *Wiener Library Bulletin* 16 (July 1962): 52–53.

[9] On this see Enno Georg, *Die wirtschaftlichen Unternehmungen der SS* (Stuttgart, 1963). Albert Speer, *The Slave State: Heinrich Himmler's Plan for SS Supremacy* (London, 1981) argues that the SS tried to infiltrate the German war economy.

[10] The most comprehensive review of the literature dealing with the Waffen-SS is provided by Bernd Wegner, "Die Garde des 'Führers' und die 'Feuerwehr' der Ostfront: Zur neueren Literatur über die Waffen-SS," *Militärgeschichtliche Mitteilungen* 23 (1978): 210–236. A comprehensive account of the Waffen-SS is given by Stein, *Waffen-SS.* Though Stein's work remains in many ways the standard treatment, it should be supplemented with Wegner's more recent *Hitlers politische Soldaten.* The best accounts on different units of the Waffen-SS are J. J. Weingartner, *Hitler's Guard: The Story of the Leibstandarte Adolf Hitler, 1933–1945* (London and Amsterdam, 1974); J. J. Weingartner, "Sepp Dietrich, Heinrich Himmler, and the Leibstandarte Adolf Hitler, 1933–1938," *Central European History* 1 (1968): 264–284; Sydnor, *Soldiers of Destruction,* Charles W. Sydnor, Jr., "The History of the SS-Totenkopf Division and the Postwar Mythology of the Waffen-SS," *Central European History* 6 (1973): 339–362. Beyond these scholarly studies there is a category of divisional and regimental histories written by former members of the Waffen-SS. Virtually all of these studies fail to address questions raised by historical scholarship and frequently eschew critical historical methods. In many instances they amount to only apologetic and rehabilitative accounts, that try to prove that members of the Waffen-SS were only soldiers like others. This latter point is argued by Paul Hausser, *Soldaten wie andere auch: Der Weg der Waffen SS* (Osnarbrück, 1966) and Fritz Steiner, *Die Armee der Geächteten* (Göttingen, 1963).

6 CHAPTER 1

other SS members were busy overseeing millions of slave laborers
and deporting millions of so-called racial inferiors to concentration
and extermination camps. As varied as its activities, so were its
personnel.

By 1945 the Waffen-SS represented a multinational army,[11] and
in its ranks could be found not only German citizens of all walks of
life and ethnic Germans from all parts of Europe, but also over
200,000 foreigners, many of whom compromised its racial exclu-
siveness.[12] At the end of the war nineteen of the thirty-eight SS
divisions consisted largely of foreign personnel,[13] including Nether-
landers, Norwegians, Danes, Finns, Swiss, Swedes, Flemings, Wal-
loons, Frenchmen, and a handful of Britons; Latvians, Estonians,
Ukrainians, Croats, Bosnians, Italians, Albanians, Romanians, Bul-
garians, Hungarians, and some Indians.[14]

The SS viewed itself as a community of kith and kin,[15] or better,
as an order with its own laws and rituals, an order of militant ideo-
logues who stood in the service of an eternally truthful idea.[16]

[11] To date, there is no authoritative work on the SS as a multinational army.
Starting points are provided, however, by Ph. H. Buss and A. Mollo, *Hitler's Germanic Legions: An Illustrated History of the Western European Legions with the SS,
1941–1943* (London, 1978); H. W. Neulen, *Eurofaschismus und der Zweite Weltkrieg. Europas verratene Söhne* (Munich, 1980); Stein, chaps. 6 and 7; Wegner,
Politische Soldaten, 263–310; Bernd Wegner, "Auf dem Wege zur pangermanischen Armee: Dokumente zur Enstehungsgeschichte des III. ('germanischen') SS-
Panzerkorps," *Militärgeschichtliche Mitteilungen* 28 (1980): 101–136.
[12] The development of the Waffen-SS into a multinational army was prompted
by wartime casualties, which were especially high among its officers and noncommissioned officers, and which in some instances threatened the existence of entire formations. Stein, 167; Wegner, "Role of the SS," 448; Wegner, *Politische Soldaten,*
282–284.
[13] Stein, *Waffen-SS,* 137.
[14] This list is reproduced from Stein, *Waffen-SS,* 287.
[15] Rede des RF-SS bei der Gruppenführerbesprechung im Führerheim der SS
Standarte Deutschland vor den SS-Gruppenführern in München am 8.11.1937, Records of the Reich Leader SS and Chief of German Police, Washington, National
Archives, Microcopy T–175/90/2612447 and "Der Sippenorden," *SS-Leitheft* 9
(1943), 14.
[16] Himmler, *Die SS.* This was, of course, not an entirely new concept. See
W. Wippermann, *Der Ordenstaat als Ideologie: Das Bild des Deutschen Ordens in
der deutschen Geschichtsschreibung und Publizistik* (Berlin, 1979).

Whereas concrete historical models for Himmler's order were always evident—the most important ones being the Society of Jesus and the Teutonic Knights—they never served as dogmatic prototypes but rather as partially valid historical examples whose individual elements could be reassembled into a new package to suit the particular needs of the SS.[17] Like all devout Nazis, the Ignatius Loyola of the SS, as Hitler referred to Himmler,[18] viewed the activities of the Jesuits as a threat to state and *Volk*. However, he was captivated by their organizational framework, their single-mindedness, their loyalty and obedience, and particularly by the fact that they recognized no outside authority other than the pope himself.[19]

As fascinated as the Black Ignatius was with the successes of the Jesuits, he found in Germany's past an even more inspiring model for his SS, the Deutsche Ritterorden (Teutonic Knights). These medieval crusading knights served as an impressive ideal because they approximated closely the SS concept of a political soldier who was involved in ideological and secular combat while conquering and colonizing the East.[20] Within the realm of Nazi ideology every activist was considered a soldier. But the notion of the political soldier, and the one-dimensional perception of the world that went with it, was particularly dear to the SS leadership. Unlike the military soldier who fights only in times of war against a clearly defined enemy, the political soldier was a *Kämpfer* (warrior or fighter) who was engaged

[17] Wegner, *Politische Soldaten*, 40 suggests that the Reichsführer-SS was willing to learn even from the foreign legion, the British diplomatic corps and civil service, the Soviet system of political commissars, the Japanese samurai, and Tito's partisans.

[18] Reitlinger, *The SS*, 14 suggests that more than one contemporary, including Hitler, likened Himmler to Ignatius Loyola. See also Henry Picker, *Hitler's Table Talks* (London, 1953), 168 and Rudolf Diels, *Lucifer ante Portas . . . Es spricht der erste Chef der Gestapo* (Zurich, 1949), 5.

[19] Höhne, *Order of the Death's Head*, 144.

[20] Wegner, *Politische Soldaten*, 40. See also Erich Maschke, *Der Deutsche Ordensstaat* (Hamburg, 1936). In an attempt to establish some historical continuity, Himmler was fond of drawing parallels between the German medieval *Drang nach Osten* and the conquest of the Soviet Union. This sort of thinking is reflected in a number of speeches. See, for instance, "Der RF-SS zu den Ersatzmannschaften für die Kampfgruppe 'Nord' am 13.7. 1941 in Stettin," T–175/109/2632683–85 and "Rede des Rf-SS auf der Ordensburg Sonthofen am 5.5.1944," T–175/92/2613449–3503.

in an eternal struggle for existence (*Daseinskampf*). The difference between external and internal enemy, the distinction between peace and war, and the separation between military and civilian life all but disappear for the political soldier.[21] Thus, the SS "is never tired, it is never satisfied, it never lays down its arms, it is always on duty, always ready to parry the enemy's blows and to fight back. For the SS, there is only one enemy, the enemy of Germany, there is only one friend, the German people."[22]

The catalogue of virtues demanded of Himmler's new knights was conventional and included items such as loyalty, obedience, honor, and decency.[23] These enviable character traits must not have been readily apparent to those outside of the SS though, as even Himmler was willing to admit: "I know there are some in Germany who get ill when they see the black tunic. We understand that and do not expect to be loved by too many people."[24] This assessment understated in the extreme how most people really felt about the SS.

It was not only a matter of being liked or disliked, however. On 30 September 1946, a little over one year after the final collapse of the Third Reich, the International Military Tribunal at Nuremberg declared the SS a criminal organization because of its perpetration of war crimes and crimes against humanity.[25] Its leader and *spiritus rector*, however, was no longer there to hear the sentence. Wearing

[21] "Der politische Soldat und das tausendjährige Reich," *Das Schwarze Korps*, 3.4.1935. The concept of the political soldier is exhaustively dealt with by Wegner, *Politische Soldaten*, part 1. For the impact of this concept see the analysis provided by Hans Buchheim, "Command and Compliance," in Buchheim et al., *Anatomy of the SS State* (New York, 1968), 303–396. See also Robert G. Waite, *Vanguard of Nazism: The Free Corps Movement in Postwar Germany, 1918–1923* (Cambridge, MA, 1952), 264–271 who examines the Nazi claim that members of the Free Corps were political soldiers and, by extension, the first soldiers of the Third Reich.

[22] The quote comes from Josef Ackermann, *Heinrich Himmler als Ideologe* (Göttingen, 1970), 156. The translation is taken from Wegner, "Role of the SS," 433.

[23] Wegner, *Politische Soldaten*, 41–44. See also *Heinrich Himmler, Geheimreden 1933 bis 1945 und andere Ansprachen*, eds. Bradley F. Smith and Agnes F. Peterson (Berlin, Frankfurt, and Vienna, 1974), 80, 220.

[24] Himmler, *Die SS*, 29. The translation in Höhne, *Order of the Death's Head*, 2 was used.

[25] International Military Tribunal, *Judgement of the International Tribunal for the Trial of German Major War Criminals (with the Dissenting Opinion of the Soviet Member), Nuremberg 30th September and 1st October, 1946* (London, 1946), 79.

the uniform of the Field Security Police, the Reichsführer-SS was arrested in hiding by British authorities on 23 May 1945. To disguise his identity he had shaved his moustache, placed a black patch over his left eye, and carried a pass in the name of Heinrich Hitzinger, a man who had been condemned by a People's Court. Two days later, Himmler committed suicide by biting his capsule of potassium cyanide, which was wedged between his gums.[26]

THE LINES OF INQUIRY

Works on National Socialism are legion, and the SS, as one of the most important and highly visible organizations of the Third Reich, has received its considerable share of attention from those who have written about Hitler's dictatorship.[27] Because the SS was such an amalgam of loosely joined branches and offices—each of which fulfilled quite different duties and frequently operated independently of each other—scholars have been consequently compelled to study a particular branch, office, or activity of the SS. In addition to its enormously varied character, the magnitude of its crimes also has posed problems for the historian by making it, at least initially, difficult to maintain a certain requisite intellectual and emotional distance from the subject. Regardless of these difficulties historians, taking advantage of the relative abundance of primary sources, have by and large succeeded in providing an almost com-

[26]Höhne, *Order of the Death's Head*, 575–576, and Reitlinger, *The SS*, 448–449.

[27]The early literature is covered by Karl O. Paetel, "The Black Order: A Survey of the Literature on the SS," *Wiener Library Bulletin* 12 (1959): 32–35. For a more recent review consult Wegner's "Die Garde." Ostensibly focusing on the Waffen-SS, the article is in reality much broader in its coverage. The most exhaustive bibliography is furnished by Wegner, *Politische Soldaten*. The first scholarly overall account of the SS comes from the pen of a journalist, Höhne, *Order of the Death's Head*. Not as lively but of more recent origin is Robert L. Koehl, *The Black Corps: The Structure and Struggles of the Nazi SS* (Madison, 1983). Though somewhat hampered by the lack of sources, earlier competent scholarly studies of the SS include Egon Kogon, *Der SS-Staat: Das System der deutschen Konzentrationslager* (Berlin, 1947); Gerald Reitlinger, *The SS: Alibi of a Nation, 1922–1945* (New York, 1957); Ermenhild Neusüss-Hunkel, *Die SS*, Schriftenreihe des Instituts für wissenschaftliche Politik in Marburg/Lahn, No. 2 (Hannover, 1956).

prehensive picture of Heinrich Himmler's organization, its aims, its activities, and its modus operandi.

Consequently during the last four decades there has evolved a relatively large and comprehensive body of literature on the SS. The resultant diversity in the literature notwithstanding, virtually all works on the SS have one thing in common—they repeatedly refer to it as an elite, thereby reflecting the self-image promoted by this organization, yet say little in a systematic fashion about those who made up this elite.[28] In its capacity as protector of the Third Reich and as architect of Hitler's New Order, the SS assumed a variety of roles, which in sum were crucial for the development of specific features and qualities so characteristic of Nazi Germany. If we disregard those elite pretensions rooted in the fanciful notion of racial superiority and view the SS as a relatively small group of individuals who, in the parlance of the social sciences, exercised very disproportionate authority in social and political control as well as in the allocation of resources, it is proper and justifiable to designate the SS as an elite.[29] But who were the men who comprised this elite of National Socialist Germany? Few scholarly works have dealt specifically with the SS membership. Information relating to the SS membership is available only in the form of cursory and anecdotal re-

---

[28] The only exceptions to this are two Ph.D. dissertations: Gunnar C. Boehnert, "A Sociography of the SS Officer Corps, 1925–1939" (University of London, 1977) and Herbert F. Ziegler, "The SS-Führerkorps: An Analysis of Its Demographic and Social Structure, 1925–1939" (Emory University, 1980); and the following articles by Boehnert, "An Analysis of the Age and Education of the SS-Führerkorps, 1925–1939," *Historical Social Research* 12 (1974): 4–17; "The Third Reich and the Problem of 'Social Revolution': German Officers and the SS," in Volker Berghahn and Martin Kitchen, eds., *Germany in the Age of Total War* (London, 1981), 203–217; "The Jurists in the SS-Führerkorps, 1925–1939," in Gerhard Hirschfeld and Lothar Kettenacker, eds., *Der "Führerstaat": Mythus und Realität, Studien zur Struktur und Politik des Dritten Reiches* (Stuttgart, 1981), 361–374. See also Herbert F. Ziegler, "Elite Recruitment and National Socialism: The SS-Führerkorps, 1925–1939," in Heinrich Best, ed., *Politik und Milieu: Wahl und Elitenforschung im historischen und interkulturellen Vergleich* (St. Katharinen, 1989).

[29] Such a definition of an elite avoids the suggestion that superior status and superior qualities necessarily accompany the elite role. John A. Armstrong, *The European Administrative Elite* (Princeton, 1973), 14. See also Amitai Etzioni, *The Active Society: A Theory of Societal and Political Processes* (London, 1962), 113ff.

marks or through specific biographies of top SS leaders or SS men who achieved some sort of special notoriety. It is in the hope of closing this gap that this book has been written.

One of the most familiar methods which has been used for the study of elites[30]—though it is by no means limited to this category—is the investigation of common background characteristics by means of a collective study of the lives of their members.[31] This approach is commonly used in an effort to identify and describe with a certain amount of precision the demographic and socioeconomic structure of a group of individuals, which is thought to have yielded a disproportionate amount of impact on the social and political life of a given society. The focus on social origins and careers of elite members reflects the assumption that the elite under investigation is characterized by intimate cohesion and homogeneity, a group identity that is derived from sources other than position or simply power. Elite members are thought to be united "not merely by similar positions of leadership, but also, for example, by the ways in which they are recruited, the course of their social biographies, significant common experiences, and the other things we mean when we say that a people speak a common language."[32]

Over the past decades, this methodological scheme—frequently labeled as collective biography—has yielded a veritable flood of empirical studies, particularly in the field of political science, although historians too have produced their share.[33] Common to all of these works is the general abundance of statistical tables and graphs detail-

[30] A research agenda for elite studies is presented by Moshe M. Czudnowski, "Towards a Second Generation of Empirical Elite and Leadership Studies," in *Political Elites and Social Change: Studies of Elite Roles and Attitudes* (1983), 250. See also William A. Welsh, *Leaders and Elites* (New York, 1979) and Lester G. Seligman, *Recruiting Political Elites* (New York, 1971).

[31] Harold D. Lasswell, Daniel Lerner, and C. Easton Rothwell, *The Comparative Study of Elites: An Introduction and Bibliography* (Stanford, 1952); Hans P. Dreitzel, *Elitebegriff und Sozialstruktur: Eine soziologische Begriffsanalyse* (Stuttgart, 1962).

[32] Ralf Dahrendorf, *Society and Democracy in Germany* (Garden City, 1967), 229.

[33] Early studies of this kind pertaining to Germany include Lewis Edinger, "Continuity and Change in the Background of German Decision Makers," *Western Political Quarterly* 14 (1961): 17–36; Maxwell E. Knight, *The German Executive, 1890–1933* (Stanford, 1952); Daniel Lerner, *The Nazi Elite* (Stanford, 1951); Ernest

ing the social background and career patterns of elite members. Unfortunately, in many instances the net effect of many such collective
biographies has been that we end up knowing much about the social
background of a particular group of persons but little about what
difference it all makes. To avoid these pitfalls, particularly since we
too will approach our subject in an empirical fashion, it is important
to state at the outset the aim, scope, and limits of this study as well
as make explicit the underlying assumptions and theoretical foundations of the methods employed.

AIMS, SCOPE, AND LIMITATIONS

In a most general sense, the principal objective of this work is to
determine which Germans joined the SS and to answer questions
such as how old were these men, where did they grow up, what
social class did they come from, and what were their educational
and occupational achievements before they joined Himmler's Black
Order? More specifically, the aim and purpose of the present study
is to:

1. determine trends and regularities in SS recruitment by comparing the
   social base of recruitment to the social makeup of the German male
   population and to the membership of the NSDAP
2. analyze the relationship between the social composition of the SS
   membership and the existing political system
3. detect transformations over time in the social base of the SS
   membership
4. explore the relationship between social background and SS rank
   attained

Upon this general framework two limitations have been imposed,
one of rank, the other of time. First the matter of rank. In discussing

Doblin and Claire Pohly, "The Social Composition of the Nazi Leadership," American Journal of Sociology 5 (1945): 42–49; Hans Gerth, "The Nazi Party: Its Leadership and Composition," American Journal of Sociology 45 (1940): 517–541. The
works on the NSDAP have been, of course, superseded by Michael H. Kater, The
Nazi Party: A Social Profile of Members and Leaders, 1919–1945 (Cambridge, MA,
1983).

the SS thus far, we have referred to it as an elite of the National Socialist regime. This is not simply because Heinrich Himmler and his men decided to take on the airs of a praetorian guard, but because, in an objective sense, the SS represented a functional elite. Based on this definition, all individuals associated with the SS should properly be viewed as elite members. Yet should each SS member from the lowly enlisted man through the ranks of noncommissioned officers up to the Reichsführer-SS himself be considered equal? Probably not, for at least in one respect members of the SS differed from each other, and that is in the amount of power they wielded. As far as power is concerned, certain members of the SS were clearly more elite than others. But how is the relative power of an individual determined?

An important insight into this problem is provided by C. Wright Mills,[34] who defined a power elite much the same way as Vilfredo Pareto defined his "governing elite," namely as those "who play some considerable part in government."[35] Using this general observation as a starting point, we can go further and define power in terms of influence whereby an individual can employ both negative and positive coercion to enforce his preferences. Negative coercion is based on the threat of varying degrees of punishment, as in demotions or court martials, whereas positive coercion is based on the prospect of gains or rewards, such as pay raises or promotions.[36] In this study we proceed on the assumption that a person's power is closely related to his position in an official hierarchy. With respect to the SS this means that at least a rough division of power existed between enlisted men and noncommissioned officers on the one hand and the commissioned officers of the SS on the other. Rank was usually associated with specific degrees of power because it was used to discipline troops, just as in any other military organization. In technical terms, therefore, the following premise is adopted: there

[34]C. Wright Mills, *The Power Elite* (New York, 1956), 23.

[35]Vilfredo Pareto, *The Mind and Society*, ed. Andrew Bongiorno, 4 vols. (New York, 1935), 3: 1423–1424.

[36]Robert A. Dahl, *Modern Political Analysis* (Englewood Cliffs, NJ, 1963), 50–52. Jack H. Nagle, *The Descriptive Analysis of Power* (New Haven, 1975), 29 defines a power relation as "an actual or potential relation between the preferences of an actor regarding an outcome and the outcome itself."

is a strong and positive correlation between rank and power, that is, the higher the rank, the more power was wielded.

It is of course recognized that the relationship is not a perfect one, for not all powerful persons hold high ranks. This approach overlooks, for instance, informal kinds of leadership since it does not necessarily uncover the éminence grise nor does it record the power of groups or classes that rule indirectly by allotting formal offices to others.[37] In defense of this approach, however, I would like to point out that in terms of feasibility a positional criterion appears to offer the only practical way of systematically locating a substantial elite group from the past. The advantage of this method is not only its simplicity, in that hierarchies are well defined, but also that records are usually extensive and information relatively easily obtained. Thus, despite the difficulties posed by the selection of rank as an indicator of power, this work proceeds from the assumption that the SS-Führerkorps—from SS-Untersturmführer to the Reichsführer-SS—was a power elite.[38] Moreover, if the SS as a whole was a functional elite, then its leadership in terms of power represented an elite within an elite.[39]

The second limitation is time. As a starting point the year 1925 has been chosen, as a terminal date 1939. Both dates are arbitrary yet natural termini, the earlier date because it is generally accepted that the SS was founded during that year and the later date because reorganization of the wartime SS reached such a point that a separate account would be required. It is true that the establishment of the SS was a gradual process which can hardly be assigned to a particular year. Its embryonic origins can be traced back to the Stabswache of 1923, yet few would disagree with the assessment that the SS did not assume its own peculiar character until 1929, when Heinrich

---

[37] Neusüss-Hunkel, *Die SS*, 21, suggests that ranks within the SS-Sicherheitsdienst were purposely kept low, under certain circumstances SS-Sicherheitsdienst Führer had *Weisungsbefugnis* vis-à-vis higher-ranking Führer, all this to camouflage the actual power of the SS-Sicherheitsdienst .

[38] Neusüss-Hunkel, *Die SS*, 23 refers to SS-Führer as a *Machtelite* (power elite) whose functions matched their elite pretensions.

[39] Dietrich Orlow, *The History of the Nazi Party, 1933–1945* (Pittsburgh, 1973), 57 suggests that shortly after the seizure of power the SS was already exhibiting its "elite of elites" feeling.

Himmler became its fourth commander. It is equally true that 1939 did not cause a sudden transformation of the SS into something very different from what it had been previously, for the SS, like the river of Heraclitus, was constantly changing. With 1939 the rate of change merely gathered momentum. It was, as one author meta-phorically states, a "swiftly moving river, fed by numerous brooks and tributaries, then overflowing its banks and separating into divergent streams."[40] If an acceptable degree of internal consistency and coherence in analysis is to be achieved, some limitation of time is unavoidable. Accordingly, this study is limited to individuals who joined the SS and received their commission before the outbreak of the Second World War.[41]

THEORETICAL ASSUMPTIONS

The aim of this work is to explore and analyze the social structure of one of the most important and visible elites of the Third Reich, Heinrich Himmler's SS. But why identify the social profile of SS leaders in the first place? What difference does it make if we were to know the average age of SS-Führer or their level of educational attainment? One reply to these questions is, of course, that any such information is intrinsically important. Surely it is of interest to find out whether or not the level of education achieved by SS members who guarded concentration camps was the same as that of those who served only in SS combat units. Still, unless statistical data on the background of SS members, or for that matter any other influential collectivity of individuals, are explicitly related to larger social or political concerns, such information will always remain much less useful than it potentially could be.

As far as this work is concerned, there are essentially two theoretical assumptions that justify a detailed analysis of the social origins and occupational backgrounds of men who joined the SS. The first

[40]Robert Koehl, "The Character of the Nazi SS," *Journal of Modern History* 34 (1962): 281.
[41]More specifically, 31 December 1938 was chosen because data for this study is based on a sample of SS-Führer who were listed in the *Dienstaltersliste der Schutz-staffel der NSDAP, Stand 31.12.1938*, bearbeitet von der Personalkanzlei (Berlin, 1938).

and overriding assumption is that, in a most general way, the recruitment of elites reflects certain salient features of the social and political order.[42] In the event that the Nazi seizure of power in 1933 and
the subsequent rule by the regime implied more than simply a new
process of establishing authoritarian power, the social or substantive
content of National Socialist rule should also be revealed at the elite
levels of society through changes in recruitment. More specifically,
it is assumed that the social composition of the SS elite can serve as
a crucial kind of seismograph of the nature and scope of the Nazi
regime, as an important indicator of elite circulation[43], social mobility, or equality of opportunity. Was National Socialism responsible for a historical change in the composition of elites?[44] Indeed,
did the SS represent a microcosm in which there was realized the
Volksgemeinschaft, "a society of equal chances where success came
from merit and achievement, and new opportunities to thrive and
prosper through letting youth and vigor have its head at the expense
of the old, the sterile, the rigid, and the decayed?"[45]

If our findings on the composition of the SS-Führerkorps were
to point to a membership that was recruited from all walks of life it
would lend support to the Nazi article of faith of open elites. A socially heterogenous SS leadership would give credence to the commitment to careers open to talent, at least within the limited realm
of the SS, a commitment that was supported by the resentment toward the traditional barriers of upward mobility posed by birth, property, and education.[46] However, if we find that the SS elite was so-

[42] Lester G. Seligman, "Elite Recruitment and Political Development," *Journal
of Politics* 26 (1964): 612–626.

[43] Armstrong, *Administrative Elite*, 13; Wolfgang Zapf, *Wandlungen der deutschen Eliten: Ein Zirkulationsmodell deutscher Führungsgruppen, 1916–1961* (Munich, 1965).

[44] Early elite investigators like Bottomore were concerned with whether and why
"there have been historical changes in the composition and cultural outlook of elites,
or in the relation between elite and the Masses." Thomas B. Bottomore, *Elites and
Society* (London, 1964), 53ff.

[45] Ian Kershaw, *The Nazi Dictatorship: Problems and Perspectives of Interpretation* (London, 1985), 147.

[46] Jeremy Noakes, "Nazism and Revolution," in Noel O'Sullivan, ed., *Revolutionary Theory and Political Reality* (London, 1983), 85.

cially homogeneous, its members tending to be drawn from the same social strata, sharing common socialization experiences and recruitment patterns, it would be a more unified or integrated elite. Such a closely integrated elite, in turn, would tend to be highly homogeneous and consensual in its beliefs and values.[47]

For many scholars such an agglutination[48] is a prima facie violation of justice and equal opportunity.[49] It is argued that elites, particularly those that are drawn only from the upper stratum of society, will not and cannot adequately represent the interests of the great majority of the population, especially the lower classes.[50] Adherents of this position fear that elite integration enables elites to act in concert contrary to the interests of ordinary citizens. The former constitute, in the words of one scholar, "a veritable ruling class, insulated from and exploiting the rest of society."[51]

The second assumption made is that social-background categories represent a taxonomy of socialization experiences that are related to elite attitudes and, ipso facto, to elite behavior.[52] An important link between social background and elite behavior is a never-ending experience of what has come to be known as socialization:

a process of learning through which an individual is prepared, with varying degrees of success, to meet the requirements laid down by other members of society for his behavior in a variety of situations. The behavior required of a person in a given position or status is considered to be his

[47] Robert D. Putnam, *The Comparative Study of Elites* (Englewood Cliffs, NJ, 1976), 107–132.

[48] Harold D. Lasswell and Daniel Lerner, *World Revolutionary Elites: Studies in Coercive Ideological Movements* (Cambridge, MA, 1965), 9 coined this descriptive term.

[49] Putnam, *Comparative Study of Elites*, 44.

[50] John D. Nagle, *System and Succession: The Social Bases of Political Recruitment* (Austin, 1977), 4.

[51] Ralph Milliband, *The State in Capitalist Society: An Analysis of the Western European System of Power* (New York, 1969), 246. See also Putnam, *Comparative Study of Elites*, 43.

[52] Donald D. Searing, "The Comparative Study of Elite Socialization," *Comparative Political Studies* 1 (1969): 471–500; Lewis J. Edinger and Donald D. Searing, "Social Background in Elite Analysis: A Methodological Inquiry," *American Political Science Review* 61 (1967): 428–445.

prescribed role. . . . If socialization is role learning, it follows that socialization occurs throughout an individual's life.[53]

Thus, an important question to ask then is, did members of the SS elite share significant common experiences prior to their recruitment into the SS and, if so, to what degree? By trying to determine the social background of the SS leadership we therefore purport to identify the context of formative experiences that contribute to explaining the behavior of SS members who have passed through it.

This assumption has been questioned because a number of empirical studies have found relatively weak and inconsistent associations between social origins and careers of policymakers on the one hand and policy preferences and decisions on the other.[54] One factor in particular, which may weaken the relationship between background and attitudes and behavior, is that background factors may measure similar environmental influences or stimuli without measuring analogous experiences, let alone attitudes and behavior. Because milieu-related influences are screened, interpreted, and integrated into diverse belief systems derived from unique past personal experiences, the same stimulus may not have the same attitudinal effect.[55] One might add, furthermore, that attitudes and behavior are difficult to assess because a historical study cannot resort to the most common way of establishing attitudes by directly questioning the proper number of persons. Consequently, one is reduced to less satisfactory operational procedures.

While recognizing this potential drawback, it nevertheless is true that social background is bound to shape the general outlook of elites

[53] Orville G. Brim, Jr., "Personality Development as Role Learning," in Ira Iscoe and Harold W. Stevenson, eds. *Personality and Development in Children* (Austin, 1960), 128. Though socialization may be a lifelong process, most experts have tended to see childhood—indeed early childhood—as the period of most significant socialization. Moreover, what is learned in childhood is difficult to change and any effort to instill new basic values (resocialization) is inordinately difficult, if not impossible. Adult socialization, therefore, focuses upon role-specific expectations, overt behavior, ability, and knowledge. See also Orville G. Brim, Jr., and Stanton Wheeler, *Socialization after Childhood: Two Essays* (New York, 1966), 22, 25.

[54] Searing, "Elite Socialization"; Putnam, *Comparative Study of Elites*, 42; Mills, *Power Elite*, 279–280.

[55] Searing, "Elite Socialization."

in an important way.[56] People from an identifiable social class are conditioned by that common experience, and they are inclined to share a set of common assumptions. Other things being equal these assumptions in turn demarcate attitudes and hence affect behavior. For instance, people are more likely to think and act in accordance with class-derived perspectives rather than against them, and ceteris paribus, they are unlikely to destroy the class from which they came. For these reasons we have also attempted to speculate about the possible connection between elite composition and attitudes and behavior.

DATA SOURCES AND SAMPLING PROCEDURES

In the effort to uncover trends and regularities in the recruitment of SS-Führer who joined the SS before 1939, an empirical approach was adopted. Although traditional historical sources have not been neglected in this work, the major conclusions reached are based primarily on the statistical analysis of biographical information. Because any conclusions are only as good as the source of information on which they are based, it is necessary to identify the source of the data, show how it was collected, and explain the coding scheme used to translate standard biographical information into numerical data.

For this study the individual SS-Führer were identified by way of the *Dienstaltersliste der Schutzstaffel der NSDAP. Stand 31.12.1938,* bearbeitet von der Personalkanzlei (Berlin, 1938), which furnished the names and other identifying information of all SS-Führer according to rank. This rank-stratified list was subdivided into three strata consisting of the SS-Totenkopfverbände (SS-TV), the SS-Verfügungstruppe (SS-VT), and the Allgemeine SS (Allg. SS). By the end of 1934 three main SS branches could be identified.[57] The original nucleus or main body of the SS was designated as Allgemeine SS (general SS) and was composed of honorary, inactive,

---

[56] Putnam, *Comparative Study of Elites,* 93–94.

[57] "Rede des Reichsführer-SS vor den SS-Gruppenführern zu einer Gruppenführerbesprechung im Führerheim der SS-Standarte Deutschland am 8.11.1938," cited in Himmler, *Geheimreden,* 30–32.

part-time members and a small number of full-time personnel.[58] At
the time this component of the SS was by far the largest, but it was
to decline not only numerically but also in significance, especially
with respect to security functions. This role was reserved for two
other SS formations, the SS-Verfügungstruppe (armed formations)
and the SS-Totenkopfverbände (death's-head units), both of which
were armed. Once the Führer were identified, biographical information on them was collected from the SS Officer and RuSHA personnel records of the Berlin Document Center.[59] Because the TV
and VT strata had relatively few cases (N = 437 and N = 766
respectively), data was collected on all those individuals who belonged to either of these groups. As to the Allg. SS, which was so
large (total population N = 12,669) as to render collection of data
on all individuals redundant, a systematic random sample of 900
men was chosen to represent this branch.[60] Because records for a very
small number of individuals could not be located and some information was not identifiable where documents had been damaged,
the final samples consist of 400 SS-TV, 692 SS-VT, and 851 Allg.
SS members (total N = 1943). Members of the SS-Sicherheitsdienst
and so-called SS-Ehrenführer (honorary commanders) are purposely
not included in the sample.[61] The former represented a separate or-

[58] *Statistisches Jahrbuch der Schutzstaffel der NSDAP, 1938* (Berlin, 1938), 10;
Günter d'Alquen, *Die SS: Geschichte, Aufgabe, und Organisation der Schutzstaffel
der NSDAP* (Munich, 1939), 18; Berlin Document Center, *Mein Weg zur Waffen-
SS* (Berlin, n.d.), 5. On the role of the Allg. SS see Werner Best, *Die deutsche Polizei*
(Darmstadt, 1941), 87.

[59] The holdings of the Berlin Document Center are described in George C. Browder, "Problems and Potentials of the Berlin Document Center," *Central European
History* 4 (1972): 362–380.

[60] Standard works on sampling include W. G. Cochran, *Sampling Techniques*
(New York, 1953) and Taro Yamane, *Elementary Sampling Theory* (Englewood Cliffs,
NJ, 1967). Also helpful are L. Kish, "Selection of a Sample," in L. Festinger and
D. Katz, eds., *Research Methods in the Social Sciences* (New York, 1953) and Bernard
Lazerwitz, "Sampling Theory and Procedures," in Hubert M. Blalock and Ann B.
Blalock, eds., *Methodology in Social Research* (New York, 1968).

[61] In order to identify Ehrenführer we relied on the judgment of Egon Burchartz,
Chief of the Evaluation Section, Berlin Document Center, who is intimately familiar
with the personnel of the SS. He was asked to identify from the *Dienstaltersliste* of
31.12.1938 any Führer who to his knowledge was an Ehrenführer.

ganization[62] that was distinct in functional terms, and the latter were not actually part of the SS organization. SS-Ehrenführer was a title granted to persons of influence and power in the Third Reich who were permitted to wear SS uniforms, usually carried high ranks, but had no direct command authority.[63]

Samples are collected as a matter of convenience, and the usual goal of statistical analysis is to make inferences about population parameters on the basis of known but intrinsically unimportant sample statistics. Thus, it is not enough merely to establish possible relationships or differences between variables, or delineate the strength or direction of relationships, but one must also determine whether or not the results found in the sample actually existed in the population represented by the sample or samples. The accepted procedure toward this end is to perform tests of statistical significance, and we have calculated the appropriate measures for all numerical relationships discussed and presented in this work. Whenever use was made of contingency-table analysis in order to establish bivariate relationships, a chi-square test was computed; when comparisons of sample means were made to test mean differences, a student's t statistic was computed. Unless otherwise indicated, the level of significance adopted was .05. As to statistical significance, the latter should not be confused with practical or substantive significance.[64]

Once individual SS men were identified in this fashion, information on their social background was collected from SS personnel

[62] Koehl, *Black Corps*, 107.

[63] Neusüss-Hunkel, *Die SS*, 15, 21; *Organisationsbuch der NSDAP* (1943), 435.

[64] For a discussion of this subject see Sanford Labovitz, "Criteria for Selecting a Significance Level: A Note on the Sacredness of .05," *American Sociologist* 3 (1968): 220–222; James K. Skipper, Anthony L. Guenther, and Gilbert Nass, "The Sacredness of .05: A Note concerning the Use of Statistical Levels of Significance," *American Sociologist* 2 (1967): 16–18; Thomas J. Duggan and Charles W. Dean, "Common Misinterpretations of Significance Levels in Sociological Journals," *American Sociologist* 3 (1968): 45–46; David Gold, "Statistical Tests and Substantive Significance," *American Sociologist* 4 (1969): 42–46; Robert F. Finch and Donald T. Campell, "Proof? No. Evidence? Yes. The Significance of Significance Tests," *American Sociologist* 4 (1969): 140–143; Denton E. Morrison and Ramon E. Henkel, eds., *The Significance Test Controversy: A Reader* (Chicago, 1970); K. W. Taylor and James Frideres, "Issues versus Controversies: Substantive and Statistical Significance," *American Sociological Review* 37 (1972): 464–472.

records and NSDAP membership files and coded into numerical data. The crucial step of coding mostly literate information into numerical form involved two factors that require explanation. First, it must be acknowledged that the coding process at once reduces the reality and complexities of an individual's social background to an artificial and limiting set of information, with the result that potentially important detail is lost for analytical purposes. This inherent shortcoming of any empirical approach is offset, is outweighed, by the increased rigor and precision that statistical and probabilistic methodologies afford. Prudently gathered and correctly analyzed, quantitative evidence adds an important dimension to historical inquiry, testing historical assumptions against historical fact. Second, the process of numeric coding entails consequential subjective judgments, all of which have a bearing on any conclusions derived from statistical manipulation of the data.

Accordingly, two guiding principles for coding data were used. First, whenever possible, the information on SS members was coded and categorized in a manner that conforms to the criteria used by the German Statistical Office and, in many instances, to those employed by other scholars. Such a coding scheme has an important advantage. It affords a direct comparison between the distributional characteristics of the SS-Führerkorps and the German population on the one hand and between the SS-Führerkorps and the general membership of the NSDAP and the SA-Führerkorps on the other, comparisons without which the presentation of any results on the SS itself becomes relatively meaningless.[65]

<hr/>

[65] Throughout this work our data on the SS are contrasted with figures compiled by Michael H. Kater and Mathilde Jamin for their studies on the NSDAP membership and the SA leadership respectively. Kater used a systematic sample of party members for the period 1925 to 1949, drawn from the Nazi Party Master File located in the Berlin Document Center, in order to construct a social profile. Because of missing data, his original sample of 18,255 cases was reduced to 15,343 cases when he constructed tables for the party class structure. For a discussion of these and other data used by him see Kater, *Nazi Party*, 13–14. By her own admission, Jamin's data do not represent a random sample of the SA leadership. Although she presents figures for two different data sets throughout her study, we made comparisons only to the larger and more "representative" data. The latter consists of biographical information for 1,134 SA members who held the rank of SA-Standartenführer or higher. Also

Relating the social profile of SS-Führer to that of Nazi party members and SA-Führer permits us to place findings on the SS within the context of other National Socialist organizations and, hence, in a more balanced perspective. For example, did the social origin of the average SS leader, who was usually also a party member, differ from that of the typical NSDAP member or SA leader and, if so, how did it differ? Likewise, comparing the SS leadership with the German population helps identify those social attributes that might have given individuals advantages or disadvantages in the quest for SS elite status. Because the incidence of characteristics in the populace can be interpreted as the distribution that would be randomly expected among SS-Führer, this method furnishes a means for assessing the degree—as well as direction—of social biases in the recruitment process. Specifically, the social profile of the SS elite is compared to the literate adult male population—or its nearest approximation.[66] This population is much more appropriate for this sort of comparison than the total population at large. Obviously, illiterates were marginal to the political system, children had no direct access to it, and women by and large played no role in it. Therefore, unless otherwise indicated, the German population is defined as the male population aged 18 to 60.

The second principle which directed the coding of information is that any variable should capture as closely as possible the social and economic realities of the time period. In most instances this was not a problem, and coding of information was relatively straightforward, as in the case of data on age, religious background, or educational achievement, for example. Problems did arise, however, in connection with the critical issue of what part of the SS support came from a given social layer (Schicht)[67] or class. The identification

---

excluded from this group were SA Ehrenführer, SA-Verwaltungsführer responsible for finances, and SA-Sanitätsführer. For a thorough discussion of her data sources see Mathilde Jamin, Zwischen den Klassen: Zur Sozialstruktur der SA-Führerschaft (Wuppertal, 1984), 56–58.

[66] Mandatory education through age fourteen and regularity of attendance based on powerful sanctions resulted in extremely low illiteracy rates for German males. See Peter Sandiford, ed., Comparative Education: Studies of the Educational Systems of Six Modern Nations (London, 1918).

[67] The more common term "class" will be employed throughout this book.

of such groups or classes, both within the population and the SS, was a major task and requires some explanation.

As far as this work is concerned, German society during the first half of the twentieth century was marked by the existence of a three-tiered social framework, a social pyramid divided into three vertically oriented sections: a large base constituting a lower class, a somewhat smaller midsection embracing a middle layer or lower middle class, and a top segment incorporating a very small upper layer composed of an upper middle class and members of the aristocracy.[68]

To be more precise, the lower class—which is synonymous with the working class—was defined as comprising propertyless, proletarian blue-collar workers. Because we proceed on the assumption that next to the class-conscious proletariat there existed a numerically large and unorganized working class, one that is defined by the objective social and economic conditions of capitalist society, which determines the position of the wage earner in the productive process,

[68] On stratification see Kater, *Nazi Party*, 2; Gerd Hardach, "Klassen und Schichten in Deutschland, 1848–1970: Probleme einer historischen Strukturanalyse," *Geschichte und Gesellschaft* 3 (1977): 501–524; Hans-Ulrich Wehler, "Vorüberlegungen zur historischen Analyse sozialer Ungleichheit," in Wehler, ed., *Klassen in der europäischen Sozialgeschichte* (Göttingen, 1979), 9–32; M. Rainer Lepsius, "Ungleichheit zwischen Menschen und soziale Schichtung," *Kölner Zeitschrift für Soziologie und Sozialpsychologie* 13 (1961): 54–64. Horst Stuke, "Bedeutung und Problematik des Klassenbegriffs: Begriffs-und sozialgeschichtliche Überlegungen im Umkreis einer historischen Klassentheorie," in Ulrich Engelhardt et al., *Soziale Bewegung und politische Verfassung: Beiträge zur Geschichte der modernen Welt* (Stuttgart, 1976), 51; Hartmut Kaelble, "Social Stratification in Germany in the Nineteenth and Twentieth Centuries: A Survey of Research since 1945," *Journal of Social History* 10 (1976): 144–165; Ralf Dahrendorf, "Industrielle Fertigkeiten und soziale Schichtung," *Kölner Zeitschrift für Soziologie und Sozialpsychologie* 8 (1956): 540; Renate Mayntz, "Begriff und empirische Erfassung des sozialen Status in der heutigen Soziologie," *Kölner Zeitschrift für Soziologie und Sozialpsychologie* 10 (1958): 62, 67; Hansjürgen Daheim, "Die Vorstellungen vom Mittelstand," *Kölner Zeitschrift für Soziologie und Sozialpsychologie* 12 (1960): 244; Harriett Moore and Gerhard Kleining, "Das soziale Selbstbild der Gesellschaftsschichten in Deutschland," *Kölner Zeitschrift für Soziologie und Sozialpsychologie* 12 (1960): 88; Dreitzel, *Elitebegriff und Sozialstruktur*; Karl Martin Bolte, *Deutsche Gesellschaft im Wandel* (Opladen, 1966), 254; Seymour Martin Lipset, "History and Sociology: Some Methodological Considerations," in Lipset and Richard Hofstadter, eds., *Sociology and History: Methods* (New York and London, 1968), 20–58; Raymond Aron, "Social Structure and the Ruling Class," *British Journal of Sociology* 1 (1950): 1–16, 126–143.

our definition of what constitutes the working class is not limited to the so-called class-conscious proletariat.[69]

Distinguishing itself from this proletariat was the so-called *Mittelstand*[70] (middle class) which, during the course of its historical evolution, underwent two subdivisions: a horizontal branching based on function and a vertical stratification based on property, education, and social status. By the mid-nineteenth century the term *Mittelstand* was applied to all those who socially stood above the worker but below the ruling aristocracy. At the end of the same century, however, this middle class was further divided into a *unterer Mittelstand* (lower middle class) and an *oberer Mittelstand* (upper middle class) by separating liberal professionals, wealthy entrepreneurs, managers of industry, finance, and commerce, and members of the higher civil service from the rest of the middle class. The resulting upper middle class of *Besitz und Bildung* (property and education) became increasingly prominent and distinct in German society, reaching a point when it was no longer counted as part of the classical nineteenth-century Mittelstand. With the opening of the twentieth century the social, economic, and political importance of this

[69] Timothy Mason, *Sozialpolitik im Dritten Reich: Arbeiterklasse und Volksgemeinschaft*, 2d ed. (Opladen, 1978), 57–58. Even Marxists tend to be confused about the relationship between occupational groups and social classes, especially with respect to the problematic distinction between the bourgeoisie and the proletariat. Alan Hunt, "Theory and Politics in the Identification of the Working Class," and Nicos Poulantza, "The New Petty Bourgeoisie," in Alan Hunt, ed., *Class Structure* (London, 1977). This problem clearly is not limited to the Weimar period, however, as is attested by recent studies which attempt to classify the class and social structure of the Federal Republic. See especially Institut für Marxistische Studien und Forschung, *Theorien, Diskussion: Sozialstatistischer Analyse*, Part 1, *Klassenstruktur und Klassentheorie* (Frankfurt, 1973); Part 2, *Klassen und Sozialstruktur der BRD, 1950–1970: Sozialstatistische Analyse*, 2 vols. (Frankfurt, 1974); Part 3, *Die Intelligenz der BRD, 1950–1970* (Frankfurt, 1975) and Project Klassenanalyse, *Materialien zur Klassenstruktur der BRD*, Part 1, *Theoretische Grundlagen und Kritiken* (Berlin, 1973); Part 2, *Grundriss der Klassenverhältnisse, 1950–1970* (Berlin, 1974).

[70] Peter N. Stearns, "The Middle Class: Toward a Precise Definition," *Comparative Studies in Society and History* 21 (1979): 377–396; Fritz K. Ringer, "Bildung, Wirtschaft, und Gesellschaft in Deutschland, 1800–1960," *Geschichte und Gesellschaft* 6 (1980): 5–35; Hermann Lebovics, *Social Conservatism and the Middle Class* (Princeton, 1969); James C. Hunt, "The Bourgeois Middle in German Politics, 1871–1933: Recent Literature," *Central European History* 11 (1978): 83–106.

haute bourgeoisie had risen in direct proportion to the diminishing power and loss of traditional privileges of the old aristocracy. During the immediate post-World War I period, this self-contained upper middle class started to blend with the aristocracy, molding in the process Germany's new upper class.[71]

Situated between the lower class and the upper class was the lower middle class, a class which has varied with time but "has always been a critical mass and, in moments of crisis, a critical swing group."[72] Although it proved itself incapable of conducting autonomous and sustained political action on its own behalf, and whereas politics in all likelihood was never carried out for its benefit, the lower middle class certainly was, in the words of one scholar, "a class in and of itself, with significant elements of autonomous class consciousness."[73] The latter manifested itself most clearly in an attitude of superiority—a sense of honorable status—felt vis-à-vis the proletariat, which marked and "gave unity to an otherwise disconcertingly heterogeneous lower middle class."[74] The numerical and economic weight of this *Kleinbürgertum*, which originally consisted of the independent small merchant, shopkeeper, handicraftsman and peasant, has declined since the mid-nineteenth century. But under the stimulus of a rapidly developing industrial, commercial, and capitalist society a "new" lower middle class of white-collar clerks and bureaucrats developed by the later decades of the nineteenth century. In numerical terms this second or new petite bourgeoisie more than compensated for the dwindling of the old. Beginning with the twentieth century, it has become customary therefore to distinguish between the two elements of the lower middle class by dividing it into an *alte Mittelstand* (old middle class) and a *neue Mittelstand* (new middle class).[75]

[71] Kater, *Nazi Party*, 11.

[72] Arno J. Mayer, "The Lower Middle Class as Historical Problem," *Journal of Modern History* 47 (1975): 418.

[73] Mayer, "Lower Middle Class," 425.

[74] Mayer, "Lower Middle Class," 418, 423.

[75] "Whereas its (lower middle class) old segments were increasingly fearful of economic and social decline, the new segments were forever anxious about their uncertain chances for the future economic and social advancement." Mayer, "Lower Middle Class," 418.

In summary, then, the social and economic cleavages of both Weimar and Nazi society were reflected in a class structure whose main segments consisted of a lower class; a lower middle class, subdivided into an old and new lower middle class; and an upper class, consisting of the upper middle class and the former aristocracy.

The single most important criterion demarcating class and status within this hierarchial system was one's occupation. Thus a vertical classification of occupational groupings was used in this study to derive a taxonomy of occupational status which, in turn, served as an indicator of class standing. There is, of course, no denying that such an approach is imperfect because any attempt to classify occupations is beset by a number of methodological obstacles such as categorizing and coding occupations in a consistent and meaningful manner. Difficulties are encountered in using occupational designations to achieve a class-based distinction. This is particularly true when a job title is descriptive only in a functional sense without providing additional, status-identifying information. Occupational designations in some instances relate to legal relations between employer and employee while in others to specific sectors of the economy. All of this is clearly illustrated among historians of National Socialism by their lack of agreement concerning occupational classification. Studies have used dissimilar systems of assigning occupations to occupational categories and therefore have ultimately differed on matching occupations to social strata and classes.

The question of social recruitment in Hitler's movement is as old as the success of National Socialism itself.[76] Theodore Abel's[77] inquiry was probably the first attempt to identify the social origins of the NSDAP. Four decades later Peter Merkl[78] produced a lengthy statistical analysis on the Abel biographies. Both works unfortunately

---

[76] A comprehensive account of published sources concerning NSDAP leaders, members, and voters is given by Eike Hennig, *Bürgerliche Gesellschaft und Faschismus in Deutschland: Ein Forschungsbericht* (Frankfurt/Main, 1977), 157–233. See also Peter D. Stachura, "Who Were the Nazis? A Socio-Political Analysis of the National Socialist Machtübernahme," *European Studies Review* 11 (1981): 293–324.

[77] Theodore Abel, *The Nazi Movement: Why Hitler Came to Power* (New York, 1934).

[78] Peter Merkl, *Political Violence under the Swastika: 581 Early Nazis* (Princeton, 1975).

28   CHAPTER 1

are based on a questionable sample. Another early attempt to provide
insights into the social structure of the party was published by the
NSDAP under the title of *Parteistatistik* (Munich, 1935). The principal shortcomings of this work are that its occupational categories
are aggregated and that it only identifies those members who were in
the party in January 1935, the year of the census. Because it only
identifies the membership at one point in time, it does not take into
account the marked fluctuations in the social composition of the party
that occurred before 1933. The same objections apply to the abbreviated version of the *Parteistatistik*, which appeared in 1938 in Hans
Volz, *Daten der Geschichte der N.S.D.A.P.* (Berlin). Hans Gerth[79]
was the first person to attempt an interpretation of the *Parteistatistik*
material. Another twenty years passed before studies appeared that
based their analyses of the social origins of party members on party
membership lists. The earliest of these studies and perhaps the least
satisfactory was by George Franz-Willing.[80] Aside from a rather un-
orthodox classification system, this work is based on only forty-five
cases, making any generalizations about the entire party membership virtually impossible. Besides, these individuals may have been
visitors rather than actual party members. A much larger data base,
but basically the same classification scheme, was used by Werner
Maser.[81] Because his "sample" was nonrandom any inference regarding the party population must be viewed with suspicion. The
most useful explorations that concentrate on the pre-1923 period are
by Michael H. Kater and Donald M. Douglas.[82] Both authors essentially conclude that the early NSDAP membership was characterized
by a high degree of middle-class support. Because they used data
supplied by members who came predominantly from South Ger-

[79] Gerth, "The Nazi Party," 517–541.
[80] George Franz-Willing, *Die Hitlerbewegung: Der Ursprung, 1919–1922* (Hamburg, 1962).
[81] Werner Maser, *Der Sturm auf die Republik: Frühgeschichte der NSDAP* (Stuttgart, 1973).
[82] Michael H. Kater, "Zur Soziographie der frühen NSDAP," *Vierteljahrshefte
für Zeitgeschichte* 19 (1971): 139 and Donald M. Douglas, "The Parent Cell: Some
Computer Notes on the Composition of the First Nazi Party Group in Munich,
1919–21," *Central European History* 10 (1977): 62–65.

many their generalizations about social structure do not necessarily apply to other parts of Germany. The most recent investigation of the early party membership of the NSDAP, and one that uses yet another classification scheme, is that conducted by Paul Madden.[83] For the post-1925 period Michael H. Kater's[84] analyses, based on a random sample of the Central Card File of the NSDAP for members who joined between 1925 and 1945, represent the most comprehensive, indeed, definitive studies of the subject. They also illustrate the crucial importance of coding occupations. All of Kater's earlier works stress the overwhelming preponderance of lower middle-class support, a finding that in no small part was the result of the fact that he only assigned unskilled laborers to the lower class while skilled workers (*Facharbeiter*) and artisans (*Handwerkergesellen*) were classified as members of the lower middle class.[85]

In spite of these obstacles, employing occupational designations as a proxy indicator for class standing carries several advantages. The information itself was readily available in standard SS personnel records, and job titles were descriptive not only in a functional sense, but also provided status-identifying information. In other words, the variable "occupation" can be evaluated and weighted in terms of prestige, the amount of training or education it required, responsibilities and authority attached to the particular job, the nature of the work performed, and the remuneration it commanded.[86]

To complicate matters further, SS personnel records carried two occupational designations for each individual: (1) the present occu-

---

[83] Paul Madden, "Some Social Characteristics of Early Nazi Party Members," *Central European History* 15 (1982): 34–56. See especially app. 2 on pp. 54–56, where he outlines his choice of occupational categories and criteria for assigning specific occupations to those categories.

[84] Michael H. Kater, "Sozialer Wandel in der NSDAP im Zuge der nationalsozialistischen Machtergreifung," in Wolfgang Schieder, ed., *Faschismus als Soziale Bewegung: Deutschland und Italien im Vergleich* (Hamburg, 1976), 25–67 and *Nazi Party*.

[85] See Mathilde Jamin, "Zur Kritik an Michael Katers Überlegungen über Quantifizierung und NS-Geschichte," *Geschichte und Gesellschaft* 4 (1978): 536–541.

[86] Jürgen Genuneit, "Methodische Probleme der quantitativen Analyse früher NSDAP-Mitgliederlisten," in Reinhard Mann, ed., *Die Nationalsozialisten: Analysen faschistischer Bewegungen* (Stuttgart, 1980), 38.

pation and (2) the occupation "trained" for. Recognizing that the occupational status might well have been exaggerated, we have nevertheless chosen the latter category. The most compelling reason for this choice is the fact that the present occupation was meaningful only with respect to part-time members of the Allgemeine SS; all others were simply listed as Führer, thereby precluding any meaningful investigation. Additionally, because the choice of occupation was probably socially and politically motivated and did not simply amount to a job description, but rather reflected the *Standesbewusstsein* (status consciousness) of the recruit, the employment label furnished was the one the recruit wanted the SS to think he held or was trained for before joining. For example, a carpenter who felt an affinity for the artisan tradition was not likely to represent himself as a woodworker, notwithstanding the fact that he was dependent on wages rather than owning his own shop. Thus, despite the obvious lack of objectivity inherent in job titles provided by the applicant, these occupational designations served as a sound basis for analytical social categories. The very subjectivity of the job description was dependent on social reality, and in this fashion it reflected the self-perception of the individual's social standing.[87]

Finally, unlike most statistical studies on National Socialism, which have focused on the social composition of the NSDAP at various stages of its development, our analysis of the SS leadership took advantage of the fact that the prospective SS recruit furnished information on his father's occupational background as well as his own. It was therefore possible, using the same coding scheme, to construct two separate occupational variables. The multitude of occupational designations associated with our sample were coded into the following fifteen exclusive occupational categories which, in turn, made up the three aforementioned social classes. They, along with information on educational achievement in the form of a separate variable, represent the single most important clue to the class origins of the SS-Führerkorps and will serve to delineate important trends in SS recruitment.

Each of the three social classes was divided into occupational

[87] Genuneit, "Methodische Probleme," 41.

subgroups. In order to compare findings on the social structure of the SS to those on the Nazi party, the definitions for the following occupational categories match those developed by Michael Kater as closely as possible.[88]

The lower class[89] is made up of three occupational categories. The first of these includes all unskilled and semiskilled urban or rural workers (1), who were listed as laborers or workers without discernible training or skills. The second subgroup consists of skilled workers (2), that is, workers who had undergone formal training in order to acquire a journeyman's certificate or a master's craftsman diploma (this includes apprentices), as well as those traditional types of skilled artisans like bakers and smiths whose crafts did not require the aforementioned diplomas. A third category was reserved for enlisted men of the military (3).

The fourth subgroup, the first of the lower middle class, consists

---

[88]Our work is much indebted to the classification scheme devised by Michael Kater, *Nazi Party*. Of particular interest here is his introductory chapter, especially pp. 6–12. Anybody attempting this sort of occupational analysis will find J. Genuneit, "Methodische Probleme," 34–66 and Konrad Jarausch, "Occupations and Social Structure in Modern Central Europe: Some Reflections on the Coding of Professions," *Quantum-Information* 11 (1979): 10–19 quite useful. To a lesser degree my work was also influenced by Karl Martin Bolte, "Die Berufsstruktur im industrialisierten Deutschland: Entwicklung und Probleme," in Karl Martin Bolte, Katrin Aschenbrenner, Reinhard Kreckel, and Rainer Schultz-Wild et al., *Beruf und Gesellschaft in Deutschland: Berufsstruktur und Berufsprobleme* (Opladen, 1970), 32–49; Theodor Geiger, *Die soziale Schichtung des deutschen Volkes: Soziographischer Versuch auf statistischer Grundlage* (Stuttgart, 1932); Michael B. Katz, "Occupational Classification in History," *Journal of Interdisciplinary History* 3 (1972): 63–88; Michael H. Kater, "Quantifizierung und NS-Geschichte: Methodologische Überlegungen über Grenzen und Möglichkeiten einer EDV-Analyse der NSDAP Sozialstruktur von 1925–1945," *Geschichte und Gesellschaft* 3 (1977): 453–484. Anthony P.M. Coxton and Charles L. Jones, *The Images of Occupational Prestige* (London, 1978) discuss previous works on determinants of social class. Also useful is another work by the same authors, *Class and Hierarchy: Social Meanings of Occupations* (London, 1979) and John H. Goldthorpe and Keith Hope, *The Social Gradings of Occupations: A New Approach and Scale* (Oxford, 1974).

[89]On the general problem of defining workers see Theodor Geiger, "Zur Soziologie der Industriearbeit und des Betriebes," *Die Arbeit* 6 (1929): 776; Dahrendorf, "Fertigkeiten"; Kater, "Quantifizierung," 472–474; Genuneit, "Methodische Probleme," 44–45.

of independent master craftsmen (4) who, as self-employed artisans
and as traditional members of the old middle class, had economic
independence in their own shops. We were able to distinguish between wage-earning and independent master craftsmen by consult-
ing the *Lebenslauf* of the individual in question.[90] The salaried
employees of small businesses, large corporations, and state and mu-
nicipal administrations were classified as lower and intermediate
employees (5).[91] This category provided the bulk of the new lower
middle class and also includes salesmen, shop and office clerks, and
technicians.

At this point it needs to be interjected that, theoretically, the
most highly trained and specialized workers such as foremen, super-
visors, and nonacademically trained engineers, the so-called labor
aristocracy, could also be classified as members of the lower middle
class rather than the lower or working class. These individuals distinguished themselves from skilled and semiskilled workers in that they
received higher wages, coupled with greater job security and job sat-
isfaction. They also found themselves exerting some authority over
fellow workers and, in all likelihood, had better chances for upward
mobility into low management positions. One might also speculate
that these labor aristocrats held higher educational aspirations for
their children than did their more common counterparts.[92] On the
flip side of this argument stands the proposition that the broad bat-
talions of average white-collar workers, because of their dependency,
subordination, and probably even income, were not unlike the industrial workers and should therefore be included in the working

[90] Kater, *Nazi Party*, 8, n. 19 used a formula to distinguish between employed
and self-employed artisans. As a result of those calculations, he defined 36.6 percent
of all artisans as independent.

[91] Jürgen Kocka, "Zur Problematik der deutschen Angestellten, 1914–1933," in
Hans Mommsen et al., *Industrielles System und politische Entwicklung in der Weimarer Republik* (Düsseldorf, 1974), 792–811.

[92] Mayer, "Lower Middle Class," 430. Geiger, *Schichtung*, 130, emphasizes the
similarity in life-style between workers and lower employees. See also Gerhard Beier,
"Das Problem der Arbeiteraristokratie im 19. und 20. Jahrhundert: Zur Sozialgeschichte einer umstrittenen Kategorie," in *Herkunft und Mandat: Beiträge zur
Führungsproblematik in der Arbeiterbewegung* (Frankfurt/Main and Cologne, 1976),
32, 51.

class.[93] Nevertheless, conventional scholarly wisdom seems to argue against both of these approaches for there were significant dissimilarities that set white-collar workers apart from the proletarian worker, including the labor aristocrats. These differences are well spelled out by Arno J. Mayer: "the clean working environment, in which they soil neither hands nor their clothing, the relaxed tempo and discipline as well as the shorter workweek of the office and salesroom as compared to the industrial plant; the opportunity to deal with people and symbols instead of material objects; the chance to associate with individuals of higher status, income, and influence both on the job and after it; and the prospects for job security, promotion, and fringe benefits."[94] It would not be unreasonable to assume, therefore, that these white-collar workers historically developed social and economic interests that differed from those of blue-collar workers.

A smaller contingent of the white-collar labor force, the lower and intermediate civil servants (6),[95] was accorded its own subgroup.

---

[93]Geiger, *Schichtung*, 57; Bolte, "Berufstruktur," 62–64; Ulf Kadritzke, *Angestellte—Der geduldige Arbeiter: Zur Soziologie und sozialen Bewegung der Angestellten* (Frankfurt/Main and Cologne, 1975), 368.

[94]Mayer, "Lower Middle Class," 428. See also Jürgen Kocka, *Die Angestellten in der deutschen Geschichte, 1850–1980: Vom Privatbeamten zum angestellten Arbeitnehmer* (Göttingen, 1981), 99, 130–140, 143–145; Erich Engelhard, "Die Angestellten," *Kölner Vierteljahreshefte für Soziologie* 10 (1932): 479–520; Bolte, "Berufstruktur," 46–47, 66–67. Also of interest in this respect is Sandra J. Conyer, "Class Consciousness and Consumption: The New Middle Class during the Weimar Republic," *Journal of Social History* 10 (1977): 310–332. She makes the point that consumption patterns of *Angestellte* resulted in a life-style that could be classified neither as working class nor middle class. Hence she views them as a "new group with its own character, its own values." Some decades earlier Heinz Hamm, *Die wirtschaftlichen und sozialen Berufsmerkmale der kaufmännischen Angestellten (im Vergleich mit denjenigen der Arbeiter)* (Jena, 1931), 17–18 pointed to a different life-style of worker, one emphasizing the mundane side of life.

[95]The genesis of the modern civil servant is succinctly explained in Bolte, "Berufstruktur," 74–75. Also of interest is J.C.G. Röhl, "Higher Civil Servants in Germany, 1890–1900," *Journal of Contemporary History* 2 (1967): 101–121. Arthur Rathke, *Wie werde ich Beamter? Ein Wegweiser durch die Vorbildungs-, Ausbildungs-, und Laufbahnvorschriften der Beamtenberufe unter besonderer Berücksichtigung der technischen und der Beamtenlaufbahnen mit Hochschulbildung* (Berlin, 1940), 19–24 lists most of the positions in question.

This second stratum of the new middle class boasted job tenure, a fixed and logical system of salaries, and symbols of authority such as uniforms and pension and social insurance benefits, not to mention professional pride. Merchants (7), representing the old middle class, made up the next subgroup. Easily identified by the designation *Kfm.* in SS records, these individuals were in most cases independent shopkeepers and innkeepers. The possibility existed that shop clerks had socially upgraded themselves by listing their occupation as *Kaufmann* instead of the more appropriate *Handlungsgehilfe.* Again, by using *Lebensläufe* we were able to screen most of such cases and classify them accordingly. For a small number of individuals, however, this procedure did not yield the required information. As a result the number of SS merchants may be slightly inflated. Another subcategory representing the old lower middle class were self-employed farmers (8). Both large landowners and entrepreneurs were easily distinguished from small farmers and merchants for the former invariably used occupational designations that reflected their professional pride and status. Finally, all those listing themselves as military personnel who could be identified as noncommissioned officers (9) were placed in a separate category.

The first subgroup of the upper class consists of white-collar workers who were classified collectively as managers (10). Because they were only salaried employees, on the surface these individuals could be linked to the white-collar workers of the new lower middle class, but they are distinguishable. These men had reached the most responsible positions in business, and *leitende Angestellten* (executives) resembled entrepreneurs or owners of businesses in life-style, political and economic philosophy, and frequently income. Moreover, in terms of function, they can also be grouped with entrepreneurs as "business leaders" and could easily be identified by titles such as Prokurist, Direktor, or Geschäftsführer.[96] Higher civil ser-

---

[96] Geiger, *Schichtung*, 45; Bolte, "Berufsstruktur," 105; Genuneit, "Methodische Probleme," 45; Kocka, *Angestellten*, 110–114. The term "business leader" is used by Hartmut Kaelble in his "Long-Term Changes in the Recruitment of the Business Elite: Germany Compared to the U.S., Great Britain, and France since the Industrial Revolution," *Journal of Social History* 13 (1980): 409. The higher grades of clerical workers, though no less dependent, identify most intensely with owners and top management. Mayer, "Lower Middle Class," 428–429.

vants (11)[97] composed the next subgroup. They differed from their lower-ranking counterparts in that they held positions of high responsibility and authority and, perhaps most importantly, could flaunt a high degree of educational attainment as demonstrated by the possession of an *Abitur* (secondary school-leaving certificate) or a university degree. Within this group were found gymnasium teachers, university lecturers and professors, as well as high-ranking civil servants in public offices. Self-employed, academically trained professionals (12),[98] including physicians, lawyers, engineers, and architects, were assigned yet another separate occupational grouping. Those SS recruits who listed their occupation as upper-school and university students (13) formed their own category. In traditional German society their educational achievement would qualify them for prestigious and well-paying positions. The next subgroup, entrepreneurs (14), comprises the prototypical "capitalists" of society who were readily identifiable by titles such as *Unternehmer* (entrepreneur), *Fabrikant* (factory owner), *Grosshändler* (wholesale dealer), and *Gutsbesitzer* (landowner). The last subgroup incorporates military personnel who identified themselves as officers (15).

Although our discussion up to this point has been limited to class groupings and occupational subgroups of German society, it should be noted that other data have also been gathered. In fact, SS personnel records, unlike simple NSDAP membership records, contained an almost overwhelming amount of information on each SS-Führer. It was possible to obtain information on time and place of birth, religious affiliation, educational achievement, spouses and children, military and paramilitary service, organizational memberships, and criminal records, as well as extensive SS service-related information such as date of joining the SS (and NSDAP), date of first commission, date of promotion, rank promoted to, SS honors and war decorations received, to mention only a few items. By the time all of this information was recorded and coded, some forty basic variables had been constructed. One might add that the number of variables fluc-

[97] Dahrendorf, *Society*, 86; Bolte, "Berufsstruktur," 160; Rathke, *Beamter*, 17–19.

[98] Bolte, *Aufstieg*, 79–80, 98–99; Bolte, "Berufsstruktur," 160; Dreitzel, *Elitebegriff*.

tuated, since they were repeatedly recorded and transformed as
called for by a particular statistical analysis. However, there is no
need to discuss the coding schemes for each of the variables at this
point, as has been done with occupation-related data, because much
of the coding was hardly controversial and, in most cases, amounted
to simply matching our variables to those of the German Statistical
Office. Nevertheless, discussion of the variables has not been neglected, but will appear in the appropriate section of this book.

2

The SS as an Elite

SS ELITE PRETENSIONS

FROM THE BEGINNING, the leadership of the SS encouraged its members to develop a *Herrenbewusstsein* (master consciousness) as individuals and an *Elitebewusstsein* (elite consciousness) as a group.[1] As early as 1925, Julius Schreck, one of the early SS commanders, insisted that only specially selected men should enter the SS, and he claimed to have worked hard to collect only "the best and most reliable party members."[2] In the following year it was demanded that SS personnel "must consist of specially selected, able, and circumspect human material."[3] Thus from its inception a feeling of superiority was promoted and existed before Heinrich Himmler assumed command of the SS, but he more than anybody else was to further that sense of exclusivity.

When Adolf Hitler installed Himmler as Reichsführer-SS on 6 January 1929, he did so with the express order to mold this organization into an elite formation of the party.[4] Indeed, it was on this

---

[1] John M. Steiner, *Power Politics and Social Change in National Socialist Germany* (Atlantic Highlands, NJ, 1979), 52. See Kogon, *SS-Staat*, 1946, 293.

[2] Höhne, *Order of the Death's Head*, 24.

[3] *IfZ*, "SABE 4.1.1926: SA und SS," FA107/1, 17.

[4] "Rede des RF-SS vor Vertretern der deutschen Justiz in Kochem am 25.5.1944," Records of the Reich Leader SS and Chief of German Police, Washington, National Archives, Microcopy T–175/91/2613780.

day that the actual history of the SS began.[5] Subsequently the new
Reichsführer-SS never missed an opportunity to stress the elite character of his organization.[6] He used all means available to instill in
the SS man the conviction that the SS was different from all other
party organizations, and that he belonged to an elite. "The SS man
is the most exemplary party member conceivable," an SS instruction
stated.[7] Under Himmler's direction the SS, according to its official
chronicler, became a formation "composed of the best physically,
the most dependable, and the most faithful men in the movement."[8]
Without a hint of modesty Himmler, in his own inimitable fashion,
proclaimed: "The SS must develop from a bodyguard to a guard of a
nation, a guard of the Nordic Race which has to lead a *Herrenvolk*
of 200 million Germans . . . every leader has about him a particular organization of men of specially high quality and who go wher-
ever things are at their worst; and those are the guards. There have
always been guards . . . and the guards in the new Germany will be
the SS."[9]

To keep alive and maintain this elitist mentality, symbols were
created and invoked which left no doubt about the extraordinary
place of the SS within the National Socialist movement and the
Third Reich. At the Second Party Rally in Weimar in July 1926,
Adolf Hitler had singled the SS out as something special. He en-
trusted to the newly created Schutzstaffel the holy symbol of the
movement, the *Blutfahne* (blood banner), whose tattered remains
made up the only swastika flag that had survived Hitler's ill-fated
putsch attempt of 9 November 1923.[10]

But this was only a beginning. Feelings of superiority were accentuated by the gradual differentiation of outward appearance. In a

---

[5] D'Alquen, *Die SS*, 8. Stein, *Waffen-SS*, xxvi.

[6] Shlomo Aronson, *Reinhard Heydrich und die Frühgeschichte von Gestapo und
Sicherheitsdienst* (Stuttgart, 1971), 10.

[7] Höhne, *Order of the Death's Head*, 27. Konrad Heiden, *Die Geschichte des
Nationalsozialismus* (Berlin, 1932), 28.

[8] D'Alquen, *Die SS*, 8.

[9] Konrad Heiden, *A History of National Socialism* (London, 1934), 125–126.

[10] Hans Volz, *Daten der Geschichte der N.S.D.A.P.*, 9th ed. (Berlin and Leipzig,
1939), 96, 122; Höhne, *Order of the Death's Head*, 25; Neusüss-Hunkel, *Die SS*, 7
gives the date of July 1926. See also d'Alquen, *Die SS*, 7.

movement and later in an entire nation dominated and indeed drowning in a sea of brown, the expensive and smartly tailored black SS uniform—enhanced as it was by black boots and black leather accessories—stood out in marked contrast to other uniforms visible in the realm of Hitler. This was especially true with respect to the brown-shirted footsoldiers of the SA (storm troopers), who had served the cause of National Socialism as a paramilitary formation since 1921.[11]

Perhaps the most memorable insignia that distinguished the SS uniform from all others was the death's head. The skull and cross-bones adorned the hat of each SS man and could also be found on the signet ring worn by virtually all SS-Führer and selected enlisted personnel. It was an important symbol because it admonished the SS member and signaled to the outsider the bearer's willingness to give and take death readily in the holy cause of National Socialism.[12] As to life, which was so often affirmed in SS rituals, the individual was important only insofar as he guaranteed the existence of the collective: kith and kin, the tribe, the SS, and the Reich.[13] "It is better that a generation dies than the Volk."[14]

Five years after receiving the blood banner, Hitler singled the SS out once again for a special honor. As a reward for services rendered in helping to put down a local SA revolt in Berlin, Hitler awarded his SS the motto "SS man, loyalty is thine honor." To symbolize the spirit of obedience within the Black Order, this motto was changed to "My honor is loyalty" and was henceforth preserved on the belt

[11] The SA, founded for the purpose of protecting party meetings, dates from August 1921, when it was known as a "Gymnastic and Sports Division" of the NSDAP. Three months later it was renamed Sturmabteilung or SA. Michael H. Kater, "Zum gegenseitigen Verhältnis von SA und SS in der Sozialgeschichte des Nationalsozialismus von 1925 bis 1939," *Vierteljahrschrift für Sozial- und Wirtschaftsgeschichte* 62 (1975): 353. Karl W.H. Koch, *Das Ehrenbuch der SA* (Düsseldorf, 1934), 17 suggests that the name "Sturmabteilung" was born on 4.11.1921. See also Heinrich Bennecke, *Hitler und die SA* (Munich and Vienna, 1962).

[12] *Das Schwarze Korps*, 26.11.1942 and 13.3.1935.

[13] Wegner, *Politische Soldaten*, 59; *Das Schwarze Korps*, 26.2.1942; "Rede des RF-SS bei der Arbeitertagung der Befehlshaber in Bad Schachen am 14.10.1943," T–175/91/2613019.

[14] "Rede des RF-SS vor den Wehrkreisbefehlshabern und Schulungskommandeuren, Jägerhöhe am 21.9.1944," T–175/92/2613640.

buckle of every SS man.[15] It should be emphasized that this inscription denoted a peculiar sort of loyalty. It did not imply loyalty to abstract ideals or their representative institutions, but related solely to the person of Adolf Hitler as Führer of the German Volk. Loyalty was reduced to blind obedience, and it was Hitler's exclusive prerogative to decide what actions or deeds this loyalty demanded.[16] Because loyalty was virtually synonymous with honor, any breach of that loyalty meant a loss of honor and was therefore an unpardonable offense within the SS.[17]

After 1935 the SS man carried as part of his uniform a dagger, which he received upon final acceptance into the Schutzstaffel, and this served as a constant reminder that it was his right and duty to defend that honor with a weapon.[18] Himmler was aware that this kind of loyalty did not always come easily, but it was rewarded. "We are not loved everywhere; . . . we should expect no thanks. But our Führer knows the value of the SS. We are his favorite and most valuable organization because we have never let him down."[19]

Special courts and the right to the duel—all vestiges of past ages—also were instituted in the SS to demonstrate to the world that the nobility of the Third Reich was the SS. This sense of exclusivity was heightened and further accentuated by the fact that members of the Black Order stood outside the jurisdiction of state courts and even party courts.[20] In 1939 the full-time members of the SS, including those individuals affiliated with the SS-Junkerschulen,

[15]T–175/15/2518681; Aronson, *Heydrich*, 53; Kater, "SA und SS," 362–363; Der Reichsführer-SS, *Dich ruft die SS* (Berlin, 1943), 5.

[16]Wegner, *Politische Soldaten*, 42; "Rede des RF-SS vor den SS-Gruppenführer zu einer Gruppenführerbesprechung im Führerheim der SS-Standarte Deutschland am 8.11.1938," T–175/90/2612195–2199 also cited in Himmler, *Geheimreden*, 43; *Das Schwarze Korps*, 10.4.1935.

[17]Wegner, *Politische Soldaten*, 43; Himmler, *Die SS*, 23.

[18]"Das Ehrengesetz der SS" (9.11.1935) T–175/15/2518682; "SS Befehl 9.11.1935," T–175/17/2520594; under this order all Führer and other SS men who had been members for at least three years had the right and duty to defend their honor with a weapon. The "SS-Befehlsblatt of 15.5.1935," T–175/209/2749353 permitted the SS man to restore lost honor through suicide.

[19]Höhne, *Order of the Death's Head*, 68.

[20]James J. Weingartner, "Law and Justice in the SS: The Case of Konrad Morgan," *Central European History* 16 (September 1983): 276–294.

the SS-Sicherheitsdienst, and the Sicherheitspolizei (Gestapo and Criminal Police), were granted by Hitler *Sondergerichtsbarkeit* (special jurisdiction) for all those accused of criminal deeds.[21] Under the direct supervision of the Hauptamt SS-Gericht (Main Office SS Court) a system of SS and police courts was established to administer the special brand of SS justice.[22] Only SS judges and superior officers were deemed capable enough and, therefore, were permitted to judge the conduct of the SS man.[23] James J. Weingartner characterized the SS judicial system better than anyone:

> In form, the SS judicial system closely followed that of the Wehrmacht. But, although paralleling the system of German military justice structurally, the SS judicial organization did not simply replicate it for within it and to a greater degree than in the Wehrmacht, law and "justice" were intended to serve the ideological goals of the Nazi movement. While the SS judicial system took cognizance of military and civilian penal law and often applied it, it was not constrained by such law. Justice had to be shaped to suit the requirements of National Socialism. . . . Accordingly, the SS judge was expected to conduct himself in a manner fundamentally different from that of the traditional judge. No slave to the letter of the law, he was, ideally, a political fighter and educator to whom principle took precedence over paragraph. Not only were his decisions expected to directly further the ideological aims of the movement, but also to serve as precepts supplementing the ideological indoctrination of SS members.[24]

There can be little doubt, then, that the SS perceived itself as an elite, and these elite pretensions were apparently accepted—though no doubt often grudgingly—by the National Socialist community and the population at large. This claim to elite status does, however, raise some important questions. In what sense, if any, did the SS represent an elite? What specific features characterized the SS as an elite? Was the elite status a function of its power vis-à-vis other insti-

[21] Weingartner, "Law and Justice in the SS," 277; Helmut Krausnick and Hans-Heinrich Wilhelm, *Die Truppe des Weltanschauungskrieges: Die Einsatzgruppen der Sicherheitspolizei und des SD, 1938–1942* (Stuttgart, 1981), 87; Buchheim, "Instrument of Domination."

[22] Wegner, *Politische Soldaten*, 269; Buchheim, "Instrument of Domination," 253–254.

[23] Höhne, *Order of the Death's Head*, 149; Neusüss-Hunkel, *Die SS*, 21.

[24] Weingartner, "Law and Justice in the SS," 278–280.

tutions and individuals? Or was the elite image tied to SS-specific
activities, activities that were of great importance to the regime and
therefore carried a great deal of prestige and authority? Or was the
SS simply a self-perpetuating, traditional, social elite of Besitz und
Bildung whose members were selected in accordance with the basic
values of bourgeois society?

THE SS AS A FUNCTIONAL ELITE

Elites can be defined in a variety of ways. Surely one of the most
salient features of any significant elite relates to the fact that it is
ultimately responsible for the realization of major social and political
goals and, once these goals have been accomplished, for their preservation.[25] In the pursuit of these important aims, elites either assume or are assigned certain necessary functions. The SS was no
exception to this development, and it derived its claim to elite status
directly from the duties it carried out on behalf of the National Socialist regime.

Particularly during its infancy the functions that were to become
the hallmark of the SS elite were not always easily discernible. As a
1926 SA directive stated, "In localities where the party organization
was still small, any differences between the duties of SA and SS
should not be stressed."[26] As a result for many years the SS, on the
surface at least, was difficult to distinguish from its mother organization, the SA. It has been argued that the SS "had few if any unique
activities in the *Machtergreifung* (seizure of power) and *Gleichschaltung* (coordination); everything it did SA units did too."[27]

In the early stages of their respective developments, both organizations evolved along similar lines and shared many of the same
experiences.[28] This was clearly evident, for example, in the organi-

---

[25] Suzanne Keller, *Beyond the Ruling Class: Strategic Elites in Modern Societies*
(New York, 1963), 4.

[26] IfZ, "SABE 4.1.1926: SA und SS," FA107/1, 17.

[27] Koehl, *Black Corps*, 63.

[28] For firsthand observation of the early SA and SS see Otto Strasser, *Hitler und
Ich* (Konstanz, 1948), 76, 97–100; Steiner, *Armee*, 35–81; Hermann Rauschning,
Gespräche mit Hitler (Vienna, 1940), 18–20; Koch, *Das Ehrenbuch*, 57–91,
92–109, and 209–221.

zational realm.[29] After November 1926 the SS was subject to control by the SA on the national level, orders from the chief of the SA as well as from Hitler applied to both SS and SA alike,[30] and the highest-ranking SS-Führer carried SA ranks until 1934.[31] On the local level they were organized in similar fashion, usually as the result of the individual initiative of a party member who frequently served as both SA and SS leader. Likewise, many of their political experiences and functions were similar.[32] Both attended the same training sessions,[33] participated in public marches shoulder to shoulder,[34] sold the party's newspaper, collected money, and canvased the population for new members. Perhaps even more memorable, SS and SA fought together in *Saalschlachten* (hall battles) as well as in the streets against the "red opposition," and during the early months of the regime they jointly guarded the first political prisoners.[35]

In spite of these similarities there existed from the beginning differences between the two organizations, which led the SS to perceive itself as something extraordinary.[36] Ever since the SS was chosen for special tasks within the party, tasks considered too difficult for the SA, it distanced itself from its mother organization. According to service regulations the SS, in contrast to the SA, was especially suited for employment in hazardous situations that required the deployment of individuals.[37] In its prototypical form in 1923—as Stoss-

[29] Kater, "SA und SS," 341.

[30] *IfZ*, "SABE 4.1.1926: SA und SS," FA107/1, 17. See also doc. 4 in Bennecke, *Hitler und die SA*, 239; doc. 140 in Albrecht Tyrell, ed., *Führer befiehl . . . Selbstzeugnisse aus der "Kampfzeit" der NSDAP: Dokumentation und Analyse* (Düsseldorf, 1969), 341.

[31] Höhne, *Order of the Death's Head*, 29; Aronson, *Heydrich*, 195.

[32] Kater, "SA und SS," 342.

[33] Jeremy Noakes, *The Nazi Party in Lower Saxony, 1921–1933* (Oxford, 1971), 187.

[34] Volz, *Daten*, 36, 46, 57, 97; William Sheridan Allen, *The Nazi Seizure of Power: The Experience of a Single German Town, 1930–1935* (Chicago, 1965), 114; Geoffrey Pridham, *Hitler's Rise to Power: The Nazi Movement in Bavaria, 1923–1933* (London, 1973), 104f.

[35] Kater, "SA und SS," 343.

[36] Julius Schreck in his Circular No. 1 of 21.9.1925 emphasized that the Schutzstaffeln were to be a formation distinct and separate from the SA. Steiner, *Power Politics and Social Change*, 50.

[37] *IfZ*, "SABE 4.1.1926: SA und SS," FA107/1, 17.

trupp and later as Stabswache—the SS was designated to serve the
leader of the party as a bodyguard, a duty that denoted a distinctive
relationship of trust between Hitler and the SS. When the NSDAP
was refounded in 1925, Hitler, as a matter of course, reassigned the
same duty to the SS,[38] which went on later to guard the party's
Brown House in Munich and finally the Reich Chancellery.[39]

While the principal duties of the SA continued to be defined as
public marching, protected by the SS, room control and the defense
of party meetings against hostile forces, as well as activities tradition-
ally associated with the dissemination of Nazi propaganda, the SS
assumed new and additional duties. After 1926 the SS was responsible not only for Hitler's personal security, but also for the protection
of prominent party leaders, the security of leadership conferences,
reporting on developments in other political parties, and most significantly, for police duties within the party.[40] The latter included
the surveillance of potential enemies within the ranks of the SA and
the party proper and, if necessary, the ferreting out of persons considered threatening.[41]

What party police duties exactly entailed was most clearly demonstrated on 30 June 1934, when on Hitler's orders SS firing squads
took aim at high-ranking comrades of the SA during the so-called
Röhm Putsch.[42] With this event the power of the SA was for all

[38] Kater, "SA und SS," 346; Buchheim, "Instrument of Domination," 140; Noakes,
Nazi Party, 187; Ernst Nolte, *Three Faces of Fascism: Action Française, Italian Fascism, National Socialism* (New York, 1966), 390.

[39] Kater, "SA und SS," 346; Aronson, *Heydrich*, 52; Höhne, *Order of the Death's
Head*, 82.

[40] Buchheim, "Instrument of Domination," 142; Höhne, *Order of the Death's
Head*, 69; Kater, "SA und SS," 347.

[41] *IfZ*, "Organisation der SA, Aufgaben und Einsatz," FA107/2, 220–22; "Sat-
zung der Sturmabteilung der NSDAP," 31.5.1927, which was a corrected version of
the 17.9.1926 original, FA101/1, 31–33; See also Wolfgang Sauer in Karl Dietrich
Bracher et al., *Die nationalsozialistische Machtergreifung: Studien zur Errichtung
des totalitären Herrschaftssystem in Deutschland, 1933–34* (Cologne and Opladen,
1960), 928; Orlow, *The History of the Nazi Party, 1933–1945*, 58; Aronson, *Heydrich*, 65, 152.

[42] Because the SA considered itself the reservoir of the future German national
army, "SA Memorandum of 3.10.1930," FA/107/1, 76, it threatened the Reichswehr.
See Hedwig Maier, "Die SS und der 20. Juli 1944," *Vierteljahrshefte für Zeitge-*

intents and purposes broken, and the main rival of the SS was rendered impotent. Its leadership emasculated, the SA never became
what Hitler publicly proclaimed on 14 July 1934, an even stronger
member of the National Socialist movement. Although brown-
shirted SA men were the principal participants in the Reichskristall-
nacht ("crystal night") of 9–10 November 1938, most of the SA's
functions after the "night of the long knives" were reduced to being
representative in nature,[43] and as an instrument of terror it became
essentially superfluous. By 1938 SA membership, as a result of
purges and voluntary separations, had declined from an high of 2.9
million members in August of 1934 to 1.2 million.[44] This remaining
numerical strength, still impressive especially in comparsion with
that of the SS, which numbered 238,159 members at the end of
1938,[45] could not, however, disguise its political powerlessness and
general impotency.

The SS was freed from all SA tutelage, its strength within the
National Socialist movement enhanced, and on 20 July 1934 Hitler
made it a totally independent organization within the NSDAP.[46] After achieving its formal independence Himmler's Black Order en-
larged its sphere of influence and power by arrogating additional
functions, all of which enhanced its image as the elite of the new
regime. Within a matter of a few years the SS achieved a virtual
monopoly in the area of security, a development that had already
been foreshadowed by its earlier police activities. Whereas Hitler's

schichte 14 (1966): 299–316, and Hermann, Mau, "Die zweite 'Revolution'—Der
30. Juni 1934," Vierteljahrshefte für Zeitgeschichte 1 (1953): 119–137.

[43] Kater, "SA und SS," 363–365.

[44] Mathilde Jamin, Zwischen den Klassen, 5, 7.

[45] Statistisches Jahrbuch der Schutzstaffel der NSDAP, 1938, 16.

[46] Stein, Waffen-SS, 7 cites the Völkischer Beobachter of 26 July 1934 carrying
Hitler's message: "In consideration of the meritorious services of the SS, especially in
connection with the events of 30 June 1934, I elevate it to the standing of an independent organization within the NSDAP." Up to this point the SS stood under the
command of the SA. Yet SS independence had for all intents and purposes been
achieved by early December 1930. At that time Hitler decreed that SA commanders
are not entitled to issue orders to the SS. Hitler, upon Himmler's recommendation,
appointed SS-Führer directly. See Höhne, Order of the Death's Head, 57; Volz, Daten, 124; Bennecke, Hitler und die SA, 153,

personal security as well as the security of party and movement had been the argued original task of the SS, the notion of security was now expanded to embrace the security of Volk and nation.[47]

The first steps in the direction of creating such a security monopoly were taken shortly after the Nazi seizure of power, when the SS began to organize armed formations. In peacetime these armed units, organized on the basis of full-time volunteers, came under the command of Heinrich Himmler who, as the Reichsführer-SS, was responsible for their organization, training, equipment, and readiness. These units were part of neither the Wehrmacht nor the police. Rather, they represented a permanent armed force exclusively at the disposal of Hitler. In the event of mobilization the armed SS units would be used by the commander in chief of the army within the framework of the army. But Hitler made it clear that insofar as they were not employed under the command of the army, the true purpose of these formations was for deployment at home. More specifically, they were retained to repress potential domestic insurrection and to prevent any possible recurrence of events similar to those of the 1918 Revolution. This also relieved the Wehrmacht of a responsibility that it had always found distasteful.[48]

Although these armed SS formations were viewed as internal security forces, their respective duties developed along different lines. The SS-Verfügungstruppe, which in the winter of 1939–40 was renamed Waffen-SS,[49] developed under the guidance of former Reichswehr officers and noncommissioned officers into elite military units[50] deployed as "fire brigades" during the Second World War. Housed in barracks and equipped with light and heavy

[47] *Organisationsbuch der NSDAP* (Munich, 1943), 417.

[48] Buchheim, "Instrument of Domination," 264–265; A Führer decree of 17.8.1938, published in Hausser, *Soldaten wie andere auch*, doc. no. 6 delineates the position of the SS and its formation within the Third Reich, especially vis-à-vis the Wehrmacht. The decree is exhaustively analyzed by Wegner, *Politische Soldaten*, chap. 8.

[49] Buchheim, "Instrument of Domination," 143, 571. Wegner, *Politische Soldaten*, 128, n. 275 suggests that by the end of 1940 the term Verfügungstruppe had disappeared.

[50] Wegner, "Role of the SS," 438, The SS-VT was headed by professional military men such as Paul Hausser and Felix Steiner. See Stein, *Waffen-SS*, 291, XXX–XXXII.

infantry weapons,[51] their training was for all intents and purposes
aimed strictly at military efficiency, as was that of their cadets, who
were trained in specially created academies in Braunschweig and
Bad Tölz.[52]

The other armed, full-time component of the SS, designated as
SS-Totenkopfverbände in 1936, assumed the duty of guarding the
inmates of concentration camps.[53] After removing them from SA
control, the SS after 1934 took command of all existing concentration camps in Germany. Under the direction of Theodore Eicke,
who used the facilities at Dachau as a model,[54] a concentration
camp system was developed which ultimately enjoyed a protected
status beyond existing laws and proper administration of justice. In
conjunction with the police, this camp system was designed to re-
move and intimidate anyone defined as an opponent or threat to the
New Order.[55]

The development of the SS as the Third Reich's supreme security
force was capped off through Hitler's decree of 17 June 1936,[56] which
invested Heinrich Himmler with the newly created office of Chief of
German Police. Himmler, who had already managed to assume control of the political police of the individual German states during the
preceding three years, was now in the position to realize his aim of
creating a *Staatsschutzkorps*[57] (state protection corps). The amal-

[51] *Statistisches Jahrbuch der Schutzstaffel der NSDAP, 1938*, 12. Service in the
SS-TV was recognized as fulfillment of compulsory military duty.

[52] Before the Second World War SS leaders were trained at two academies,
one established at Bad Tölz in 1934 and the other at Braunschweig in 1935. See
"Rede des Reichsführer-SS am 23.11.1942, SS-Junkerschule Bad Tölz," T–175/94/
2614803–805, and Steiner, *Armee*, 86–102, 129–132.

[53] Although they were required to enlist for twelve years, their service was not
counted as fulfilling the compulsory military duty. *Statistisches Jahrbuch der Schutzstaffel der NSDAP, 1938*, 14.

[54] See Martin Broszat, "National Socialist Concentration Camps, 1933–1945,"
in Buchheim et al., *Anatomy of the SS State* (New York, 1968), 397–504, and
F. Pingel, *Häftlinge unter SS-Herrschaft: Widerstand, Selbsbehauptung, und Vernichtung im Konzentrationslager* (Hamburg, 1978).

[55] Wegner, "Role of the SS," 436.

[56] *Reichsgesetzblatt* 1: 487, 1936.

[57] Werner Best, "Die Schutzstaffel der NSDAP und die deutsche Polizei,"
Deutsches Recht (edition A) 9 (1939), 44–47, furnished a contemporary comment on
this concept.

48 CHAPTER 2

gamation of SS and police under Himmler who, in the parlance of the Third Reich, was henceforth known as RFSSuChdDtPol (Reichsführer-SS und Chef der Deutschen Polizei) had several other important implications. To begin with it meant the centralization of the police, who until this time had been under the jurisdiction of the states, thus abrogating the remaining vestiges of German federalism. It also meant that authority over the police was transferred from state or administrative authority to party and SS control, thereby creating a totally independent machinery.

Himmler, in his capacity as Chief of the German Police, was ostensibly subordinate to Wilhelm Frick, the Minister of the Interior. In reality, however, Himmler could always circumvent Frick's authority. As Reichsführer-SS he received his orders directly from Hitler, and in the event of conflicting orders there was never any question as to which took precedence.[58] Serving as a security force that was both loyal to and entirely at the disposal of Hitler, the SS became "both an instrument and an expression of Hitler's absolute personal dictatorship"; this function became "the hallmark of the further development of the SS and of its *de facto* and *de jure* position in the Third Reich."[59]

There is no denying that, from the perspective of power politics, the security-related functions of the SS established this organization as a major force within the realm of the Third Reich and thereby promoted its image as an elite. But the SS did not rest on its accomplishments. After the outbreak of the war it continued to assume additional functions, ironically reaching the apex of its power at a time when the outcome of Hitler's war was no longer in question. There is no need to undertake a survey of these activities, as this would require far larger compass than this study provides. It is sufficient to note that the extent of the influence of the SS is quite well mirrored in some of the offices and titles that Himmler acquired after 1938.[60] In October 1939, for instance, he was appointed Reichskom-

---

[58]Buchheim, "Instrument of Domination," 143, 160–162, and Karl Dietrich Bracher, *The German Dictatorship: The Origins, Structure, and Effects of National Socialism* (New York, 1970), 352–353.

[59]Buchheim, "Instrument of Domination," 143.

[60]Although Himmler never tired of expanding the scope of SS functions, the very diversity of these functions also made him anxious. He feared that particularly

missar für die Festigung deutschen Volkstums (Reich's Commissar
for the Strengthening of the German Race) and less than four years
later, in August 1943, Minister of the Interior. In the following year
he assumed command of the Volksgrenadier divisions and German
prisoner of war camps and, after the events of 22 July 1944, he became Befehlshaber des Ersatzheeres und Chef der Heeresrüstung
(Chief of the Reserve Army and Head of Army Armaments).[61]

The diverse and at times seemingly incompatible, indeed conflicting, activities of the SS have led some historians to view this
organization as a haphazard conglomerate, "a bizarre nonsensical
affair," which was the "product of accident and automatism, . . .
and devoid of any logic."[62] Unfortunately such a view denies the SS
any functionally specific character and fails to recognize that this
was an organization sui generis, which achieved a unique position
among the agencies and foci of power in Nazi Germany. The SS did
not exist without purpose within a *System der Systemlosigkeit*[63] (ab-
sence of system), adapting itself simply to the polycratic[64] realities of
the Third Reich. Rather, it was the result of "a conscious, precon-
ceived and central concern of Himmler's social thinking,"[65] which

---

during the war one branch or another would strive and succeed in achieving organizational independence. Such fragmentation, he realized, would endanger the
powerful position of the SS within the National Socialist state. These concerns are reflected in his speeches of 4.10.1943, as cited in Hans Buchheim, "Die Höheren SS-
und Polizeiführer," *Vierteljahrshefte für Zeitgeschichte* 11 (Munich, 1963): 379 and
"Rede des RF-SS vor den SS-Gruppenführer zu einer Gruppenführerbesprechung im
Führerheim der SS-Standarte Deutschland am 8.11.1938," T–175/90/2612195–
2199, also cited in Himmler, *Geheimreden*, 29. To prevent the drifting apart of individual SS parts Himmler tried to link the individual activities as closely as possible.
Wegner, "Role of the SS," 441. "The Waffen-SS will live only when the entire SS
lives, only when the entire corps is an order, and only when all parts realize that
existence without the other parts is inconceivable." Steiner, *Power Politics and Social
Change*, 67.
    [61] Himmler's reflections on his career are presented in a speech to the Gauleiter
of August 3 1944, in *Vierteljahrshefte für Zeitgeschichte* 1 (1953): 357–394.
    [62] Höhne, *Order of the Death's Head*, 13.
    [63] Ibid., 409.
    [64] Peter Hüttenberger, "Nationalsozialistische Polykratie," *Geschichte und Ge-
sellschaft* 2 (1976): 417–442.
    [65] Yoash Meisler, "Himmler's Doctrine of Leadership," *Jahrbuch des Instituts für
Deutsche Geschichte* 8 (1979): 400–401.

envisaged the SS as a new elite destined not only to secure Hitler's New Order but also to sire it.[66]

Ever since Himmler assumed tutelage of the SS in 1929, it assumed a creative mission, a mission that went beyond the security of the German Volk and had as its ultimate aim the creation of the Germanic Empire of German Nations.[67] Himmler left no doubt that this would be "the greatest empire ever created by man and ever seen on earth."[68] We have only glimpses, albeit horrific glimpses, revealing the specifics of this glorious future pursued by an organization reckless enough to attempt its realization. Suffice it to say that his vision of the future Reich bore a close affinity to his racist and *völkisch* views and simultaneously embodied and expressed some of the fundamental values and myths of National Socialism.[69]

Although this vainglorious goal was never reached, Himmler left little doubt that the end not only justified but even sanctified all SS actions, including those normally considered criminal. He was prepared to go to any length to realize this future Reich, even if it re-

[66] For a Marxist view of the SS and its role see Hans-Otto Fleischner, "Einige Bemerkungen zur besonderen Rolle der SS innerhalb des Systems der faschistischen Organisationen, 1935–1945," *Jenaer Beiträge zur Parteingeschichte* 37/38 (1976): 74–94.

[67] Meisler, "Himmler's Doctrine," 409.

[68] Himmler speech of 8.11.1938 in Himmler, *Geheimreden*, 49.

[69] Racism and the conquest of Lebensraum were two complementary aspects of National Socialist ideology and war aims. Eberhard Jäckel, *Hitlers Weltanschauung: Entwurf einer Herrschaft* (Tübingen, 1969). Himmler's concept of Lebensraum, moreover, was connected to a vision of an ever eastward-expanding world empire. "Die Hauptkolonie unseres Reiches ist aber der Osten: Heute Kolonie, morgen Siedlungsgebiet, übermorgen Reich!" "Rede des RF-SS vor den Junkern der SS-Junkerschule Tölz vom 23.11.1942," T–175/90/2612781. For additional glimpses of the future see: "Himmler Rede vor den OA-Führern und Hauptamtchefs im Haus der Flieger in Berlin vom 9.6.1942," T–175/90/2612706; "Rede des RF-SS vor den Gauleitern in Posen vom 6.10.1943," T–175/85/2610227; "Rede des RF-SS auf dem Truppenübungsplatz Bitsch vom 26.7.1944," T–175/93/2614198–99; Rede Himmler's vom 3.8.1944 in Posen, cited in *Vierteljahrshefte für Zeitgeschichte* 1 (1953): 357–394; "Himmler Ansprache vom 24.5.1944 vor Generalen in Sonthofen," T–175/94/8194609–46; Josef Ackermann, *Heinrich Himmler als Ideologe* (Göttingen, 1970), 187, 194; Felix Kersten, *Totenkopf und Treue—Heinrich Himmler ohne Uniform* (Hamburg, 1952), 31–316. In contrast to these images stood the reality as detailed by Alexander Dallin, *German Rule in Russia, 1941–1945. A Study of Occupation Policies* (London and New York, 1957).

quired him "to go out and rob and steal Germanic blood throughout the world."[70] It is equally apparent that his methods in pursuing these utopian goals were opportunistic to the extreme. This opportunism, which was necessitated to a certain extent by the conditions prevailing in the Third Reich, should not be construed, however, as a tergiversation of his revolutionary ideals.

Because the attainment of the future kingdom hinged entirely on SS activities, the Black Order insisted on the right to embrace and fuse all those forces of state and society viewed as indispensable to its designs. More precisely, this creative agenda dictated a threefold calling to the SS. First, it would serve as the implement responsible for the establishment of the Greater Reich as a political fact.[71] In this capacity, SS activities collectively referred to as police or security duties would be emphasized and would, at the same time, become "steps in a comprehensive process of creation."[72] Second, the SS would embark upon the task of bringing back into the racial fold all the racially valuable Germanic peoples of Europe.[73] Finally, the SS would assume the role of a vanguard, indeed model community, in which the Greater Germanic Empire was already realized in some measure.[74] As one historian put it, the SS was "at one and the same time both means to another end, and also the end which is realized in the means."[75]

As stated earlier, elites usually owe their existence to the fact that they are needed for the realization of major social and political goals, and the SS was no exception to this. Himmler's organization was intended not simply for the purpose of completing certain circumscribed and tangible tasks, but was perceived as the principal agent charged with the creation of the future Reich.[76] "The SS already

[70] Himmler speech of 8.11.1938 in Himmler, *Geheimreden*, 38.

[71] "Rede des RF-SS auf dem Truppenübungsplatz Bitsch vom 26.7.1944," T–175/93/2614198–99 and Himmler, *Geheimreden*, 236–237.

[72] Meisler, "Himmler's Doctrine," 409 and Karl. D. Bracher, *The German Dictatorship*, 353–354.

[73] "Himmler Rede vor den OA-Führern und Hauptamtchefs im Haus der Flieger in Berlin vom 9.6.1942," T–175/90/2612706 and Himmler, *Geheimreden*, 157.

[74] "Rede des RF-SS vor den Gauleitern in Posen vom 6.10.1943," T–175/85/2610227 and Himmler, *Geheimreden*, 182.

[75] Meisler, "Himmler's Doctrine," 409.

[76] Wegner, "Role of the SS," 431.

marches down the corridor of the heavenly kingdom, or rather, the SS is that corridor, for the realization of this kingdom is completely dependent on SS activity."[77] It is within this context, therefore, "that the different activities of the SS—however varied they may seem at first sight—take on their proper significance." Moreover, it is also from this creative mission that the SS inexorably inferred its elite pretensions and elite status, seeing itself unequivocally as an elite of the society as a whole.[78]

The SS as a Racial Elite

The SS epitomized the evolution of an idée fixe directed toward the creation of a racially determined elite. For the foundation of this totally New Order Heinrich Himmler, through *Auslese* (selection) and *Zucht* ("breeding"),[79] wanted to cultivate a new human type—a loyal, duty-committed, tough, and self-sacrificing warrior, leader, scholar, and administrator all in one[80]—who was capable of coping with the enormous tasks that lay ahead. In the words of the Reichsführer-SS, "we want to create an upper class for Germany, selected constantly over centuries, a new aristocracy, recruited always from the best sons and daughters of our nation, an aristocracy that never becomes old."[81]

Himmler's own racial views had received their proper ideological veneer in large part from his friend, Richard Walther Darré—the proponent of *Blut und Boden* (blood and soil) mysticism—whom he

---

[77] Himmler, *Geheimreden*, 48; Meisler, Himmler's Doctrine," 410.

[78] Wegner, "Role of the SS," 434.

[79] Meisler, "Himmler's Doctrine," 398–400 detects in the development of the SS "a consistent and continual employment of *Zucht* methods in the pursuit of *Bildungs* ends." Whereas the term Zucht is essentially defined as any process of socialization "based on 'automatic,' irreflective appropriation of characteristic habits," norms, and behavior patterns, *Bildung* is viewed as a process focusing on "the acquisition of knowledge" and "like methods of reflective and intellective activity."

[80] Meisler, "Himmler's Doctrine," 420–422 views the SS as a synthetic aristocracy, a synthesis of the traditional aristocracy whose foci of identity were "blood" and "land."

[81] "Rede des Reichsführer-SS vor SS-Gruppenführern am 8.11.1937," T–175/ 90/2612447.

had met during his student days in the League of Artamanen.[82] Darré, through a number of publications,[83] had earned himself a reputation as an expert on "human breeding" before he was appointed chief of the SS Race and Settlement Main Office (SS Rasse und Siedlungs Hauptamt) in 1931. His brand of biological determinism glorified German farmers, for he believed that among them could be found the remnants of the true Nordic race. These original Germans were, in his view, destined to play a pivotal role as the elite of the Germanic Reich of the future. Although Himmler agreed with Darré that the German farmer was the ideal recruiting ground for the future aristocracy, his search for "qualified" recruits was never limited to this segment of the population.[84]

In place of a traditional social elite, Heinrich Himmler envisioned a racial elite based on the purity of blood, equating superior racial traits with manifest ability as well as character. Old elites based on transmitted social privileges were to be replaced by a new synthetic aristocracy, created in the mold of a community organized and determined along racial lines. Thus, to insure the continued existence of a politically reliable leadership class characterized by superior human qualities and capabilities, Himmler reinforced the pretensions of a functional elite with the concept of a nobility of blood.

Attempts to put into practice the vision of an elite of blood were mirrored in the fervent exertion expended in the biological screening of potential SS candidates.[85] The racial evaluation of recruits was conducted within a medical and pseudoscientific environment by

---

[82]The league Artam e.V. was founded in 1923, refounded in 1931 as the Nationalsozialistische Bundes der Artamanen, and finally closed its doors in 1934. *Völkischer Beobachter*, 9.10.1934. See also "Was sind und was wollen die Artamanen?" *Völkischer Beobachter*, 19/20.3.1929 and Michael Kater, "Die Artamanen— Völkische Jugend in der Weimarer Republik," *Historische Zeitschrift* 213 (1971): 577–638.

[83]Richard Walther Darré, *Neuadel aus Blut und Boden* (Munich, 1930); *Das Bauerntum als Lebensquell der nordischen Rasse* (Munich, 1933). See also his two-part essay published in the *Völkischer Beobachter*, 19/20 and 21 April, 1931.

[84]Barbara Miller Lane, "Nazi Ideology: Some Unfinished Business," *Central European History* 7 (1974): 27–28.

[85]Steiner, *Power Politics and Social Change*, 75–77.

"white-coated technician[s] with calipers and measuring tape."[86]
After 1933 the experts of the SS Race and Settlement Main Office
began to screen applicants according to a system developed by SS-
Hauptsturmführer, Professor Dr. Bruno K. Schultz. The latter had
devised two measuring devices; one consisted of a nine-point model
intended to aid the examiner in the assessment of physical build and
appearance of SS candidates, while the second comprised a five-
point scale designed to gauge the degree of the individual's admixture
of blood and human worth.[87]

These evaluations were supplemented by genealogical proof of
unblemished Aryan ancestry as far back as 1800 and 1750 for enlisted personnel and Führer respectively, as well as by a battery of
tests whose purpose it was to determine a minimum degree of physical endurance, agility, speed, dexterity, and courage. Juxtaposed
with such "racial" appraisals was a twenty-minute "intelligence test"
which consisted of, among other items, three mathematical problems and three lines of dictation.[88] To ensure the preservation of all
this genetic material winnowed in such a fashion, Himmler issued
his infamous Marriage Order of 1931.[89] This eugenic edict required
a clean bill of racial worth for the prospective brides of all SS men.

In addition to these overtly physical barriers the SS also featured
more traditional entry requirements, including evidence of good
conduct and character. Former members of the armed forces who
held a dishonorable discharge were normally not welcome, nor were
convicted criminals unless, of course, they were convicted of crimes
committed for the sake of the movement. The only other item of
concern to SS recruiters was the political attitude (*politische Hal-
tung*) of the potential recruit. In practice this meant that former
members of the SPD and KPD were as a rule excluded (their immediate families were also considered unreliable), as were theolo-
gians, Freemasons, and former members of the Foreign Legion.

[86] Koehl, *Black Corps*, 83.

[87] Robert A. Gelwick, "Personnel Policies and Procedures of the Waffen-SS"
(Ph.D. dissertation, University of Nebraska, Lincoln, NE, 1971), 200; Wegner, *Politische Soldaten*, 136.

[88] Wegner, *Politische Soldaten*, 136.

[89] D'Alquen, *Die SS*, 9–10, 18–19; "Verlobungs und Heiratsbefehl"
(31.12.1931), T–175/15/2518681.

Most of this is quite familiar by now, and there is no need to elaborate any further upon the tendentious racial entry requirements. The much-heralded biological sifting never functioned or at most functioned incompletely; the "principle of biological selection was . . . applied at best to the broad mass of followers and was to this extent merely a technique for imbuing the followers with a contrived elite mentality and an esprit de corps."[90] It could not function because the choice of SS volunteers was determined by certain realities that not even Himmler and the SS could sidestep.

One dilemma facing the Black Order—one that was never resolved—was the contradiction created by the desire to promote organizational growth while simultaneously trying to enforce stricter entry requirements. Expansion of the SS dictated the induction of additional personnel which, in turn, resulted in the acceptance of individuals exhibiting little or no affinity to the SS vision of the perfect Nordic man.

Recognizing that a massive influx of inferior joiners would dilute the basis of his future elite, Himmler imposed a temporary moratorium on recruitment between April and November 1933. Beginning in 1933, but especially after the events of 30 June 1934, he even started a thorough housecleaning, resulting in the expulsion of some 60,000 recent but "useless" SS members by the end of 1935.[91] In the final analysis, however, Himmler's effort to purify the ranks of the SS in this fashion proved unsuccessful.

The need for more men caused the contradiction between SS intentions and social reality to become quite visible. A good case in point are the armed SS formations which, along with the entire SS, expanded rapidly during the latter part of the prewar decade. Physical qualifications for enlistment in the armed SS were relaxed and modified as early as December 1938 when the door to further SS expansion was opened. Himmler decreed that for the next five years entry requirements would be less demanding, with the exception of racial or hereditary shortcomings. Particularly those men born between 1919 and 1923, who were assumed to have suffered physically

[90] Neusüss-Hunkel, *Die SS* 18, 67.
[91] Ibid., 18. Himmler issued this order on 10 July 1933, and it remained effective until September 1934. Steiner, *Power Politics and Social Change*, 67.

from growing up in those years, were able to join the racial elite as long as any physical defects were not attributable to hereditary or racial causes.[92]

The outcome was a far cry from what Himmler had envisioned. Young men who were nearsighted or had lost their vision in one eye through accident were no longer automatically rejected, whereas in previous years even recruits needing spectacles were not considered.[93] The perfect physical specimens of the elite force were now permitted to lack as many as six molars, have tooth decay, and varicose veins, not to mention bad posture, bone abnormalities, and poor muscular coordination, and were often below height and weight standards. During the war years the racial and physical requirements governing acceptance into the Waffen-SS continued to suffer strains and modifications,[94] and the SS actually never was a reflection of the "great reservoir of pure racial stock"[95] for which the Reichsführer-SS strove.

In an attempt to disguise these tendencies and to enhance the outward appearance of his organization, Himmler appointed influential public officials, diplomats, scientists, and party notables to the position of SS-Ehrenführer (honorary SS commander). Little pretense was made of enrolling these individuals on the basis of racial characteristics. These persons of influence and power received an SS-Führer rank with the right to wear the corresponding uniform, yet they never served one hour or had any command authority within the SS. By doing this Himmler not only hoped to enhance the elite image of the SS but, quite naively, also sought to influence or even capture the "commanders" for the objectives of the SS. The latter ambition was particularly unrealistic because many of the hon-

[92]See the Himmler memorandum dated 14.12. 1938, *IfZ*, FA127/3, 417.

[93]Gelwick, "Personnel Polices," 184.

[94]High personnel losses during the war prompted the SS to look to manpower outside the Reich borders. At first this meant the recruitment of ethnic Germans and non-German "Germanic" volunteers from virtually all parts of Europe. This manpower reservoir was supplemented by the induction of foreigners, most of whom did not meet the racial and ideological standards of the SS. Thus the creation of a multinational force accelerated the decline of enlistment standards. See Stein, *Waffen-SS*, chaps. 6 and 7; Wegner, *Politische Soldaten*, 263–310.

[95]Gelwick, "Personnel Policies," 203–204.

orary commanders—including Rudolf Diels, Martin Bormann, and Signora Ciano, wife of the Italian foreign minister—were hardly friends of the Black Order.[96]

Himmler's racist views were never dogmatic, and he always found room for a good dose of pragmatism.[97] As a result in the SS—just as in any other organization of the Third Reich—"racial standards are established and upheld in a way that is . . . capricious, arbitrary, and open-ended. Few men are automatically excluded by these standards, and the possibility of exceptions is held forth."[98] The open-endedness of racial concepts hence was used to suggest different, and often contradictory, demands; these facilitated SS recruitment needs by legitimizing the power of the existing leadership, who in the past had demonstrated its worth, while removing any tangible restrictions upon the recruitment of those who possessed much-needed expertise. The SS was quite willing to take advantage of the best bourgeois society had to offer in terms of talent and positive traits.

At this point it hardly bears emphasizing that racial purity could not be made the elite principle within the SS. There is one item, however, that emerges from these considerations and must be stressed. Whatever the recruitment priorities, traditional elite norms—be they educational achievement or social origins—were intentionally abandoned and were not a prerequisite for entering the SS.

Because the substitution of a racial selection mechanism for a social one was arbitrary, inconsistent, and ultimately doomed to failure does not mean the SS erected social barriers before its recruits. It has in fact been suggested that "racism in the SS, as in other institutions and practices during the Third Reich, provided an often transparent veil for other standards, of which one of the most clearly stated was ability or achievement."[99] *Das Schwarze Korps* defined

[96] Höhne, *Order of the Death's Head*, 137; Neusüss-Hunkel, *Die SS*, 15, 21; *Organisationsbuch der NSDAP 1943*, 435.

[97] Jeremy Noakes, "Nazism and Revolution," in Noel O'Sullivan, ed., *Revolutionary Theory and Political Reality* (London, 1980), 79–80.

[98] Walter Struve, *Elites against Democracy: Leadership Ideals in Bourgeois Political Thought in Germany, 1890–1933* (Princeton, 1973), 425.

[99] Struve, *Elites*, 425.

the views and policies of the SS as follows: "We have new standards, a new way of appraising. The little word "von" no longer means to us the same thing it once did. We believe that a nobility has the right to exist, not a nobility of class, not a nobility of birth or of property, but a nobility of achievement (*Leistung*) . . . the best from all classes, . . . that is the nobility of the Third Reich.[100]

Heinrich Himmler's order was to serve as a new elite, but not as one which would assume a class structure of its own. Despite its attempts at exclusivity vis-à-vis the outside world, the SS aimed at a fundamental equality among its members;[101] everyone was above all else an "SS man"! To all appearances—and this requires further investigation—men did not need to come from a family of high status or income in order to embark on a career in the SS. Those willing to join Himmler's new knighthood were provided with *la carrière ouverte aux talentes*.

[100] *Das Schwarze Korps*, 13 May 1935, "Zweierlei Adel." See also an article by Gunter d'Alquen, "Unsere Aufgabe," *Das Schwarze Korps* (Werbenummer) February 1935.

[101] SS recruitment publications repeatedly stressed that the career of SS-Führer was open to all irrespective of social origins or formal education. Likewise decisive for promotions within the corps were one's character as a German man and proven performance as National Socialist, SS man, and soldier. *Dich ruft die SS*, "Laufbahnbestimmungen der Waffen-SS während des Krieges," 24–25; *Mein Weg zur Waffen-SS*, 4–5. This was also reflected in Himmler's speeches. See, for example, "Rede des Reichsführer-SS vor den SS-Gruppenführer zu einer Gruppenführerbesprechung im Führerheim der SS-Standarte Deutschland am 8.11.1938," T–175/90/2612397 where Himmler stated that all he is interested in recruiting is the "best blood." Experience has shown him that it does not matter whether a young man has the Abitur or attended a *Volksschule*, whether recruits come from the nobility or working class, they are all welcome.

3

Elite Structure: Ascribed Attributes

GENERATIONAL FACTORS

MODERN SCHOLARSHIP seems to confirm what contemporary Nazi notables were saying all along, that is, "National Socialism is the organized will of Youth."[1] According to an observer of the early NSDAP, "the most striking single social fact about the National Socialist Party is that it was a party of the young."[2] Observations such as this have been made repeatedly by historians who have studied the rise of National Socialism[3] and, if there exists any consensus among scholars, it has to do with the age structure of its following. Virtually all the available evidence, but especially that coming from works on the social composition of the NSDAP, overwhelmingly supports

[1] Peter D. Stachura, "German Youth, the Youth Movement and National Socialism in the Weimar Republic," in Peter D. Stachura, ed., *The Nazi Machtergreifung* (London, 1983), 70. This is a revised version of an earlier article entitled "Deutsche Jugendbewegung und Nationalsozialismus: Interpretationen und Perspektiven," *Jahrbuch des Archivs der deutschen Jugendbewegung* 12 (1980): 35–52.

[2] Harold J. Gordon, *Hitler and the Beer Hall Putsch* (Princeton, 1972), 68.

[3] Many of the references made to the youthful character of the National Socialist movement are anecdotal in nature and not based on critically examined empirical evidence. See, for example, Joachim C. Fest, *Hitler* (Frankfurt/Main, 1973), 386; Bracher, *The German Dictatorship*, 96; David Schoenbaum, *Hitler's Social Revolution: Class and Status in Nazi Germany, 1933–1939* (Garden City, NJ, 1966), 11, 30; Martin Broszat, *The Hitler State* (New York, 1981), 50. One of the earliest studies of the social structure of the NSDAP, including its age structure, was furnished by a sociologist, Hans Gerth, "The Nazi Party," 525–530.

the contention that Adolf Hitler's party "came to power as a party of youth."[4]

The actual age structure of the party, not surprisingly, fluctuated over the years. The average age of party members during the early membership in 1919 to 1921[5] was 32 to 33 years, but dropped to 27 years just shortly before the November 1923 Putsch.[6] After the refounding of the NSDAP in the spring of 1925, the average age rose again to 29 years.[7] From that point on the party continued to age somewhat so that its membership averaged about 35 years by 1932.[8] This picture remains essentially the same when the age structure of the party is compared to the age of new joiners; between 1925 and 1932 the average age of incoming recruits was 31 years.[9] Whether the data pertain to the existing membership at any given time or to new joiners or whether the sample comes from this or that region[10] of Germany, there is no escaping the conclusion that the Nazi party was much younger than one would expect considering the age distribution then prevalent in the population of the Reich.[11]

[4] Walter Z. Laqueur, *Young Germany: A History of the German Youth Movement* (London, 1962), 191.

[5] Douglas, "The Parent Cell," 71; Madden, "Social Characteristics," 50 calculates the median age of the early Nazi party as follows: 1919, 32; 1920, 31; 1921, 30; 1922, 28; 1923, 27. The average age for the entire period hovered around 28 years. In view of the figures calculated by Douglas and Madden, those provided earlier by Georg Franz-Willing, *Die Hitlerbewegung: Der Ursprung, 1919–1920* (Hamburg and Berlin, 1962), 129, 202, and Werner Maser, *Die Frühgeschichte der NSDAP: Hitlers Weg bis 1924* (Frankfurt/Main and Bonn, 1965), 175 are now outdated.

[6] Kater, "Zur Soziographie," 155, 157.

[7] Joseph Nyomarky, *Charisma and Factionalism in the Nazi Party* (Minneapolis, 1967), 74 and n. 8.

[8] Lawrence D. Stokes, "The Social Composition of the Nazi Party in Eutin, 1925–1932," *International Review of Social History* 23 (1978): 18.

[9] Kater, "Sozialer Wandel," 27 and Michael M. Kater, "Quantifizierung," 467.

[10] Noakes, *The Nazi Party in Lower Saxony, 1921–1933* 60 illustrates regional differences in the age structure of the NSDAP on the basis of figures obtained from 1925 membership lists. "In Hamburg, for example, 64.5% of the new members were under 25, in Halle 61.1% were under 30 and of these 65.1% were under 25, in East Prussia 68% were under 30." For local deviations from the national norm see Kater, *Nazi Party*, 140 and H. Grill, *The Nazi Movement in Baden, 1920–1945* (Chapel Hill, 1983), 81.

[11] In order to put their findings into proper perspective, most works that deal with the age distribution of the NSDAP have compared their calculations to the age distri-

The NSDAP was young not only in comparison to the German population [12] of the time but, more important, this was especially true when its age profile is held up against that of the established political parties of the Weimar Republic. The image the NSDAP presented, namely that of an active, youthful, even virile organization, was further accentuated by the fact that the bourgeois parties in general and the Social Democrats in particular exhibited a distinctly and notably aging membership structure. Only the extreme party of the Left, the KPD, could hope to match the attractiveness of the Nazis vis-à-vis the young. [13]

Because the origins and development of the Sturmabteilung (SA), the paramilitary wing of the NSDAP, were closely tied to those of the parent party, the age structure of the storm troopers was very much in keeping with the pronounced youthfulness of the party as a whole. [14] This at least is the theme of the three most recent studies on the SA membership. Conan Fischer in his study concluded that

---

bution of the German population. Even the Nazis adhered to this convention. See, for example, the *Parteistatistik, Stand 1 Januar 1935*, vol. 1 where the age distribution of the party is compared to that of the population, as determined by the 1933 occupational census.

[12] The youthfulness of the NSDAP vis-à-vis the population holds even when allowances for the demographic trends of the period—that is, the cohort of those born between 1900 and 1914 was unusually large in comparison to older and younger cohorts—are made. It seems with the exception of Kater, *Nazi Party*, 141 these trends have often been overlooked by other scholars. See also Herbert Möller, "Youth as a Force in the Modern World," *Comparative Studies in Society and History* 10 (1968): 243–244.

[13] See Gerth, "The Nazi Party," 530; Richard N. Hunt, *German Social Democracy, 1918–1933* (New Haven, 1964), 107; Hermann Weber, "Einleitung," in Ossip. K. Flechtheim, *Die KPD in der Weimarer Republik* (Frankfurt, 1969), 65; and Hans Mommsen, "National Socialism: Continuity and Change," 187 and Juan J. Linz, "Some Notes toward a Comparative Study of Fascism in Sociological Historical Perspective," table 1, 45 in Walter Laqueur, ed., *Fascism, A Reader's Guide: Analyses, Interpretations, Bibliography* (Los Angeles, 1976), 187. W. L. Guttsman, *The German Social Democratic Party, 1875–1933: From Ghetto to Government* (London, 1981), 156 and table 4.4 also suggests that the SPD membership during the Weimar period was somewhat overaged when compared with the population as a whole. Likewise the SPD was markedly older than the KPD; in 1927, 31.8 percent of the KPD membership was below 30 years compared with 17.3 percent for the SPD in 1926, 158.

[14] Michael M. Kater, "Ansätze zu einer Soziologie der SA bis zur Röhmkrise, in Ulrich Engelhardt et al., eds., *Soziale Bewegung und Politische Verfassung* (Stuttgart,

"the active SA appealed decisively to the young, . . . most stormtroopers were younger than 30 and, until 1933, younger than 25."[15]
Similar sentiments are echoed in Eric Reich's work on the Nuremberg SA, which examines the age structure in more detail than did
Fischer. According to the author, "the majority of the stormtroopers
joined predominantly while in their teens and twenties"[16] and, "by
the end of 1932, nearly half of the members were less than 31 years
of age."[17] This pattern changed, however, during 1933–34 when the
SA assimilated other paramilitary organizations and by doing so grew
older. It was common for the new storm troopers to be in their thir-
ties and forties, as opposed to men who joined before 1933, who
were predominantly under 31 years of age. The average age of those
joining the SA between 1925 and 1932 was roughly 30.7 years
whereas those joining the organization in 1933–34 did so at an average age of 35.9 years.[18] The result of these developments was that
by June 1934 the average age for all SA members who had joined
between 1925 and 1934 had climbed to 35.7 years.[19] These age patterns, with some modifications, are mirrored in the age structure of
the higher SA-Führerkorps. According to Mathilde Jamin, roughly
74 percent of the SA leadership was under age forty in 1935. Although this meant that the SA-Führer was on the average ten years
older than the common SA man, he was still younger than the typical NSDAP member or German adult.[20]

With its ideological predilections and its expansive capacity, the
SS offered an attraction for the young, and an examination of statistics compiled by the SS supports this contention. According to the
statistical yearbook of the SS,[21] the average age for members of
the SS-Totenkopfverbände (SS-TV), SS-Verfügungstruppe (SS-VT),

1976), 808 and Conan Fischer, "The Occupational Background of the SA's Rank and
File Membership during the Depression Years, 1929 to mid-1934," in Peter D. Stachura, ed., *The Shaping of the Nazi State* (London, 1978), 150.

[15] Conan Fischer, *Stormtroopers: A Social, Economic, and Ideological Analysis,*
1929–35 (London, 1983), 49.

[16] Eric G. Reiche, *The Development of the SA in Nürnberg, 1922–1934* (New
York, 1986), 222.

[17] Ibid., 114.

[18] Ibid., 195.

[19] Ibid., 197.

[20] Jamin, *Zwischen den Klassen,* 85–86.

[21] *Statistisches Jahrbuch der Schutzstaffel der NSDAP, 1938,* 19, 62, 74, 80.

and Allgemeine SS (Allg. SS) was given as 21, 23, and 29 years of age respectively in 1938. The mean age for the entire organization was 28.7 years.

This general pattern is reflected in the leadership of the SS as well.[22] Even the most cursory examination of our data reveals that the men in charge of the SS-TV and SS-VT relative to the male population, the NSDAP, and the SA and its leadership were consistently as overrepresented in the thirty-years-or-younger age bracket as they were underrepresented in over-forty age groups. In fact, approximately two-thirds of the SS-TV and SS-VT members were under age thirty in 1938, with the average age being thirty-one and twenty-nine respectively. The leadership of the Allg. SS on the other hand was considerably older than its siblings; its average age was thirty-eight years. Except for the fifty-one-and-older age categories, however, the Allg. SS was similar in its age structure to that of the population, NSDAP, and the SA, with over half of its individuals being under forty years of age. The age pattern of SS leaders therefore corroborates the findings of other scholars, that is, the SS leadership, like the membership of the NSDAP and the SA, was much younger than could be expected from the age distribution of the male population at large. But what exactly is the implication or significance of this demonstrable youthfulness?

Although scholars have often treated the youthfulness of Nazi supporters more or less as a curiosity rather than a central or perhaps even significant aspect of National Socialism,[23] there are exceptions to this rule. Generally speaking, two different approaches have been taken in examining the connection between youth and National Socialism. Whereas one directs attention to certain segments of the German youth movement and its possible role in the rise of the Third Reich, the other focuses on the role of crucially important generations of young people.

Because National Socialism seemed to have held a special attraction for the middle-class youth of the interwar period, academic

[22] Boehnert, "SS-Führerkorps, 1925–1939," 8–10 also maintains that the "SS was successful in attracting the younger elements of German society." See also Wegner, *Politische Soldaten*, 214–216.

[23] For the relationship between youth and fascism in general see Linz, "Comparative Study of Fascism," table 1, 45 and Michael A. Ledeen, "Fascism and the Generation Gap," *European Studies Review* 1 (1971): 275–283.

TABLE 3.1

Age Distribution of the SS Leadership in 1938 Compared to the Membership of the NSDAP, the Leadership of the SA, and the Male Population, Relative Frequency Distribution

Age Groups Adult Male Population[c]	SS-TV	SS-VT	Allg. SS	NSDAP[a]	SA[b]	SA Leaders	Population
30 or less	71.0	57.6	19.6	37.6	36.2	26.1	34.6
31–40	22.5	28.6	47.2	27.9	31.0	30.4	21.3
41–50	5.5	10.5	27.0	19.6	24.5	31.1	15.8
51–60	1.0	2.9	5.4	11.2	5.8	8.1	14.1
over 60	0.0	0.4	0.8	3.7	2.5	4.3	14.2
	100.0	100.0	100.0	100.0	100.0	100.0	100.0
Total N =	400	688	853	2,493,890	161	326	23,736,188

SOURCES: The figures for SA leaders are based on Reiche, *The Development of the SA*, 197 Table 6.3. Because Reiche's data pertain to Nüremberg only, generalizations to the entire organization are probably hazardous. The *Partei-Statistik. Stand 1. Januar 1935*, Vol. 1. 5 provided the basis for the NSDAP figures. Finally, the information for the population figures come from German census data for all age groups 15 to 60 and over, obtained from the *Statistisches Jahrbuch für das deutsche Reich*, 1935, 11. The data reflect only males, and those below age 15 and above age 80 were excluded from the calculations.

[a] These figures are from the *Parteistatistik. Stand 1. Januar 1935*, Vol. 1, 5.

[b] The figures for the SA and SA leaders are from Reiche, *Development of the SA*, 197, table 6.3. Fischer, *Stormtroopers*, 49 provides age-related data on the SA. Unfortunately, his age categories do not match those employed in table 3.1. Furthermore, it is not entirely clear whether his data refer to age at a specific point in time or the age at the time of joining the SA. Lastly, we could not determine what kind of sample the figures represent. Relevant to these matters is an article by Richard Bessel and Mathilde Jamin, "Nazis, Workers, and the Use of Quantitative Evidence." *Social History* 4 (1979): 111–116.

[c] The figures are based on the *Statistisches Jahrbuch für das deutsche Reich*, 1935, 11.

TABLE 3.2
AGE STRUCTURE OF THE SS LEADERSHIP IN 1938, MEASURES OF CENTRAL TENDENCY

	SS Branch		
	SS-TV	SS-VT	Allg. SS
Mean	31	29	38
Median	29	25	37
Mode	27	27	38

scholarship has concentrated much attention on the German Youth Movement or, more specifically, the independent sector of the German Youth Movement. The latter made up the nucleus of the five-million-member-strong Greater German Youth Movement and was "represented before the First World War by the *Wandervögel* and after 1918 until the *Machtergreifung* by Free German Youth and, more importantly, *Bündische Jugend.*" [24] Virtually all historians writing on the subject have implicitly or explicitly tried to assess how much the Youth Movement contributed to the successful rise of the Third Reich.

Not surprisingly, the Youth Movement's role vis-à-vis National Socialism is subject to considerable debate and has resulted in sharply divided opinions. Some scholars have repudiated the entire notion of an affinity between the NSDAP and the Youth Movement, [25] others more specifically deny that the *Bündische Jugend* was a precursor of the Hitler Youth, [26] while still others point only to some sort of indirect responsibility for the rise of the NSDAP on the part

[24] For an historiographical discussion of the subject see Stachura, "German Youth," 68–84. Our own cursory overview of the role of the Youth Movement leans heavily on Stachura's account.

[25] Jakob Müller, *Die Jugendbewegung als deutsche Hauptrichtung neukonservativer Reform* (Zurich, 1971), 290ff. This work is not to be confused with the apologetic type that appeared in the immediate post-1945 period, written by former members of the Youth Movement. The aim of these works was simply to absolve the Youth Movement from any responsibility for National Socialism. See, for example, Hans Ebeling, *The German Youth Movement: Its Past and Future* (London, 1945).

[26] Fritz Borinski and Werner Milch, *Jugendbewegung: The Story of German Youth, 1896–1933* (London, 1945), 43; Karl O. Paetel, *Jugend in der Entscheidung, 1913–1933–1945* (Bad Godesberg, 1963), 5; Karl Seidelmann, "War die Jugend-

of the *Bündische Jugend*.[27] Conversely, a formidable body of scholarship has maintained that the Youth Movement not only made a significant contribution to the rise of Hitler,[28] but that the *Wandervogel-Bündische* tradition was inherently prefascist or fascistoid. The latter term is employed by Michael H. Kater,[29] who asserts that the underlying currents within the Youth Movement were compatible with the essential nature and views of the Nazi movement.

The variety of conclusions notwithstanding, mention must be made of the fact that the independent Youth Movement represented a very small fraction of organized youth—leaving out Catholic, socialist, and communist organizations, among others—and therefore exempts from consideration the majority of young people of the Weimar Republic. Consequently, whatever the findings of the various studies, they are limited in value because any generalizations they support can apply only to the minority of young Germans.[30]

Theoretically transcending these limitations and much broader in its scope and potential explanatory power is another body of literature that posits a relationship between Germany's youth and the rise and victory of National Socialism. Notably representative of this "generational approach" are the studies by Peter Loewenberg,[31] Peter Merkl,[32] Paul Madden,[33] and most recently, Michael Kater.[34] What

bewegung präfaschistisch?" *Jahrbuch des Archivs der deutschen Jugendbewegung* 7 (1975): 74; Gerhard Ziemer, "Die deutsche Jugendbewegung und der Staat," *Jahrbuch des Archivs der deutschen Jugendbewegung* 5 (1973): 46–48.

[27] Felix Raabe, *Die Bündische Jugend: Ein Beitrag zur Geschichte der Weimarer Republik* (Stuttgart, 1961), 200; Werner Klose, *Generation im Gleichschritt: Eine Dokumentation* (Oldenburg, 1964), 38. Although Laqueur, *Young Germany*, 234 denies that the Bündische Youth was a precursor of the Hitlerjugend, he points, nevertheless, to its intellectual responsibility.

[28] George L. Mosse, *The Crisis of German Ideology: Intellectual Origins of the Third Reich* (New York, 1971), 188, 310.

[29] Michael H. Kater, "Bürgerliche Jugendbewegung und Hitlerjugend in Deutschland von 1926 bis 1939," *Archiv für Sozialgeschichte* 27 (1977): 127–174.

[30] This point has been made by Stachura, "German Youth," 73–74.

[31] Peter Loewenberg, "The Psychohistorical Origins of the Nazi Youth Cohort," *American Historical Review* 76 (1971): 1457–1502.

[32] Merkl, *Political Violence*.

[33] Paul Madden, "Generational Aspects of National Socialism, 1919–1933," *Social Science Quarterly* 63 (1982): 445–461 and "Social Characteristics," 34–56.

[34] Michael H. Kater, "Generationskonflikt als Entwicklungsfaktor in der NS-Bewegung vor 1933," *Geschichte und Gesellschaft* 11 (1985): 217–243.

these works all have in common is that they identify the youthful aspect of National Socialism as a crucial feature and, more important, assert that during the Weimar period there existed a causal connection, indeed, a positive correlation, between the conflict of generations and the ascendancy of National Socialism. Accordingly, the NSDAP—professing to be not only a party of youth, but also emphasizing that it embodied the rebellion of youthful Germany against the Weimar gerontocracy—capitalized on deep-seated disaffection and successfully mobilized German youth.

THE CONCEPT OF GENERATIONS

The notion of generations as an analytical tool is not new, of course; its roots reach back to the nineteenth-century legacy of the young generation as the vanguard of cultural transformation and national renewal.[35] But it was roughly the 1920s and early 1930s that saw the conception and formulation of the most innovative and pivotal generational theories of cultural change. Leaving its mark in literature, memoirs, and the writings of social scientists, generational thinking of the time portrays youth as a clearly defined and demographically significant group to which was commonly attributed a sense of collective historical destiny.[36] Although clearly owing an

[35] See Laqueur, *Young Germany*; Peter D. Stachura, *The German Youth Movement, 1900–1945: An Interpretative and Documentary History* (New York, 1981).

[36] Robert Wohl, *The Generation of 1914* (Cambridge, MA, 1979), 208, 222–223. The group most often identified with a historical mission was the "front generation" of the First World War. It was believed that the young soldiers, the men who had been closest to the war, should play an important role in postwar affairs because only they were capable of overcoming the antagonisms within the nation and giving to a seemingly absurd time its true meaning. The veterans movements established all over Europe—not just in Germany—were inspired by these hopes and were meant to make the survivors' weight felt in national politics. Edgar Jung, "Die Tragik der Kriegsgeneration," *Süddeutsche Monatshefte* 26 (May 1930) and *Die Herrschaft der Minderwertigkeiten* (Berlin) first published in 1927 and expanded into a second edition in 1929 vigorously argued for the significance of the front generation. According to him, those born between 1885 and 1900 had the authentic war experience, had rediscovered heroism, and would therefore make up not simply a new generation but a levy of "new men." On Jung's role within the new German Right see Struve, *Elites*, 317–351. Prospects and promises for the revival of the war generation are also voiced in Franz Schauwecker, *Aufbruch der Nation* (Berlin, 1930); Ernst Jünger, ed., *Krieg und Krieger* (Berlin, 1930); and Edwin Erich Dwinger, *Wir rufen Deutschland* (Jena,

intellectual debt to José Ortega y Gasset,[37] Wilhelm Pinder,[38] Eduard Spranger,[39] Eduard Wechssler,[40] and others, most contemporary empirical studies of generations proceed from the theoretical contributions of Karl Mannheim and accept his classic formulation: "The social phenomenon of 'generations' represents nothing more than a particular kind of identity of location, embracing related 'age groups' embedded in the historical-social process."[41]

1932). The center of much of the discussion of the importance of the war generation was the so-called *Tat-Kreis* and its monthly magazine *Die Tat* under the editorship of Hans Zehrer. See, for example, the latter's article, "Die zweite Welle," *Die Tat* 21 (1929–30): 577–582 in which he argued that the core of the "young generation" were young war veterans like himself and it was only they who were capable of rebuilding Germany. In his subsequent article, "Absage an den Jahrgang 1902," *Die Tat* 21 (1929–30): 740–748 he attacked the postwar youth contending that they, in contrast to his own age group of war veterans, had aged beyond their years. The class of 1902, he concluded, is more like our fathers than like us. This provoked a reply by Utmann von Elterlein, "Absage an den Jahrgang 1902?" *Die Tat* 22 (1930–31): 202–206 which seemed to insinuate that the concept of generation could not be defined solely in terms of age. See Wohl, *Generation of 1914*, 62–65. For a study of Hans Zehrer and the *Tat* circle see Kurt Sontheimer's article, "Der Tat-Kreis," *Vierteljahrshefte für Zeitgeschichte* 7 (1959): 229–260 and Struve, *Elites*, 353–376.

[37] José Ortega y Gasset, *Man and Crisis* (New York, 1958) and *The Modern Theme* (New York, 1961).

[38] Wilhelm Pinder, *Das Problem der Generation in der Kunstgeschichte Europas* (Berlin, 1926).

[39] Eduard Spranger, *Psychologie des Jugendalters* (Leipzig, 1911).

[40] Eduard Wechssler, *Die Generation als Jugendreihe und ihr Kampf um die Denkform* (Leipzig, 1930).

[41] Karl Mannheim, "The Problem of Generations," in his *Essays on the Sociology of Knowledge* (London, 1959): 292. The following works deal with the utility, validity, and definitional problems of the generational concept: Richard Alewyn, "Das Problem der Generation in der Geschichte," *Zeitschrift für deutsche Bildung* 10 (1929): 519–527; Günther E. Gründel, *Die Sendung der jungen Generation: Versuch einer umfassenden revolutionären Sinndeutung der Krise* (Munich, 1932), 14; Yves Renouard, "La notion de géneration en histoire," *Revue Historique* 209 (1953): 1–23; S. N. Eisenstadt, *From Generation to Generation: Age Groups of Social Structure* (Glencoe, IL, 1956); Bennet M. Berger, "How Long Is a Generation?" *British Journal of Sociology* 11 (1960): 10–23; Marvin Rintala, "A Generation in Politics: A Definition," *Review of Politics* 25 (1963): 509–522; Marvin Rintala, "Generations: Political Generations," in the *International Encyclopedia of the Social Sciences* 18 vols. (New York, 1968), 6: 92–96; Herbert Butterfield, *The Discontinuities between the Generations in History* (Cambridge, 1972); Allen B. Spitzer, "The Historical Problem of

With these suppositions in mind, historians have envisaged generations as groups of coevals of the same age whose common historical conditioning profoundly differentiates them from contemporaries in other age groups and who are marked by a particular and characteristic type of generational behavior. The latter reflects the distinctive collective experience of given age groups who tend to assume a separate and permanent identity of their own as they move through time.[42] Such generational behavior—often identified with reference to major historical traumas such as wars, revolution, and economic disasters—is frequently accompanied by an articulation of a shared generational ideology. As Mannheim wrote, "individual members of a generation become conscious of their common situation and make this consciousness the basis of group solidarity."[43] Like class consciousness, generational consciousness is a form of collectivism and determinism leading to common values and, most important, to clearly identifiable common action. But unlike the concept of class consciousness, generational consciousness stresses temporal rather than socioeconomic location. Consequently the real confrontation in society, the generational approach implies, is not between religious factions, regional sentiments, or social classes, but between the young and the old.

Moreover, scholars have usually been compelled to make distinctions between coevals of a particular generation if they want to isolate particular social groups with reference to birth dates. Thus the historical treatment of generations invariably refers only to segments of the age group under consideration,[44] generational sub-

---

Generations," *American Historical Review* 78 (1973): 1353–1385; Hans Jaeger, "Generationen in der Geschichte: Überlegungen zu einer umstrittenen Konzeption," *Geschichte und Gesellschaft* 3 (1977): 429–452.

[42] Implicit in a generations approach to history and politics is the supposition that political attitudes of individuals do not get modified significantly way in the course of a lifetime. Once set, political convictions are presumed to remain constant. Instead of changing a previous political view on the basis of new information, the individual either embraces or repudiates new facts depending on whether their are congruous with his or her previous outlook. Marvin Rintala, "Generations in Politics," in A. Esler, ed., *The Youth Revolution: The Conflict of Generations in Modern History* (Lexington, MA., 1974), 15–20.

[43] Mannheim, "Problem of Generations," 290.

[44] Spitzer, "Historical Problem," 1355–1356.

groups that theoretically are akin to Mannheim's "generation unit."
"Youth experiencing the same concrete historical problems may be
said to be part of the same actual generation; while those groups
within the same actual generation which work up the same material
of their common experiences in different specific ways, constitute
generation units"[45] [emphasis added]. Consequently it is possible
that members of the same generation may develop contrasting views.
Still, regardless of their differences on specific concerns, even the
most diverse generation units are presumed to have more in common with each other than with the members of older or younger
generations.

GENERATIONAL REVOLT AND NATIONAL SOCIALISM

Scholars of National Socialism who avail themselves of a generational framework typically view those born between 1880 and 1920
as a significant generation because their youth was bifurcated by the
Great War.[46] The trauma of the Great War served as a watershed and
defining experience for a generation of young people who were
haunted by the memory of an experience that would overshadow
everything that would happen during their lives.[47] Although differing
in their exact definitions of a generation, it is usually assumed that
the latter comprised two distinct subgroups consisting of (1) those

[45] Mannheim, "Problem of Generations," 304.
[46] This is only a rough definition of this "war generation." Wohl, *Generation of
1914*, 64–84 is without a doubt the most thorough and comprehensive study on this
subject, providing as it were a survey of virtually every definition ever attempted. One
particular merit of his work is that he places the generation of 1914 in a European-
wide context. For the variety of recent definitions associated with studies on the
German war generations see the previously cited works by Loewenberg, "Psychohistorical Origins," Merkl, *Political Violence*, Madden, "Generational Aspects," and Kater, "Generationskonflikt." Also of interest is Phillipe Bénéton, "La géneration de
1912–1914: Image, Mythe, et Réalité," *Revue Française de Science Politique* 21
(1971): 981–1009.
[47] Implicit in the claim that National Socialism represented a "generational revolt" is that the historical experience that binds members of an age group together is
more important than any social differences that might divide them.

who experienced the war at the front and (2) those who experienced it at home.[48]

The first group, collectively referred to as the "front generation," traces its conflict with the older generation back to the days of the prewar German Youth Movement, especially the *Wandervogel* ideal of the autonomy of youth.[49] What had begun as a distancing between sons and fathers turned, under the impact of the war, into outright opposition and hostility. Whereas the majority of those who had risked their lives at the front were young, those who had provided the reasons for the slaughter and directed the war from home, then only to sign a humiliating armistice and peace, tended to be older. The negative image of fathers was reinforced by the disillusionment that came with peace. Once again it was the older men who were able to return to their jobs, their professions, and their wives, but the young had nothing to return to. To be sure, disillusionment was felt by many young men and women, but the feeling of betrayal and defeat was especially strong among the young returning veterans. Thus the dichotomy, indeed the conflict, between young and old received a new and potent emotional impetus.[50]

While one group of young men developed their animosity toward the older generation during their baptism of fire at the front, a cohort of adolescents cultivated its own peculiarly determined alienation, rancor, and resentments toward their fathers.[51] Because of their young age, these individuals had to remain at home with their

[48] Merkl, *Political Violence*, 479–480, for example, speaks of a war and a postwar generation. Kater, "Generationskonflikt," 218 works with the concept of two related subcohorts whose oldest members were born in 1884 and its youngest in 1918. Thus, between the end of the First World War and the beginning of Hitler's Third Reich these two groups make up a young and not-so-young generation whose age ranges from 15 to 35.

[49] Kater, "Generationskonflikt," 218–219. For general accounts of the movement see Hans Blüher, *Wandervogel: Geschichte einer Bewegung*, 2 vols. (Jena, 1912) and Ulrich Aufmuth, *Die deutsche Wandervogelbewegung unter soziologischem Aspekt* (Göttingen, 1979).

[50] Wohl, *Generation of 1914*, 222–223.

[51] This is the age cohort singled out by Loewenberg, "Psychohistorical Origins," described on 1480, 1485–1496, 1499.

mothers and, as the war progressed, increasingly endured the psychological and psychosomatic consequences of the conflict. Marked by sickness, nutritional deprivation, even starvation, they became estranged from their fathers and developed an abnormally close relationship with their mothers, becoming in fact rivals to their fathers for the love of their mothers. The defeat of their fathers represented nothing short of a catastrophe to them.[52] Confused and hateful, these young individuals viewed their returning fathers in 1918 as the ones responsible for losing the war and as traitors to the national honor.

At the time of the Paris Peace Settlement, these two groups of young men coalesced into a generation[53] of young Germans who—because of their highly conscious dissatisfaction with the social order—rejected the bourgeois world of their elders and held idealistic notions of a new community. Their antibourgeois feelings[54] expressed themselves in a variety of ways, but found their most fundamental expression in the desire for destruction of the Weimar system and all that came with it, for these were the fruits of parental misdeeds. The enthusiasm, energy, and elan of National Socialism, it is argued, appealed especially to this segment of the population, which believed that political problems are best resolved by violent methods rather than deliberation and reason.[55] Thus it was the hopes and disillusionment of young individuals which, in the final analysis, helped destroy the Weimar Republic. As Peter Merkl metaphorically observed, "German youth set up the storm ladders against the republic and helped one of its false alternatives, the Nazi party, to power."[56]

[52] Kater, "Generationskonflikt," 221–222.
[53] Kater, "Generationskonflikt," 222.
[54] A. E. Günther, "Der Bürgerhaß der jungen Generation," Deutsches Volkstum (1930): 89–95.
[55] Irmtraud Götz von Olenhusen, "Die Krise der jungen Generation und der Aufstieg des Nationalsozialismus," Jahrbuch des Archivs der deutschen Jugendbewegung 12 (1980): 53–82, esp. 61.
[56] Merkl, Political Violence, 13. The resentments of the young were accentuated by the world economic crisis that began in 1929. It was the young who suffered disproportionately more than the old from economic dislocation for they were the last ones to be hired but the first to be let go. Thus, an above-average rate of unemployment was a crucial factor in the progressive radicalization in the political out-

TABLE 3.3
AGE DISTRIBUTION OF THE SS LEADERSHIP AT THE TIME OF JOINING THE SS,
RELATIVE FREQUENCY DISTRIBUTION

Age Groups	SS Branch		
	SS-TV	SS-VT	Allg. SS
30 or younger	83.6	73.8	48.0
31–40	14.1	17.2	37.2
41–50	2.0	7.1	12.5
51–60	0.3	1.9	2.3
61 and over	0.0	0.0	0.0
	100.0	100.0	100.0
Total Number of Cases	396	667	788

TABLE 3.4
AGE STRUCTURE OF THE SS LEADERSHIP AT THE TIME OF JOINING THE SS,
MEASURES OF CENTRAL TENDENCY

	SS Branch		
	SS-TV	SS-VT	Allg. SS
Mean	24	26	32
Median	22	23	31
Mode	20	19	34

On the surface at least, data on the SS-Führerkorps seem to mesh nicely with the concept of a generational analysis. In view of the 1938 age structure examined earlier, Himmler's elite must have commenced its activity at an early age, and that was indeed the case, as is demonstrated by the data summarized in Tables 3.3 and 3.4.

look of youth. Kater, "Generationskonflikt," 226; Joachim Bartz and Dagmar More, "Der Weg in die Jugendzwangsarbeit—Massnahmen gegen Jugendarbeitslosigkeit zwischen 1925 und 1935," in Gero Lenhardt, ed., *Der hilflose Sozialstaat: Jugendarbeitslosigkeit und Politik* (Frankfurt, 1979), 28–94; Loewenberg, "Psychohistorical Origins," 1468; Dieter Petzina, "Germany and the Great Depression," *Journal of Contemporary History* 4 (1969): 59–74.

More than three-fourths of the future SS-TV and SS-VT leaders were under thirty years of age when they joined the SS, over half of them being 23 years or younger. In fact, so young were the majority of them that they could not have fought in the First World War.[57] In 1914 the mean age of the men who would later serve in SS-TV and SS-VT was only three and seven years respectively; measured modally the age of most of them was only between one and three years when the conflict began. Thus the so-called front generation was in a decided minority among the leaders of the prewar full-time SS branches. Only 14.7 percent of the SS-TV members and 24.3 percent of the SS-VT were born before 1903, the earliest date of birth that made one eligible to join in the front experiences of their elder counterparts. The figures then leave no doubt that the men who would provide the leadership of the armed SS formations and those guarding the prewar concentration camps comprised for the most part a generation of young individuals who fit Loewenberg's[58] description of the Nazi Youth Cohort, rather than a war generation seeking to turn the trench experience into a metaphor and general model of life.[59] As Robert Wohl put it, "Hitler's coming to power and the creation of the Third Reich signified not the victory of the war generation, as the Nazis claimed, but the victory of one part of the war generation over its opponents and the imposition of one interpretation of the war generation's experience on the population as a whole."[60]

If members of the front-line generation played a role in the formation of the SS, they have to be located among the older and mostly part-time[61]—though admittedly numerically the largest[62]—

[57] See Stokes, "NSDAP in Eutin," 18 whose findings verify this.

[58] Loewenberg, "Psychohistorical Origins."

[59] As early as 1931 Leopold Dingräve [Ernst Wilhelm Eschmann], *Wo steht die junge Generation?* (Jena, 1931), 11 suggested that a new mentality based on the war experience was impossible because this experience did not have a universal validity.

[60] Wohl, *Generation of 1914*, 80–81.

[61] Only 26.5 percent or 3,640 out of a total of 13,746 SS-Führer of the Allgemeine SS were full-time as of 21.1.1938. T–175/123/649254.

[62] In December 1938 91.3 percent of all SS-Führer belonged to the Allgemeine SS, 5.5 percent to the SS-Verfügungstruppe, and 3.2 percent to the SS-Totenkopfverbände (*Statistisches Jahrbuch der Schutzstaffel der NSDAP. Stand 31.12.1938*, 18).

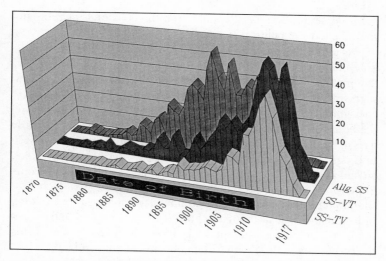

FIGURE 3.1   Absolute Frequency Distribution of Date of Birth. (For Leaders of the Allgemeine SS, the SS-Verfügungstruppe, and the SS-Totenkopfverbände.)

TABLE 3.5
DATE OF BIRTH OF THE SS LEADERSHIP, MEASURES OF CENTRAL TENDENCY

	SS Branch		
	SS-TV	SS-VT	Allg. SS
Mean	1908	1906	1900
Median	1913	1911	1900
Mode	1910	1909	1900

segment of the Black Order. And so they were. Most members of the Allgemeine SS were born at the turn of the century, some 57 percent before 1903. It is therefore accurate to conclude that the majority of these men—as a result of general conscription—were participants in the Great War, and one might agree with the assessment that "spiritually, they stemmed from the front officers and front soldiers of the Great War . . . [they were] *anti-bürgerlich* from their experience at the front; anti-November Republic from their natural tradition and from the force of political events."[63]

Yet another consequence of the age differential between the full-time branches of the SS and the Allgemeine SS is that it was predominantly members of the Allgemeine SS (see Figure 3.1) who supplemented their military experience with a postwar paramilitary background.[64] It is precisely this cohort of SS men who, by joining the Freikorps[65] and other paramilitary formations[66] during the early days of the Republic, became the so-called political soldiers who, in turn, are credited with preparing the physical environment in which violent political movements such as National Socialism could come to power.[67] According to James Diehl, "the militarized SS state in which political violence was institutionalized and legalized was the historical and logical, though not inevitable, conclusion to the practice of paramilitary politics introduced by the volunteer forces during the early years of the Weimar Republic and continued by their successors, the *Wehrverbände* and *Kampfverbände*."[68]

"Either unable or unwilling to demilitarize psychologically,"[69] these men felt betrayed and deceived by the Republic they had

[63] Friedrich Wilhelm von Oertzen, *Die deutschen Freikorps, 1918–1923*, 5th ed. (Munich, 1939), xv as cited in Waite, *Vanguard of Nazism*, 268.

[64] See Reiche, *The Development of the SA*, 115, table 4.9 for the paramilitary experience of the Nürnberg SA rank and file and leadership corps.

[65] Karl O. Paetel, "The Reign of the Black Order," in Maurice Baumont, ed., *The Third Reich* (New York, 1955), 671. See also Waite, *Vanguard of Nazism*, 281 and Höhne, *Order of the Death's Head*, 54–56.

[66] If the SS recruited its members with an eye to paramilitary experience, it did so also from the ranks of National Socialism. As early as 1929, Heinrich Himmler began to recruit SA men for his organization and thereby set in motion a system of social mobility which had a negative sifting effect on the SA. The Reichsführer-SS apparently succeeded in recruiting the "best men" and despite objections raised by the SA leadership, continued his recruiting efforts unabashedly until 1934. Kater, "SA und SS," 363. See also Höhne, *Order of the Death's Head*, 57–58. Whether it was because of Himmler's efforts or in spite of them, by the end of 1938 about one-third of the SS leadership, regardless of the branch they belonged to, had previously been associated with the SA. It should be noted, however, that these figures may already include individuals who belonged previously to other paramilitary formations.

[67] James M. Diehl, *Paramilitary Politics in Weimar Germany* (Bloomington, 1977), ix.

[68] Ibid., 291.

[69] Ibid., 18, 47–48, 54.

helped save. They turned against it and, lacking their own political concepts, joined forces with the emerging counterrevolutionary forces. Their common agenda for action, insofar as they shared one, included the destruction of the Republic, the denunciation of the Treaty of Versailles, and the elimination of those responsible for fostering social strife and frustrating the harmony of the Volk. The leader of the Stahlhelm stated their objective directly, if less than delicately: "We must fight to get the men into power who will depend on us front soldiers for support—men who will call upon us to smash once and for all these damned revolutionary rats and choke them by sticking their heads into their own shit."[70] Such a highly developed propensity for aggressive behavior on the part of fascists in general, and Freikorps members in particular, has been linked to their misogynist fantasies about women, their bodies, and their sexuality. As their fantasies allegedly demonstrate, these activists fought wars and engaged in excessive violence in order to escape women.[71]

The generational approach promises great explanatory power. On the surface, at least, it is an approach to politics that is convincing in its logic and seductive in its analytical parsimony. But can one identify age groups with a given type of politics? Is age really more important than geographic, religious, and occupational origins in determining political attitudes and behavior? The answer, though qualified, must be a no.[72]

Leaving aside methodological considerations such as how to define exactly the spatial and temporal location of a particular generation, it would seem that in the long run no political movement can rely solely on young people in its recruitment. In order to become significant, it must attract people of many age groups, both old and young. There was obviously many an older individual who was important to the growth and development of National Socialism. Another and perhaps even more acute problem is that it is quite difficult, if not impossible, ever to demonstrate that a young traumatized generation was more attracted to the SS or National Social-

---

[70] Cited in Waite, *Vanguard of Nazism*, 267.

[71] Klaus Theweleit, *Male Fantasies*, vol. 1, *Women, Floods, Bodies, History* (Minneapolis, 1987).

[72] For recent reflections on the general validity of the generational approach to the history of National Socialism see Kater, "Generationskonflikt," 241–243.

ism than a nontraumatized youth. Surely there were many traumatized youths who opposed the Weimar system, but did not fall under
the spell of Adolf Hitler and Himmler's Black Order. In fact, many
of these very young men could and indeed did join the ranks of the
Communist party. Furthermore, no one has adequately explained
why the factors that impelled older men to join the SS do not sufficiently account for the attractiveness the SS held for the young, for
they may well be similar. Finally, just because a large proportion of
SS members came from one significant generation does not necessarily mean that a correspondingly large segment of this generation
joined the SS.

Perhaps the utility of a generational explanation of National Socialism should be limited to the well-known conclusion that it is the
young in general, and students in particular, who exhibit the propensity to turn to extreme solutions when traditional alternatives seem
to have failed.[73] In other words, during this period young people in
general were inclined toward antiliberal politics and commonly were
more open to radical political ideologies. Although individuals could
be attracted toward political movements of both Left and Right, it is
also true that most found it difficult to make a commitment to the
Left because its tenets represented, above all, a class ideology. The
idea of a class-based ideology was a precept that went against the
predisposition and ideals of many young people.[74] They were instead
captivated and enticed by an ideology that promised a revolution that
would overcome class divisions. The Nazis benefited enormously
from the fact that they offered the generation of young men up to 35
years of age or so the opportunity not only of employment, but of
appointments and promotions to positions of considerable responsibility. "The Nazis provided a vehicle for the ambitions of a younger
generation which, during the Weimar period, had felt frustrated by
what they regarded as the ossified structures and hidebound estab-

---

[73] See Möller, "Youth as a Force," 237–260; Phyllis H. Stock, "Students versus
the University in Pre-War Paris," *French Historical Studies* 7 (1971): 93–110; William J. McGrath, "Student Radicalism in Vienna," *Journal of Contemporary History*
2 (1967): 183–201; and the entire issue of *Journal of Contemporary History* 5 (1970)
which is devoted to the "Generations in Conflict."

[74] Wohl, *Generation of 1914*, 230–232.

lishment of the older generation which was no longer capable of providing Germany with the dynamic leadership that was required to solve a grave national crisis."[75] It is in this sense fair, then, to say that National Socialism was the great temptation of the young generation.

REGIONAL AND URBAN/RURAL DIMENSIONS OF RECRUITMENT

If individuals have no control over the time of their birth, the same can be said about the place of their birth. The latter is an important source of information because it indicates, within limits, the milieu in which the family of the SS leader moved.[76] More specifically, information on birthplace can reveal important regional dimensions in SS recruitment and, beyond that, help assess the relative degree of urban and rural backgrounds within the SS elite. Accordingly, information on the place of birth for each SS-Führer was coded into two distinct variables, one measuring the size of the birthplace and another gauging the regional source of the SS recruit.

Our first consideration is the size of the communities in which future SS leaders spent their early years, that is, the time of childhood socialization. For ease of comparison, data for this particular variable were grouped into community sizes that are comparable to those employed by the German Statistical Office.[77] To minimize any biases, particularly upward biases, the size of the birthplaces was coded according to the population residing in that community at the time of birth of an individual.[78] Rather than choosing an arbitrary

[75] Jeremy Noakes and Geoffrey Pridham, eds., *Nazism, 1919–1945*, 2 vols., vol. 2, *State, Economy, and Society, 1933–39: A Documentary Reader* (Exeter, 1984), 2: 379.

[76] Linz, "Comparative Study," 50.

[77] The following is the official classification: less than 2,000—rural communities; 2,000 to 4,999—rural towns; 5,000 to 19,000—small cities; 20,000 to 99,999—medium-sized cities; 100,000 and over—large cities. See *Statistisches Jahrbuch des deutschen Reiches, 1935*, 10.

[78] This point is less trivial than it first might appear when one considers that Germany was still in the process of becoming a highly urban nation and that some communities experienced rapid population growth during the period under discus-

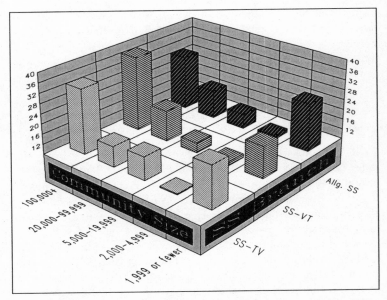

FIGURE 3.2   Relative Frequency Distribution of Place of Birth according to Community Size. (For Leaders of the Allgemeine SS, the SS-Verfügungstruppe, and the SS-Totenkopfverbände.)

date for the census return and then classifying the community according to population figures at that time, care was taken to use the census return closest to the time of birth for each Führer. The same place of birth, therefore, could have been assigned a different population figure depending on the date of birth. One final word of explanation. The data collected by the German census bureau on community size refer to the resident population at the time of the census whereas our data relate to the size of a community at the time an

sion. To cite but one example, the city of Mannheim experienced a rise of population from 79,058 in 1890 to 193,002 in 1910. That amounts to a 145 percent population increase in twenty years or the differing environmental influence of a youth spent in a medium-sized city or a sizable urban area.

individual was born.[79] Our data consequently is a proxy indicator, though the only one that is available.[80]

Despite the aforementioned margin of error, there is no doubt that the SS-Führerkorps as a whole tended to be more urban in its roots than would be expected from the distribution of the population.[81] Indeed, the most decisive difference between the SS elite and the German population in general is the smaller percentage of elite members growing up in a rural environment. To illustrate this point, a breakdown according to size of the birthplaces confirms a high proportion of city origins; while 21 percent of the general population lived in large cities in 1919, almost every third Führer came from such an area and over half from cities larger than 20,000. Conversely, the number of men coming from the countryside was accordingly small. Only about one-fourth originated in communities of 2,000 or less, compared to some 40 percent of the German people. This urban origin clearly contrasts with the SS's agrarian ideology so much propagated by the SS leadership.[82] The apparently limited enthusiasm for this sort of ideology— which held the prospect of settling in the East after a victorious

[79]The obvious solution to this problem would have been to record the address of residence for each SS recruit and code those according to community size. Unfortunately such an approach creates more problems than it solves because the home address of SS-Führer, especially the full-time members of the SS-TV and SS-VT, was the address where they were stationed.

[80]The community size for towns with a population of less than 10,000 was taken from the *Statistik des deutschen Reiches*, vol. 151 (1903), 392–744, 775–789.

[81]This also confirms the findings of Wegner, *Politische Soldaten*, 220 and, with some deviations, those of Boehnert, "Sociography," 85, table 3.5. Jamin, *Zwischen den Klassen*, 100–102 points to an overrepresentation of "urbanites" among the SA leadership. Although our data are not strictly comparable because Kater, *Nazi Party*, 225, table 9 elected to use a tripartite division of community size, this relatively high degree of "urbanism" does not hold for the rank and file of the NSDAP in 1930–1932. The proportion of men coming from cities with a population above 100,000 was 26 percent, the same proportion found in the general population. See also Kater, "Sozialer Wandel," 27, table 2.

[82]Totally unsubstantiated is the claim by Steiner, *Armee*, 96–97 that 90 percent of the Waffen-SS commanders were raised on the land. See also Höhne, *Order of the Death's Head*, 136 who suggests that the rank and file of the Totenkopfverbände was drawn from the young peasantry.

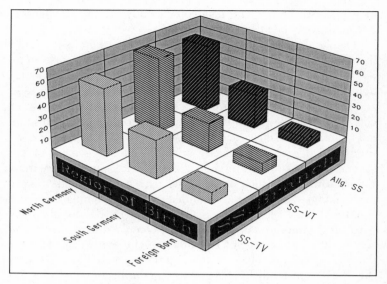

FIGURE 3.3   Relative Frequency Distribution of Place of Birth according to Region of Birth. (For Leaders of the Allgemeine SS, the SS-Verfügungstruppe, and the SS-Totenkopfverbände.)

war—must be connected to the limited agricultural roots in the leadership corps of the SS.

As to regional patterns, the data on place of birth were coded into three major categories. Using the river Main[83] as a rough dividing line between northern and southern Germany, places of birth were coded as South Germany if they fell into the *Länder* Bavaria, Würtemberg, Baden, and Hessen. The Prussian *Regierungsbezirke* of Wiesbaden, Koblenz, Trier, and the Saarland were also considered South Germany. With the exception of foreign places of birth, which were coded separately, the remaining ones were assigned the category North Germany. The so-called *Ostgebiete*, which later became part of Poland, were classified as North Germany as well.

The regional distribution of the place of birth does not point to

[83] Kater, "Soziographie," 136.

any extreme or, for that matter, notable deviation from the general population.[84] This leaves no other conclusion than that the leadership personnel of all three SS branches were recruited more or less evenly from all areas of the Reich. The slight underrepresentation of the northern parts of the country is accounted for by the fact that a minority of SS men came from areas outside of Germany. The men who were born on foreign soil comprised two distinct groups: (1) German Austrians and (2) German citizens living abroad in countries other than Austria. This would seem to suggest, first, that SS leaders were recruited from Austria long before its incorporation into the Reich in 1938 and, second, that the SS held "a striking appeal for *Auslandsdeutsche*, Germans who had spent the impressionable years of their lives in a German community abroad."[85]

RELIGIOUS AFFILIATIONS

Although Adolf Hitler, as Führer of the German people, never failed to give the impression of a pious and devout being—he often invoked the Almighty or Providence—the gospel of Christianity was, in the final analysis, irreconcilable with that of National Socialism. The Christian churches of Germany existed during the first two or three years of National Socialist rule under the illusion that all was well.[86] Because he was dependent upon the toleration of his regime on the part of the churches Hitler, during the first few years after

---

[84] This substantiates the findings of Wegner, *Politische Soldaten*, 219–220. The figures by Boehnert, "Sociography," 82, table 3.4, however, suggest an overrepresentation of southern Germany as a region of birth for members of the Totenkopfverbände. Again, Jamin, *Zwischen den Klassen*, 92–93 also finds that the regional distribution among SA leaders is essentially identical to that of the population.

[85] Schoenbaum, *Hitler's Social Revolution*, 44. See also Linz, "Comparative Study," 29–30.

[86] Klaus Scholder, *Die Kirchen und das Dritte Reich: Vorgeschichte und Zeit der Illusionen, 1918–1934* (Frankfurt/Main 1977). One of Hitler's achievements in 1933 was his success, through the Concordat, in persuading the Catholic church to adopt a more positive attitude toward the regime. But relations rapidly cooled when it became clear that the National Socialist regime systematically set out to obstruct and consequently to coordinate or suppress all activities of the church apart from pastoral care. John J. Hughes, "The Reich Concordat 1933: Capitulation or Compromise," *Australian Journal of Politics and History* 20 (1974): 164–175.

1933, minimized or explained away the fear that the Third Reich was anti-Christian. In reality, the Nazis simply needed to establish their rule more firmly before embarking on policies that could conceivably lead to another *Kulturkampf*.

It is well established, and not only with hindsight, that beginning in 1936 the regime embarked on a policy of severe encroachment against the Christian churches. The smoldering antagonism between the Nazis and the Roman church, for example, came to a head in 1937 when Pope Pius, dismayed at the situation of the Catholic church in Germany, attacked the Third Reich with the encyclical *Mit brennender Sorge* of 14 March 1937. The same year saw a more pronounced conflict between the Nazi regime and Protestant opposition. After the outbreak of the war this antichurch policy was outwardly modified in order to avoid social tension, but in reality it held to its previous line with the intention of suppressing the churches altogether once victory was achieved. In the meantime arbitrary actions against the church could be disguised and legitimized as necessary for the conduct of the war.[87]

The hostility of National Socialism vis-à-vis Christianity and its established denominations meshed conveniently with Heinrich Himmler's own aim to provide the SS with an ideology that would remain unchanged over the centuries. Fundamental to this goal was the obliteration of religion. The relationship of the SS to religion can thus be readily identified above all as a bitter struggle against the Christian churches. Articulated in Himmler's speeches, decrees, and orders, this struggle varied in form and intensity according to tactical considerations, but there is no doubt that the Reichsführer-SS fought a tenacious fight. The morality of the church, if nothing else, stood in clear opposition to that of the SS, and Himmler's own values can only be interpreted as the antithesis of central Christian values.[88] Not surprisingly, then, the loyal Heinrich intended his SS to be in

---

[87] Ackermann, *Ideologe*, 93. See also John S. Conway, *The Nazi Persecution of the Churches, 1933–1945* (London and New York, 1968); Friedrich Zipfel, *Kirchenkampf in Deutschland, 1933–1945: Religionsverfolgung und Selbstbehauptung der Kirchen in der nationalsozialistischen Zeit* (Berlin, 1965); Ernst Christian Helmreich, *The German Churches under Hitler: Background, Struggle, and Epilogue* (Detroit, 1979).

[88] Wegner, *Politische Soldaten*, 50.

the vanguard in the fight against Christianity. Although he endeavored to camouflage his real intentions,[89] he did not mince words when discussing the issues of religion among his own men. According to his "deepest convictions" Himmler viewed all of Christianity and the priesthood as nothing but an indecent union, with the majority of its priesthood constituting "an erotic homosexual league of men" whose only purpose was to create and maintain a "twenty-thousand-year-old Bolshevism."[90] To the Reichsführer-SS Christianity was the greatest plague delivered by history, and he demanded that it be dealt with accordingly.[91] A perennial favorite song of the storm troopers had this refrain: "Storm Trooper Comrades, hang the Jews and put the priests against the wall."[92]

However, Himmler was determined to avoid under all circumstances the impression that the SS promoted atheism,[93] and according to him the National Socialist state recognized that individuals have the right to exercise "personal freedom in spiritual matters."[94] In the SS, he announced, "we believe in a God Almighty who stands above us; he has created the earth, the Fatherland, and the Volk, and he has sent us the Führer. Any human being who does not believe in God should be considered arrogant, megalomaniacal, and stupid and thus is not suited for the SS."[95] The Reichsführer-SS, on the occasion of Reinhard Heydrich's burial, confessed in front of a group of high-ranking SS leaders that he believed in a God.[96] It apparently

[89] Ostensibly to avoid becoming embroiled in any religious disputes, Himmler ordered that the SS must never participate in any religious ceremonies. *SS-Befehls-Blatt* 25 November 1934 T–175/209/749380.

[90] Ackermann, *Ideologe*, 92; "Rede des Reichsführer-SS anlässlich der Gruppenführer-Besprechung in Tölz am 18.2.1937," T–175/89/2611833–1836.

[91] "Rede des Reichsführer-SS auf der Tagung der Auslandsorganisation in Stuttgart am 2.9.1938," T–175/90/2612588.

[92] Richard Grünberger, *The 12-Year Reich: A Social History of Nazi Germany, 1933–1945* (New York, 1971), 442.

[93] Berlin Document Center, *SS-Handblätter für den weltanschaulichen Unterricht*, "Als Nationalsozialisten glauben wir an eine göttliche Weltanschauung."

[94] *SS-Befehls-Blatt* 25 November 1934 T–175/209/749380.

[95] Heinrich Himmler, *Die SS*, 27; "Die innere Sicherung des Reiches," *Das Schwarze Korps* 21.11.1935, 2. This a reproduction of Himmler's speech given at the Reichsbauerntag in Goslar.

[96] Wegner, *Politische Soldaten*, 53; Himmler, *Geheimreden*, 160.

did not matter to him, however, what label was assigned to this
God—God Almighty, the Ancient One, Destiny, "Waralda," Nature, or some such; all would do nicely—as long as there was demonstrated a belief and acceptance of the concept of a higher power,
a power that had created this world and endowed it with the laws of
struggle and selection that guaranteed the continued existence of nature and the natural order of things.[97] With such a pantheistic notion
of what constitutes a supreme being, something which Schoppen-
hauer might have defined as noble atheism, Heinrich Himmler and
the SS attempted to overcome the personal God of Christianity, indeed, Christianity itself.[98]

So-called *Gottlosigkeit* was consequently prohibited within the
Black Order, while the SS indoctrination publication *SS-Leithefte* was
permitted to announce: "We are *gottgläubig!*"[99] What it meant to be
gottgläubig was defined as follows: "Only he who opposes the belief
in a higher power is considered godless."[100] Thus, the God-believing
Ignatius of the SS, who had left the Catholic church, tried to make
certain that the number of SS members who still admitted to being
church members declined while the proportion of God believers—if
necessary under the threat of expulsion[101]—increased accordingly.[102]

[97] Ackermann, *Ideologe*, 83. See also "Entwurf der 9 Lebens-Leitsätze für die
SS," 25.6.1935, T–175/155/5468.

[98] Ackermann, *Ideologe*, 83. In the *SS-Befehls-Blatt*, 15 October 1934 T–175/
209/749375 it was stated that clergy men should not be accepted into the SS. Those
SS men who are priests [sic] will be asked to leave the SS in the most tactful and
honorable fashion possible.

[99] "Der politische Katholizismus hat das Wort," *SS-Leitheft* 7, 1 November 1937,
42. There was no substantial decline in religious practice and church membership
between 1933 and 1939. In 1939, 94.5 percent belonged to a Christian church,
while 3.5 percent claimed to be Gottgläubig, and only 1.5 percent were without a
faith. Wolfgang Zorn, "Sozialgeschichte, 1918–1970," in H. Aubin and W. Zorn,
eds., *Handbuch der deutschen Wirtschafts-und Sozialgeschichte*, 2 vols. (Stuttgart,
1976), 915.

[100] Ackermann, *Ideologe*, 82–83; "Der politische Katholizismus hat das Wort,"
SS-Leitheft 7, 1 November 1937, 42.

[101] See Himmler, *Die SS*, 27.

[102] The *Das Schwarze Korps* 3.9.1936, with an article entitled "Vorsicht Büro-
kratie" threatened those bureaucrats who would place obstacles in the way of proven
National Socialists who did not belong to either the Catholic or Evangelical church.

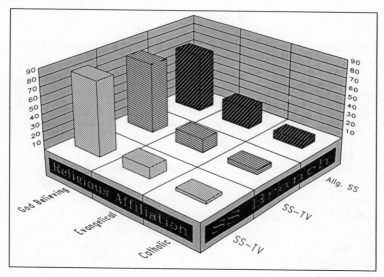

FIGURE 3.4   Relative Frequency Distribution of Religious Affiliation. (For Leaders of the Allgemeine SS, the SS-Verfügungstruppe, and the SS-Totenkopf-verbände.)

To find the majority of SS-Führer describing themselves as gottgläu-big (see Figure 3.4) comes, therefore, as little or no surprise.[103] Judg-ing from the entries in the personnel records, the SS man who was listed as "God-believing" left the church of his birth usually just before entering the SS or shortly after entering Himmler's organiza-tion. Whether these men left the church before or after joining the SS, one must conclude that under either circumstance they were hardly men of deep religious conviction.

The term gottgläubig was, of course, politically an astute tactic.

[103] Apparently the leadership of the SS was setting an example for the rest of the organization. Official records for the entire SS (including enlisted personnel) in-dicate that in 1938 some 51 percent of the SS membership was affiliated with the Evangelical church, 26 percent with the Catholic church, while 23 percent were listed as *gottgläubig* (God-believing). *Statistisches Jahrbuch der Schutzstaffel der NSDAP, 1938*, 99.

It made possible a broad recruitment basis for the SS among the
more religious strata of the middle class while at the same time creating better prospects for an antichurch struggle because the term
suggested a differentiation between a belief in a God and church
membership. The anti-Christian orientation of the SS could, in
other words, be justified as a struggle against the clergy as an institution rather than against the acceptable religiosity of human beings
in general. The roots of SS hostility were to be found in the political
misuse of Christianity by the church.[104]

In an effort to ascertain the religious upbringing of the men who
so willingly left the church and became God believers in black uniform, we have also constructed a variable measuring the "religious
background"[105] of individual SS leaders. The distribution of this
variable, especially in comparison to the religious distribution of the
general population,[106] indicates a preponderance of Protestants and,
conversely, a certain underrepresentation of Catholics in the SS-
Führerkorps.[107] As to the reasons why Catholics were more hesitant

[104] Wegner, *Politische Soldaten*, 53. See Reinhard Heydrich, *Wandlungen unseres Kampfes* (Berlin, 1936), 7. The same argument was used during the war as an
alibi vis-à-vis the public. See a letter by the Reichsführer-SS of 19.12.1942 to Frau
Schneider, reproduced by Ackermann, *Ideologe*, 258.

[105] The variable religious background refers to the denominational affiliation of
SS leaders before joining the SS. Once they had become formal members, the standard personnel records usually indicated that the individual was *Gottgläubig*. It was
therefore necessary to canvas a number of different sources on each individual, including membership applications, family trees, and birth certificates. In addition,
records were scrutinized for entries that had been altered. For example, some records
exhibit the religious denomination of an individual before he had left the church,
while others had the original entries crossed out and replaced by the term *Gottgläubig*. In the rare instance (less than 4 percent of the time) when no information was
available on the individual in question, the religious affiliation of the father was
recorded.

[106] *Statistisches Jahrbuch*, 1928, 18.

[107] This pattern remains when controls are made for regional origins. See Wegner, *Politische Soldaten*, 221 whose data also established a higher proportion of Protestants than would be expected from the standard prevailing in the population.
Jamin, *Zwischen den Klassen*, 90 confirms these findings for the SA leadership, where
67 percent of its members were Evangelical and only roughly 14 percent were
Catholic.

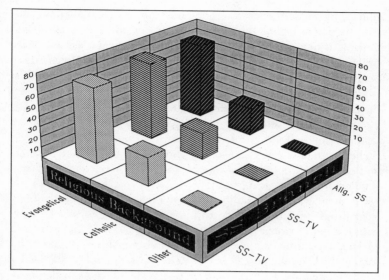

FIGURE 3.5   Relative Frequency Distribution of Religious Background. (For
Leaders of the Allgemeine SS, the SS-Verfügungstruppe, and the SS-Totenkopfverbände.)

to join the Black Order, we can only speculate. But one possible
explanation might lie in the different relationship between National
Socialism and Catholicism on the one hand and the relationship
between Protestants and Nazis on the other.[108]

In the conflict between Christianity and National Socialism
the antagonism toward Catholicism was always more pronounced
than that against Protestantism.[109] Despite the fact that it was impos-

[108] William Sheridan Allen, stressing the importance of religion as an explanatory
variable in electoral analysis, suggests that "Germans responded differently to Nazi
appeals according to their religion, at least in areas where one religion or the other
predominated strongly and in communities under 25,000." "Farewell to Class Analysis in the Rise of Nazism: Comment," *Central European History* 17 (1984): 57.

[109] See for example, Klaus Scholder, "Die evangelische Kirche in der Sicht
der Nationalsozialistischen Führung," *Vierteljahrshefte für Zeitgeschichte* 16 (1968):
15–35.

sible to reconcile the teachings of Christianity and National Socialism, the Hitler regime found Catholicism considerably more objec-
tionable if not more threatening than Protestantism "because of its
universal, supra-national character, its stronger institutional independence and spiritual authority."[110] "In the eyes of the Nazis a
trilogy had been set up—Rome, Judah and Moscow"[111] and after
the other two, Rome was considered the severest enemy of the nordic
Germanic Weltanschauung. Unlike Marxism, Jewry, and political
Catholicism—all three rated their own sections within the SS-
Sicherheitsdienst and Gestapo departments for countersurveillance
and counteraction—the Protestant church was never identified as a
fundamental ideological enemy.[112]

   If there was less hostility between Protestantism and National
Socialism it might have to do with the fact that the former brought
with it a more sympathetic understanding for the mission of the SS,
making recruitment among Protestants comparatively easier than
among the Catholic population.[113] Religious indifference that facilitated indifference to Nazi policies was probably more widespread
among Protestants than Catholics; thus they were able to ignore the

[110]Broszat, *The Hitler State*, 222. Heydrich characterized political clerical-
ism, next to Jewry, as the principal enemy of National Socialism. Heydrich, *Wandlungen*, 7.

[111]Robert d' Harcourt, "National Socialism and the Catholic Church in Germany," in Maurice Beaumont, John H.E. Fried, and Edmund Vermeil, eds., *The
Third Reich* (New York, 1955), 808.

[112]Broszat, *The Hitler State*, 222.

[113]Richard V. Pierard, "Why Did German Protestants Welcome Hitler?" *Fides
et Historia* 10 (1978): 8–29. Both Richard F. Hamilton, *Who Voted for Hitler?*
(Princeton, 1980) and Thomas Childers, *The Nazi Voter: The Social Foundations of
Fascism in Germany, 1919–1933* (Chapel Hill, 1983) agree that Catholics were less
likely to vote for the NSDAP than Protestants. Walter Dean Burnham, "Political
Immunization and Political Confessionalism: The United States and Weimar Germany," *Journal of Interdisciplinary History* 3 (1972): 29 argues that "if substantial
parts of the electorate have been active adherents of political churches, they tend
to be far more immunized against radical political contagion from a fascist 'radical middle' movement than are the middle classes who support traditional bourgeois—especially left-liberal—cadre parties." See also Karl-Wilhelm Dahm, "German Protestantism and Politics, 1918–1939," *Journal of Contemporary History* 3
(1968): 29–49.

religious implications of National Socialism and act as though they did not exist. If that was not enough, the Nazis could also count on an active following in the camp of Protestantism. The Glaubens-bewegung Deutscher Christen (Confessional Movement of German Christians), founded in 1932, provided, as it were, active support for the Nazis.[114] Finally, because of the historically close and cozy association between Protestantism and the state, Protestants in general enjoyed strong support in the conservative Prussian leadership of the Wehrmacht, judiciary, and civil service, which were capable of establishing limits to persecution simply by disapproval.[115]

In conclusion one might also note that because SS ideology was deeply anchored in antirational mysticism and since Himmler realized only too well the need for and effects of symbols and rituals, the SS—while fighting Christianity—not unwillingly slipped into the ban of religion.[116] Not satisfied with the open attack against institutionalized Christianity and the promotion of God believers, the Reichsführer-SS attempted to create his own spiritual substitute. The latter amounted to an ersatz religion whose main elements included the "germanization" of German history,[117] a form of ancestor worship, a general dislike for the concept of a life hereafter,[118] and

[114] Jonathon R. Wright, "The German Protestant Church and the Nazi Party in the Period of Seizure of Power, 1932–33," *Studies in Church History* 14 (1977): 393–418. Wright (397) maintains that "rank and file church members were predisposed to welcome the Third Reich and this attitude was seen to be quite consistent with their religious beliefs." For the *Glaubensbewegung* see especially 403–412. Also of interest on the same subject is Günther von Norden, "Die Stellung der evangelischen Kirche zum Nationalsozialismus, 1930–1933," in Gotthard Jasper, ed., *Von Weimar zu Hitler, 1930–1933* (Cologne, 1968).

[115] Broszat, *The Hitler State*, 283, 285, 294.

[116] Wegner, *Politische Soldaten*, 52; Ackermann, *Ideologe*, 253; the introduction by John M. Steiner, "Über das Glaubensbekenntnis der SS," in J. Hutter, R. Meyers, and D. Papenfuss, eds., *Tradition und Neubeginn* (Cologne, 1975), 317. For the social function of cults under National Socialism in general see K. Vondung, *Magie und Manipulation* (Göttingen, 1971), 193; D. J. Diephouse, "The German 'Catastrophe' Revisited: Civil Religion in the Third Reich," *Fides et Historica* 7 (1975): 54–74.

[117] Ackermann, *Ideologe*, 53–64.

[118] Ackermann, *Ideologe*, 64–71. See also "Verwirrung im Blut," II. "Die artfremde Ewigkeit," *Das Schwarze Korps* 22 June 1939, 11–12.

the ardent veneration of Adolf Hitler as the völkische Messiah and tool of destiny.[119]

Led by a man who talked publicly about executing the pope,[120] the SS more than any other formation of the Third Reich tried to replace traditional Christianity with a neo-paganism, which was but an improvised adjunct to National Socialist ideology in the "spiritual" sphere. With the local SS-Führer taking the place of traditional clergy, this neo-paganism centered chiefly on "de-Christianizing the rituals surrounding birth, marriage, and death, and on reconverting Christmas into a pagan solstice festival."[121] Nevertheless, the trappings of this ersatz religion never replaced the old customs, and the SS policy of enmity toward Christianity in general and the established churches in particular was never quite successful.[122] Although professional disadvantages could be incurred for not being listed as a God believer,[123] nominal church membership was tolerated. During the war it was even possible to fight in the ranks of the Waffen-SS and to receive the sacraments of one's church.[124]

[119] Ackerman, *Ideologe*, 71–81; Kersten, *Totenkopf*, 148–156.

[120] Ernst Röhm, *Die Geschichte eines Hochverräters* (Munich, 1933), 275.

[121] Grünberger, *The 12-Year Reich*, 44–445.

[122] Höhne, *Order of the Death's Head*, 156–157.

[123] Ackermann, 83. The promotion to the rank of Führer frequently depended upon whether or not the candidate had left the church, Steiner, *Power Politics*, 118. An internal memorandum, dated 14.6.1941, spelled out the minimum qualifications necessary to hold the position of Chef des Hauptamtes SS-Gericht. There were only two principal conditions: the individual must have a military *Ausbildung* and should hold the rank of a Waffen-SS general, and he must not belong to any church. The latter qualification was necessary to avoid any conflict of interest in judgments concerning punishable offenses that touched upon religious matters. This memo came from the Chief and was sent to Himmler (T–175/123/648724).

[124] Steiner, *Power Politics*, 114.

4

Elite Structure: Achieved Attributes

ADOLF HITLER, along with most of his disciples and supporters, professed and indeed believed that National Socialism was a revolutionary movement. Ostensibly the Third Reich would usher in "a new social order in which class conflict and ideological cleavages would disappear and be replaced by a sense of national solidarity and by a commitment on the part of every individual to put the interests of the nation before self (Gemeinutz vor Eigenutz)."[1] The abstraction employed by National Socialism to portray its social model was the backward ideal of a racial community, or Volksgemeinschaft, where social hierarchy was determined by function, not status. The antimodern aspects of this ideal must be understood, however, as more than simply the resurrection of premodern conditions or as a revolution from above, because National Socialism was an attempt to find a *Sonderweg*. Such a special path would afford an escape from the problems of modernity into a utopia which would avoid the crises and conflicts that were inherent in parliamentary-democratic, capitalist society on the one hand, and the fears and aggressions engendered by the reality of a socialist revolution on the other. Since this Sonderweg was to take place within the framework of capitalistic and industrialized development, the split personality of the reality we call National Socialism was characterized by partially modern and partially antimodern manifestations.[2]

---

[1] Noakes and Pridham, eds., *Nazism*, 2: 376.
[2] Horst Matzerath and Heinrich Volkmann, "Modernisierungstheorie und Na-

These claims and visions notwithstanding, historians of National
Socialist Germany have been at odds over what this revolution exactly entailed.[3] While some assert that the Nazi seizure of power
represented not only a real break with the past but should in reality
be classified as a revolution,[4] others contend that Nazi rule embodied
the unwitting and unwilling implementation of a social modernization that opened the way to a modern liberal-bourgeois society that
found its realization in postwar West Germany.[5] But most scholars

tionalsozialismus," in Jürgen Kocka, ed., Geschichte und Gesellschaft, Sonderheft 3:
Theorien in der Praxis des Historikers (Göttingen, 1977), 99.
   [3] For a discussion of of the concept of revolution in relation to fascism see Eugene
Weber, "Revolution?" Counterrevolution? What Revolution?" in Walter Laqueur,
ed., Fascism: A Reader's Guide: Analyses, Interpretations, Bibliography (Berkeley,
1976), 435–467.
   [4] Horst Möller, "Die nationalsozialistische Machtergreifung: Konterrevolution
oder Revolution?" Vierteljahrshefte für Zeitgeschichte 31 (1983): 47 suggests that a
revolution need neither be associated with fundamental changes in social structure
nor qualify a priori as a progressive historical event. See also Karl Dietrich Bracher,
"Tradition und Revolution im Nationalsozialismus," in his Zeitgeschichtliche Kontroversen: Um Faschismus, Totalitarismus, Demokratie (Munich, 1976), 66–70.
   [5] Although this so-called social revolution represented an admittedly complex
process, it appears to be intimately connected to changes in social stratification as a
consequence of the weakening of class cohesion, the leveling of social strata, and the
enforcement of more egalitarian social behavior as Volksgenossen. Dahrendorf, Society, 402–418.
   Like Dahrendorf, Schoenbaum, Hitler's Social Revolution, maintains that Nazism did produce a social revolution whose substance was modernity. He argued that
"in the Third Reich, relative approximation of class and status came to an end" (292),
amounting to unprecedented social mobility and, in terms of status, to the "triumph
of egalitarianism" (284–285). This argument was picked up by Henry A. Turner,
"Fascism and Modernization," World Politics 24 (1972): 558. He basically accepts
National Socialist intentions to destroy modern society through a successful war,
which was fought with modern means. The Nazis "practiced modernization inadver-
tently in order to pursue their fundamentally antimodern aims." The usefulness and
applicability of modernization theories for historians is evaluated by Hans-Ulrich
Wehler, Modernisierungstheorie und Geschichte (Göttingen, 1975). For an application of modernization models to German development see Hartmut Kaelble et al.,
Probleme der Modernisierung in Deutschland: Sozialhistorische Studien zum 19. und
20. Jahrhundert (Opladen, 1978). Thomas Nipperdey, "Probleme der Modernisierung in Deutschland," Saeculum 30 (1979): 292–303 maintains that although
National Socialism never wanted equality or abolishment of traditional class structure, the unintended outcome was accelerated equalization and leveling of German
society.

have been hesitant at best to identify the Nazi *Machtergreifung* and the subsequent creation of the Third Reich as a revolution or force of modernization. The principal objection often voiced by those who resist the equation is that the regime only slightly changed the substance of the social structure.[6] Perhaps equally important, they also protest that the term "revolution" is ordinarily reserved for events and developments of a "progressive nature," something of which National Socialism can hardly be accused. Not surprisingly, the same historians regard the creation of the Third Reich as nothing more than the establishment of an essentially socially reactionary or counterrevolutionary regime.[7]

The diversity of opinions reflects, of course, the problematic nature of the subject itself and the fact that the debate itself is often conducted in confused terms. To begin with, the term "social revolution" defies any consensual definition because personal and ideological predilections of individual historians inevitably come into play. When speaking of modernization scholars invariably do not distinguish between political, social, or economic modernization and consequently fail to demarcate disparate indexes of change. Further, even more acute problems are encountered when one tries to measure significant societal change effected by a regime which lasted only twelve out of its projected one thousand years, six of which were

---

[6] For the failure or partial success of Nazi modernization see Matzerath and Volkmann, "Modernisierungstheorie und Nationalsozialismus," 95–98. See also Kershaw, *Problems and Perspectives*, 146 who concludes: "It seems clear, then, that Nazism did not come remotely near producing a 'social revolution' in Germany during the period of the Third Reich—whether one of 'objective' or of 'interpreted' reality." Kater, *The Nazi Party*, 238, likewise suggests that "the Nazi revolution remained unfinished." Heinrich A. Winkler, "Vom Mythos der Volksgemeinschaft," *Archiv für Sozialgeschichte* 17 (1977): 484–490 echos these sentiments by judging, "Die Volksgemeinschaft blieb ein Mythos" (489). A survey on the recent research in the field by Richard Bessel, "Living with the Nazis: Some Recent Writing on the Social History of the Third Reich," *European History Quarterly* 14 (1984): 211–220 concurs with the assessments that National Socialism did not affect a social revolution.

[7] Because Marxists usually restrict their analyses of social change to transformations in the structure of capitalism and the state of the class struggle, they reject bourgeois modernization theories. See Gerhard Lozek and Rolf Richter, "Zur Auseinandersetzung mit vorherrschenden bürgerlichen Faschismustheorien," in Kurt Gossweiler and Dietrich Eichholz, eds., *Faschismusforschung. Positionen, Probleme, Polemik* (Berlin, 1980), 417–451.

war years. Besides, how do we discriminate between transmutations brought about directly and deliberately by the Nazis and those that were indirect or unintentional changes? If there was measurable change, should it be assessed and compared to what in our understanding the Nazis tried to do? Or do we compare changes occurring during the Third Reich to those of other societies, to some counterfactual model that assumes National Socialism never did exist, or simply to some concept of ideal development?[8] One might also ask, as has Charles S. Maier, "what the plausible trajectory of the development would have been had the respective regimes remained nonauthoritarian."[9]

In the final analysis, however, the polycratic nature of Nazi rule and system of government virtually negates efforts to gauge the effects of modernization in their economic and social totality. The Third Reich was not a closed system, but was characterized by a multiplicity of frequently contradictory developments and autonomous power structures.[10] Thus using an overarching modernization concept to measure changes runs the very real danger of ignoring the historical realities of National Socialism. The danger does not come from the application of modernization theory per se, but from the diffuse nature and breadth of the theory. What one must do is concentrate on partial aspects of National Socialist structures. Indeed, what is needed is a more differentiated analysis, one that focuses on specific entities of the regime in order to analyze quantitatively the dependence of changing social processes on National Socialist political measures.[11]

NATIONAL SOCIALISM AND SOCIAL MOBILITY

While it is fair to state that Adolf Hitler never promised—nor did his supporters, or anybody else, expect—a "revolution in the form of a sudden major social upheaval leading to a drastic redistri-

---

[8] Kershaw, *Problems and Perspectives*, 130–131; Matzerath and Volkmann, "Modernisierungstheorie und Nationalsozialismus," 109.

[9] Charles S. Maier, *In Search of Stability: Explorations in Historical Political Economy* (New York, 1987), 88.

[10] Peter Hüttenberger, "Nationalsozialistische Polykratie," 417–442.

[11] Matzerath and Volkmann, "Modernisierungstheorie und Nationalsozialismus," 106.

bution of political, economic and social power between existing social classes," it is equally plausible to suggest that the Nazis aimed to go beyond a mere reorganization of political power.[12] And while it is true that the Nazis sought their model in the past—not a historical past, but a mythical past embracing cults of blood, soil, and sword—there is no denying that part and parcel of the Nazi concept of the Volksgemeinschaft[13] was also a disdain for and aversion to the rigid immobility of traditional social hierarchies, coupled with the resolve to conquer the antiquated and restrictive elite criteria of inherited birthright and social rank. Despite the obvious and often noted "archaic and atavistic"[14] ingredients of Nazi ideology and the alleged backward-looking, reactionary character of Nazism's mass support, there can be detected in Hitler's movement an undeniably modern appeal proffering social mobility.[15] Irrespective of the explanation of Nazism that is championed, "the authenticity of the revolutionary impulse is undeniable."[16]

National Socialism, in essence, envisaged a new type of community, a community that offered upward social mobility and advancement through merit and *Leistung* (achievement) and appealed to a broad spectrum of the population.[17] "One of the keys to the

[12] Noakes, "Nazism and Revolution," 75.

[13] John Hiden and John Farquharson, *Explaining Hitler's Germany: Historians and the Third Reich* (London, 1983), 86 suggest that the concept of the people's community must be taken more seriously than it sometimes has been.

[14] Kershaw, *Problems and Perspectives*, 147.

[15] Kershaw, *Problems and Perspectives*, 134, 147. Noakes, "Nazism and Revolution," 85 states that the concept of careers open to talent had been an article of faith since the very earliest days, reflecting a resentment at the traditional barriers of upward mobility posed by birth, property, and education. For modern aspects of Nazism see also Martin Broszat, "Zur Struktur der NS-Massenbewegung," *Vierteljahrshefte für Zeitgeschichte* 31 (1983): 52–76 and Timothy W. Mason, "Zur Entstehung des Gesetzes zur Ordnung der nationalen Arbeit, vom 20. Januar 1934: Ein Versuch über das Verhältnis 'archaischer' und 'moderner' Momente in der neusten deutschen Geschichte," in Hans Mommsen et al., eds., *Industrielles System und politische Entwicklung in der Weimarer Republik* (Düsseldorf, 1974), 322–351.

[16] Leonard Krieger, "Nazism: Highway or Byway?" *Central European History* 11 (March 1978): 14.

[17] Hiden and Farquharson, *Explaining Hitler's Germany*, 86, 109; George L. Mosse, "The Genesis of Fascism," in Nathanael Greene, ed., *Fascism: An Anthology* (Arlington Heights, IL., 1968), 9. The latter was originally published in the *Journal of Contemporary History* 1 (1966): 14–65.

successes of the Nazis in gaining electoral support before 1933 and in consolidating the regime afterward was their ability to project a credible image of a deep commitment to democracy of personnel selection."[18] Because National Socialism sought and indeed delivered increased social opportunity, the Nazis, it has been argued, "must be placed within a long European tradition of struggle by the lower orders against the restraints imposed upon them by their 'betters.' "[19]

The promise, and potential realization, of upward social mobility[20] then is a nexus, indeed, a pivotal concept, between social revolution and the establishment of a people's community. If there is any substance to Hitler's utterances that the task of a *Volksstaat* was "not to preserve the decisive influence of an existing social class, but . . . to pick out from the sum of all fellow citizens the most able" and "that the Reich opened the way for every qualified individual—whatever his origin,"[21] the concept of social mobility explains to a very large extent the appeal of National Socialism. It explains why the NSDAP was a broad movement compared to con-

---

[18] Struve, *Elites*, 425.

[19] William J. Jannen, "National Socialists and Social Mobility," *Journal of Social History* 9 (1975–76): 339–340. For a dissenting view see Mason, *Sozialpolitik im Dritten Reich*, 274.

[20] Social mobility in the twentieth century has been for the most part the scholarly preserve of nonhistorians. However, an excellent introduction to the subject by a historian is given in Hartmut Kaelble, *Historical Research on Social Mobility. Western Europe and the USA in the Nineteenth and Twentieth Centuries* (New York, 1981). In "Social Mobility in Germany, 1900–1960," *Journal of Modern History* 50 (1978): 439–461, Kaelble maintains that the social origins of German university students did not change in favor of more open recruitment between 1900 and 1960 (458). The Nazis, in other words, did not introduce any effective educational reforms that might have changed these long-term trends. On the contrary, by cutting educational expenditures and reducing university enrollments, they even reduced opportunities (450). For a survey of the period up to the First World War see the author's "Sozialer Aufstieg in Deutschland, 1850–1914," *Vierteljahrschrift für Sozial- und Wirtschaftsgeschichte* 60 (1973): 41–71, and more recently, *Historical research on Social Mobility*. A theoretical approach to the subject of social mobility is provided by Franklin Mendels, "Social Mobility and Phases of Industrialization," *Journal of Interdisciplinary History* 7 (1976): 193–216. An early account is Josef Nothass, "Sozialer Aufstieg und Abstieg im deutschen Volk," *Kölner Vierteljahrshefte für Soziologie* 9 (1930/31): 61–81.

[21] Adolf Hitler, *Mein Kampf* (New York, 1941), 640–641.

temporary parties, able to win support from all sectors of the population to such a degree that it could profess to represent the whole community as a bona fide *Volkspartei*, and why fascism in the final analysis was not the expression of a specific social class, but found supporters and adversaries among all classes.[22] It answers the questions of why "the NSDAP always had a respectable number of workers in its ranks,"[23] why millions of unorganized manual workers gave their vote to a party that set out to destroy the gains of the German working class,[24] and why the slogan of Volksgemeinschaft was one of the most effective elements of Nazi propaganda,[25] striking a responsive chord with the disillusioned segments of society whose demands for a real community and the abolition of a class-oriented society articulated genuine democratic and human needs.[26] Finally, the promise of upward social mobility may well have played a significant role in the consent to Nazi rule, a consent that was as important to the stability of the regime as was fear and terror.

If the concept of the people's community with its emphasis on social mobility was more than simple election rhetoric or a cosmetic veneer of National Socialist ideology, the social or substantive content of the Nazi revolution should be readily discernible in the recruitment practices of German elites. In the event that the Nazis were truly committed to the idea of an open elite they, in the aftermath of the seizure of power, should have begun to practice something akin to a democracy in personnel selection. As it turned out they probably did no such thing, and traditional elites continued to

---

[22] Hiden and Farquharson, *Explaining Hitler's Germany*, 91.

[23] Mason, *Sozialpolitik im Dritten Reich*, 56, 62.

[24] The role workers played in the success of National Socialist electoral politics is delineated by Jürgen W. Falter, "Warum die deutschen Arbeiter während des Dritten Reiches zu Hitler standen: Einige Anmerkungen zu Günther Mais Beitrag über die Unterstützung des nationalsozialistischen Herrschaftssystems durch Arbeiter," *Geschichte und Gesellschaft* 13 (1987): 217–231 and Jürgen W. Falter and D. Hänisch, "Die Anfälligkeit von Arbeitern gegenüber der NSDAP, 1928–1933," *Archiv für Sozialgeschichte* 26 (1986): 179–216.

[25] See Gunther Mai, "Worum steht der deutsche Arbeiter zu Hitler? Zur Rolle der Deutschen Arbeitsfront im Herrschaftssystem des Dritten Reiches," *Geschichte und Gesellschaft* 12 (1986): 21–34.

[26] Reinhard Kühnl, *Formen bürgerlicher Herrschaft: Liberalismus—Faschismus* (Hamburg, 1971), 86 and Broszat, "Struktur der NS-Massenbewegung," 66.

recruit in the old ways, especially from the educated strata of society. Because Hitler was only too aware that, initially at least, he needed the expertise and skills of existing elites, he was consequently unwilling to upset the status quo by introducing changes in the way elites acquired their recruits. The predictable outcome of this attitude was that in the Third Reich

> the most important factor governing the recruitment into the officer corps, the higher ranks of the civil service, and the professions continued to be the requirement that candidates had to be in possession of the school-leaving certificate (the *Abitur*) and, in the case of the civil service and the professions, of a university degree as well. . . . Similarly, industry, big business, and the banks continued to recruit their executives from the same social strata as before.[27]

What was true of traditional elites, however, did not necessarily hold for the new elites of Brown Germany, for if the regime introduced changes into the structure of elites it took place within the new organizations of the party.[28] A recent study supports the proposition that the National Socialist Machtergreifung entailed a change in leadership that was much more radical than the one following the events of 1918–19. "The National Socialist revolution," according to its author, "continued the revolution of 1918–19 with incomparable intensity and, as paradoxical as it may sound, effected a social democratization of leadership groups, forever replacing the old power elites of the empire."[29] An examination of the social makeup of Nazi Gauleiter supports this general thesis by concluding that "in

---

[27] Noakes, "Nazism and Revolution," 82–83. It has been argued that Nazi attempts to train new elites in NAPOLAS and Ordensburgen and Adolf Hitler schools proved largely ineffective; the single largest obstacle to upward mobility—educational qualifications—remained. See Dietrich Orlow, "Die Adolf Hitler Schulen," *Vierteljahrshefte für Zeitgeschichte* 13 (1963): 272–284; Horst Uberhorst, ed., *Elite für die Diktatur: Die nationalpolitischen Erziehungsanstalten 1933 bis 1945; Ein Dokumentarbericht* (Düsseldorf, 1969); Harald Scholtz, "Die NS-Ordensburgen," *Vierteljahrshefte für Zeitgeschichte* 15 (1967): 269–298; and by the same author, *Nationalsozialistische Ausleseschulen: Internatschulen als Herrschaftsmittel des Führerstaates* (Göttingen, 1973).

[28] Noakes, "Nazism and Revolution," 83, 84.

[29] Möller, "Konterrevolution oder Revolution?" 47, 50.

its internal affairs, the NSDAP practiced an egalitarianism that was extraordinary by the standards of our time, and claimed to foreshadow the rule of merit that would apply universally in a rejuvenated Germany."[30]

In an effort to test empirically the notion of "openness" of National Socialist elites and the closely related subject of fostering social mobility, we have analyzed three variables which serve as proxy indicators of class standings of the prewar SS-Führerkorps. These highly interrelated variables are "father's occupation," the "Führer's learned occupation," and the "Führer's educational attainment." The distributions of these variables and comparable distributions for members of the NSDAP and the general population are summarized in Table 4.1. By establishing with as much precision as possible the social base of the prewar SS leadership, we hope to answer one principal question: what proportion of SS leaders came from any given segment of society?[31] Put differently, do the social origins of Himmler's recruits justify the characterization of SS policies as emphasizing the selection of the able for high posts regardless of social position, as policies that opened up new possibilities for the lower classes while eschewing the privileges of the upper classes? Indeed, was SS-Obergruppenführer Mathias Kleinheißterkamp correct when he remarked, "This is how it is in the SS, a coachman is Untersturmführer (Second Lieutenant) while an educated person is Scharführer (Sergeant)."[32]

[30] Ronald Rogowski, "The Gauleiter and the Social Origins of Fascism," *Comparative Studies in Society and History* 19 (1977): 427.

[31] The scope of our analysis is limited, therefore, to the attributes, circumstances, and motives of the individuals from each social class who decided to join the SS. Though frequently overlooked, the reason for this limitation is obvious. There is the temptation to make generalizations about an entire class based on the findings on the social makeup of a particular organization when in fact only a proportion of a given class belonged to the organization in question. Put simply, because a particular fraction of the SS membership was recruited from a certain section of society does not mean that the entire class responded en bloc. Should we find, for instance, that some 30 percent of the SS leadership was recruited from the upper stratum of German bourgeois society, this does not imply that 30 percent of the entire upper class joined the SS, but only a minute minority. This point has been made by Richard F. Hamilton, "Reply to Commentators," *Central European History* 27 (1984): 73.

[32] Berlin Document Center, Personnel File of Mathias Kleinheissterkamp.

OCCUPATIONAL STRUCTURE

If there exists any consensus regarding the mass following of fascism in general and National Socialism in particular, it pertains to the view that the swelling of fascist ranks cannot for the most part be attributed to successful recruitment from the working class. It is generally held that after the Nazis' initial attempts to penetrate the socialist and organized working class, workers were essentially immune to the siren call of fascism.[33] There have, of course, been exceptions to this general outlook, although they have generally not been well received.[34] A recent example of this is Conan J. Fischer's assessment that the SA was largely of working-class origin, serving as an instrument for the penetration of the working class.[35] In the words of the author, "The SA's ordinary membership was largely working class during the early 1930s, albeit with a sizable lower middle class minority," and "the expanding SA maintained and possibly even enhanced its working class character after Hitler's accession to power."[36]

[33] Kater, *Nazi Party*, 20; Kurt Gossweiler, "Faschismus und Arbeiterklasse," in Dietrich Eichholtz und Kurt Gossweiler, eds., *Faschismus—Forschung: Positionen, Probleme, Polemik* (Berlin, 1980), 123. On the attempts of the DAP/NSDAP to win workers, see Max H. Kele, *Nazis and Workers: National Socialist Appeals to German Labor, 1919–1933* (Chapel Hill, 1972), 31–66; Geiger, *Die soziale Schichtung*, 110; Dietrich Orlow, *The History of the Nazi Party: 1919–1933* (Pittsburgh, 1969), 19; Theodore Abel, *Why Hitler Came to Power*, 170.

[34] Kele, *Nazis and Workers*, 215 has maintained that the NSDAP always had a respectable number of workers in its ranks; by 1932–33 workers alone constituted about one-third of the membership. For a criticism of this work see H. Katz, "Arbeiter, Mittelklasse, und die NSDAP," *Internationale wissenschaftliche Korrespondenz zur Geschichte der deutschen Arbeiterbewegung* 10 (1974): 300–304. Other scholars who have pointed to working-class components within the NSDAP include Gordon, *Hitler and the Beer Hall Putsch*, 74–76 who, on the basis of eyewitness reports, deduced that the Nazis before 1924 drew substantial support from the ranks of the proletariat, and Nyormarkay, *Charisma and Factionalism*, 58 who judged that "the DAP at its inception . . . was composed of people of working class origins."

[35] Fischer, "Occupational Background," 131–59, esp. 139, 152. For a methodological criticism of Fischer's thesis see Richard Bessel and Mathilde Jamin, "Nazis, Workers, and the Use of Quantitative Evidence," *Social History* 4 (1979): 111–116.

[36] Fischer, *Stormtroopers*, 35–36. Peter Stachura, *Nazi Youth in the Weimar Republic* (Santa Barbara and Oxford, 1975), 58–62 suggests that the Hitler Youth was characterized by strong working-class ties; 65 to 70 percent of its membership came from the working class.

Still, that the Nazis made certain inroads among the nonorganized working class after 1930 can by now be regarded as equally well established as the fact that workers were always underrepresented in the party vis-à-vis the general population.[37] While this obviously means that the working class could not have served as the principal recruiting ground for National Socialism, it has never been adequately explained why the NSDAP should have had a sizable proportion of workers in its ranks in the first place[38] or why the NSDAP attracted more workers than any other contemporary non-Marxist party.[39]

The first notable feature of our data on both paternal occupation and the occupation cited by each Führer is the relatively high proportion of individuals who can be classified as manual workers.[40] To be more precise, if we designate the sum of the first three categories in Table 4.1 as the lower class or working class, we find that roughly one-quarter of the SS elite was recruited from this segment of society. This finding contradicts much conventional wisdom as exemplified by the view of Timothy Mason, who declared: "One of the grandest claims of the Nazi leadership was to have created a national community in which talent and not social background determined a

[37] Kater, *Nazi Party*, 35, 154–155. The only local study on the NSDAP that suggests that workers were overrepresented in the party is Stokes, "NSDAP in Eutin," 1–32.

[38] Ernst Nolte, "The Problem of Fascism in Recent Scholarship," in Henry A. Turner, ed., *Reappraisals of Fascism* (New York, 1975), 29. Data presented by Kater, *Nazi Party*, 252–253, table 7 establishes clearly that workers constituted approximately between 30 and 40 percent of party joiners during the period 1933 to 1939. See also Detlef Mühlberger, "The Sociology of the NSDAP: The Question of Working Class Membership," *Journal of Contemporary History* 15 (1980): 473–511.

[39] Hiden and Farquharson, *Explaining Hitler's Germany*, 90.

[40] This contrasts greatly with the findings of Wegner, *Politische Soldaten*, 225, table 17 who found a 9.8 percent combination of *Arbeiter* and *Angestellte* among the SS leadership. To put these findings into perspective, Wegner collected data only on the upper ranks of the SS-Führerkorps. Thus, he collected data on all Führer from the rank of Standartenführer and upward, and sampled approximately one-fourth of the Sturmbannführer and Obersturmbannführer who belonged to the field units of the Waffen-SS (see 208). An even lower estimate of working-class origins for SS leaders is cited by Boehnert, "Sociography." Although tables 6.1 and 6.3 show 6.3 percent under the rubric "skilled workers," Boehnert (165) concludes that only 1.1 percent of the sampled officers belonged to the *Arbeiterschicht*.

TABLE 4.1

Occupational Structure of the SS Leadership, Fathers of SS Leaders, the Membership of the NSDAP, the Leadership of the SA, and the German Population, Relative Frequency Distribution

Occupational Groups	SS-Führer in 1938			Fathers			SA-Führer in 1935	NSDAP in 1933	NSDAP in 1938	Population in 1933
	SS-TV	SS-VT	Allg. SS	SS-TV	SS-VT	Allg. SS				
Unskilled Workers	2.6	1.1	4.2	7.4	5.5	7.9	7.2	12.6	13.7	37.2
Skilled Workers	22.6	16.8	21.7	19.8	17.3	18.8	5.7	18.1	19.5	17.3
Military: Enlisted	0.5	3.6	0.8	0.3	0.2	0.0	0.4	—[b]	—	—
LOWER CLASS	25.7	21.5	26.7	27.5	23.0	26.7	13.3	30.7	33.2	54.5
Independent Craftsmen	0.3	0.1	0.1	5.8	5.0	3.5	2.6	8.9	9.1	9.6
Farmers	5.0	4.3	7.6	6.3	6.8	8.7	6.8	8.9	8.1	7.7
Small Businessmen	0.3	1.4	0.5	6.0	6.6	7.6	10.5	12.8	5.1	6.0
Salaried Employees	31.1	30.2	30.8	17.6	20.1	19.9	40.5	10.6	21.8	12.4
Civil Servants	2.4	4.4	3.6	18.4	19.8	13.4	10.3	11.7	10.3	5.2
Military: NCO	2.1	1.7	0.1	1.1	0.5	0.3	1.3	—	—	—
Nonacademic Professionals	—	—	—	—	—	—	—	4.2	3.4	1.8
LOWER MIDDLE CLASS	41.2	42.1	42.7	55.2	58.8	53.4	72.0	57.1	57.8	42.7

Managers	0.8	0.3	1.6	2.5	1.5	1.4	3.8	2.3	1.7	0.5
Higher Civil Servants	1.0	1.1	2.1	6.0	7.2	5.9	3.7	2.8	0.0	0.5
Professionals	12.6	12.5	19.9	3.0	4.6	8.5	1.8	3.0	2.6	1.0
Students	17.4	16.3	1.9	—	—	—	—	1.7	4.3	0.5
Entrepreneurs	0.0	0.0	0.0	2.2	2.0	3.2	2.5	2.4	0.4	0.3
Military: Officers	1.3	6.2	5.1	3.6	2.9	0.9	0.5	—	—	—
UPPER MIDDLE CLASS	33.1	36.4	30.6	17.3	18.2	19.9	12.3	12.2	9.0	2.8
Total	100.0	100.0	100.0	100.0	100.0	100.0	97.6[a]	100.0	100.0	100.0
N of Cases	380	657	858	364	586	656	951	3,316	234	27,047,899

SOURCES: (1) Percentages of occupations and classes of gainfully employed German population (except in the case of students) and percentages of NSDAP joiners in the Reich are calculated on the basis of data in Michael H. Kater, *The Nazi Party: A Social Profile of Members and Leaders, 1919–1945* (Cambridge, MA: Harvard University Press, 1983), 152, 241; (2) Percentages of occupations and classes for SA-Führer are based on "standardized" occupations for men who joined the SA between 1925 and 1933, as calculated by Mathilde Jamin, *Zwischen den Klassen: Zur Sozialstruktur der SA-Führerschaft* (Wuppertal, 1984), 194–95.

[a] This column does not add up to 100% because one of Jamin's categories, *mithelfende Familienangehörige* (2.3%), was not included in this table.

[b] In cases marked by a dash (—), the figures for this particular category could not be ascertained. However, the particular subgroup with the exception noted above, has always been included as the total of another.

man's career; but on the question of advancement from within the working class there is no evidence upon which generalizations can be based."[41]

Admittedly, men of working-class background were underrepresented vis-à-vis the general population,[42] but there is no escaping the conclusion that the SS and its leadership corps were extraordinarily successful in attracting support from workers. No traditional German elite could boast such representation from a class whose occupational and social status was equally low in both Imperial and Weimar Germany. It remains a remarkable accomplishment to have recruited a significant number of workers into the leadership of the most notorious and antisocialist elite formation of the Third Reich.

Because the working class did not provide a mass basis, conventional wisdom holds that it was the lower middle class that figured as the principal font of fascism, including the German variety. According to this view the German lower middle class, threatened by capitalism and organized labor during a period of severe economic crisis and social luxation, provided the necessary votes for the NSDAP, swelled the ranks of the party membership, and furnished the requisite leadership and functionaries.[43] Although current scholarship often concedes that the NSDAP's supporters were socially more di-

[41]Timothy W. Mason, "Labor in the Third Reich, 1933–1939," *Past and Present* 33 (1966): 112.

[42]Depending on the definition, the proportion of workers hovered around 46 to 50 percent of the total population in the 1920s and 1930s. See, for example, *Statistisches Jahrbuch für das deutsche Reich* (Berlin, 1935), 17 where the proportion of workers in the population (excluding military) is cited as 46 and 46.3 percent in 1925 and 1933 respectively. Hardach, "Klassen und Schichten," 518 cites the proportion of workers as 55, 49, and 49 percent in 1907, 1925, and 1939 respectively. Bolte, "Berufsstruktur," 43 suggests that the proportion of male workers in the 1925, 1933, and 1939 population was 53.9, 55.3, and 53.4. respectively.

[43]Stanley G. Payne, *Fascism: Comparison and Definition* (Madison, 1980), 181 contends that the "middle class thesis" was first suggested by Luigi Salvatorelli in his *Nazionalfascismo* (Turin, 1923). The first German proponent of this thesis probably was Theodor Geiger, "Panik im Mittelstand," *Die Arbeit* 7 (1930), 637, and by the same author, *Die soziale Schichtung*, 117–122. This argument received further impetus in the postwar era through Seymour M. Lipset, "Fascism—Left, Right, and Center," in *Political Man* (London, 1960), esp. chap. 5, who defined fascism as "the radicalism of the center." For a modifications of this thesis, see Heinrich A. Winkler, "Mittelstandsbewegung oder Volkspartei? Zur sozialen Basis der NSDAP," in W. Schiederer, ed., *Faschismus als soziale Bewegung* (Hamburg, 1976), pp. 97–118,

verse than has been commonly held[44]—especially as the result of a
considerable upper middle class presence[45]—there is still agreement
on the basic conclusion that the important nucleus of the party's
constituency was recruited predominately from components of the
lower middle class.[46] The significance of this class in the success of
National Socialism is well stated by Michael H. Kater:

> The historically important role that representatives of the lower middle
> class played in the foundation of the party, their continued numerical
> strength in it, and the specific value system with which they imbued it
> mark this class as the single most important influence in the development
> of the NSDAP from 1919 to 1945. Judged from the point of view of party
> membership (both rank and file and leadership corps), the National So-
> cialist movement was indeed a preeminently lower middle class phe-
> nomenon. . . . Not only is there no "need to abandon the middle-class
> thesis of Nazism," as has most recently been urged, but it would be folly
> to do so.[47]

---

and by the same author, "Extremismus der Mitte? Sozialgeschichtliche Aspekte der
nationalsozialistischen Machtergreifung," *Vierteljahrshefte für Zeitgeschichte* 20 (1972):
175–191. Winkler argues that National Socialism came to power only with the support of the traditional Right, whose support Hitler acquired because the latter ap-
proved of his attacks against the Left. Although they have never judged the class
character of fascism by the social composition of its mass following but instead on the
basis of the class content of its policies, Marxist scholars also point to the middle class
as the mass basis for fascist movements. See for example Wolfgang Ruge, "Monopolbourgeoisie, faschistische Massenbasis, und NS-Programmatik in Deutschland vor
1933" in Dietrich Eichholtz and Kurt Gossweiler, eds., *Faschismus—Forschung: Positionen, Probleme, Polemik* (Berlin, 1980), 125–155. Also of interest are Jakub Banaszkiewicz, "German Fascism and People of the Social Fringe," *Polish Western Affairs*
8 (1967): 251–288 and Evelyn Posisil, "Diskussionsbeitrag: Die Massenbasis des Faschismus," *Jenaer Beitrag für Parteiengeschichte* 31 (1969): 31–40.

[44]Thomas Childers, "National Socialism and the New Middle Class," in Reinhard Mann, ed., *Die Nationalsozialisten. Analysen faschistischer Bewegungen* (Stuttgart, 1980), 19 characterizes the NSDAP as "a catch-all party of middle class protest"
and "party of bourgeois integration."

[45]See Hamilton, *Who Voted for Hitler?*, 393 and Kater, *Nazi Party*, 236.

[46]Childers, *The Nazi Voter*, 262–269 and Thomas Childers, "Who Indeed, Did
Vote for Hitler?" *Central European History* 17 (1984): 49–50. While Kater, *Nazi
Party*, 19–71, 234–239 emphasizes the importance of the lower middle class, his
data also point to a heavy overrepresentation of Germany's elite within the membership of the party. On this see esp. 97–108.

[47]Kater, *Nazi Party*, 236. The quotation within Kater's comes from Mühlberger,
"The Sociology of the NSDAP," 504.

Our own data on the SS-Führerkorps indicates that in terms of
absolute numbers at least, the largest segment of the prewar SS leadership was recruited from the lower middle class.[48] To put this finding into the proper perspective, note should be made of the fact that
the case for the preponderance of lower middle class origins is compelling only with respect to data on the occupations of fathers. As far
as the occupational structure of SS recruits is concerned, this social
stratum was neither underrepresented nor overrepresented in the
leadership of the SS. The proportion of SS members with a lower
middle class background matched almost precisely the proportion
this class constituted in German society in general.

Another important missive provided by the same data is that the
majority of SS recruits coming from a lower middle class milieu held
white-collar jobs before joining Heinrich Himmler's organization.[49]
Among the Führer's occupations, roughly 30 percent were classified
as salaried employees. The number of civil servants, on the other
hand, was quite small.[50] In comparison to the population, where
approximately 5 percent were classified as lower or intermediate civil
servants, the same occupations were underrepresented in the SS

[48] Boehnert, "Sociography," 163–164, 206 and tables 6.1 and 6.3 respectively
calculated that some 59 percent of SS leaders came from the lower middle class.

[49] On the economic situation of white-collar workers in general see Winkler, "Extremismus," 185; Hans Speier, Die Angestellten vor dem Nationalsozialismus: Ein
Beitrag zum Verständnis der deutschen Sozialstruktur, 1918–1933 (Göttingen, 1977),
93; Kocka, "Zur Problematik," 792–811, and by the same author, Die Angestellten,
142–176.

[50] From the mid-1920s to Hitler's assumption of power lower civil servants were
overrepresented in the NSDAP. Kater, Nazi Party, 41–42. For the position of civil
servants before Hitler's assumption of power see Hans Mommsen, "Die Stellung der
Beamtenschaft in Reich, Länder, und Gemeinden in der Ära Brüning," Vierteljahrshefte für Zeitgeschichte 21 (1973): 151–165, and Wolfgang Ruge, Politik und
Beamtentum im Parteistaat: Die Demokratisierung der politischen Beamten in Preussen zwischen 1918 und 1933 (Stuttgart, 1965). The ambivalence of the NSDAP towards Germany's civil service has been noted by Jane Caplan, "Speaking the Right
Language: The Nazi Party and the Civil Service Vote in the Weimar Republic," in
Thomas Childers, ed., The Formation of the Nazi Constituency, 1919–1933 (London, 1986), 182–201. For the Hitler era see Hans Mommsen, Beamtentum im
Dritten Reich: Mit ausgewählten Quellen zur nationalsozialistischen Beamtenpolitik
(Stuttgart, 1966), and Jane Caplan, "The Politics of Administration: The Reich Inte-
rior Ministry and the German Civil Service," Historical Journal 20 (1977): 707–736.

leadership. As to the fathers' occupations, a total of about 40 percent fell into the categories of white-collar employees and civil servants, with each category making up about 20 percent respectively. The strong presence within the NSDAP and its electorate of salaried employees who faced much economic uncertainty and lower civil servants who were likely to be disgruntled by salary reductions and disenchanted by a parliamentary democracy which seemingly became increasingly Marxist-oriented has been noted.[51] Because of the high proportion of salaried employees among the recruits (and civil servants among the fathers), occupations of the old lower middle class were correspondingly scarce. Among SS-Führer independent craftsmen and owners of small shops could hardly be found, and even farmers were notably underrepresented.[52] The sum of all occupations that embraced the alte Mittelstand amounted to 5 to 8 percent of all occupations cited by SS members.[53] By comparison, the same categories of independent craftsmen, small businessmen, and farmers constituted about 24 percent of all occupations in the German population. The same pattern holds for the occupational structure of fathers. Although the proportion of old middle-class-type occupations tended to be higher than they were among their

[51] Kater, *Nazi Party*, 41–43; Pridham, *Hitler's Rise to Power*, 193; Thomas Childers, "The Social Bases of the National Socialist Vote," *Journal of Contemporary History* 11 (1976): 23; Noakes and Pridham, eds., *Nazism*, 2: 90; Hans Mommsen, "Die Stellung," 154–155; Mommsen, *Beamtentum*, 197–199.

[52] These figures must have been disappointing to Himmler, who was so fond of dreaming of the Greater Germanic Empire in which German peasant settlers would play an important role. For Himmler's interest in the plight of the German farmer and his personal role in the propaganda efforts of the NSDAP see Johnpeter Horst Grill, "The Nazi Party's Rural Propaganda before 1928," *Central European History* 15 (1982): 171–173.

[53] The prevailing view among many historians is that the Nazis no longer paid heed to the demands of the alte Mittelstand after the seizure of power. This argument has been most forcefully presented by Heinrich A. Winkler, *Mittelstand, Demokratie, und Nationalsozialismus: Die politische Entwicklung von Handwerk und Kleinhandel in der Weimarer Republic* (Cologne, 1972), 146, 149, and by the same author, "Vom Mythos der Volksgemeinschaft," 484–490. A more differentiated view is offered by Adelheit von Saldern, "Alter Mittelstand im Dritten Reich: Anmerkungen an einer Kontroverse," *Geschichte und Gesellschaft* 12 (1986): 235–243. See also by the same author, *Mittelstand im Dritten Reich: Handwerker-Einzelhändler-Bauern*, 2d ed. (Frankfurt/Main, 1985).

sons, they were either less than or equal to the proportion of occupations that would be expected from the distribution in the population. Thus, although it may well be true that shopkeepers and craftsmen were harmed by the growth of factories and department stores and suffered from a feeling of neglect and sociopolitical isolation,[54] and despite the fact that farmers faced economic plight in the form of declining income and foreclosures,[55] the old lower middle class did not serve as an important recruiting reservoir for the SS-Führerkorps.

The upper ranks of the Mittelstand as represented by the occupational categories of "managers," "high-level civil servants," "military officers," and "professionals" (and students in the case of Führer) are all heavily overrepresented in the SS leadership relative to their strength in the Reich.[56] Compared to the Reich, where only about 3 percent of the population would have been classified as upper middle

[54] Kater, Nazi Party, 24. Noakes, The Nazi Party In Lower Saxony, 1921–1933, 110–111 argues that the feeling of neglect and isolation drove these people away from the conservative right toward the Nazi radical right. The economic suffering of shopkeepers and craftsmen has been put into proper perspective by Winkler, Mittelstand, Demokratie, und Nationalsozialismus, 30, 79, 104–106.

[55] According to Kater, Nazi Party, 39–41 farmers flocked to the NSDAP after 1928 and bore a major responsibility for Hitler's victory in 1930. See also, Werner T. Angress, "The Political Role of the Peasantry in the Weimar Republic," Review of Politics 21 (1959): 538–540; Johann Dorner, Bauernstand und Nationalsozialismus, 2d ed. (Munich, 1930), 12–13, 22, 40–41; Onno Poppinga, Bauern und Politik (Frankfurt/Main and Cologne, 1975), 44–45; Hans-Jürgen Puhle, Politische Agrarbewegungen in kapitalistischen Industriegesellschaften: Deutschland, USA, und Frankreich im 20. Jahrhundert (Göttingen, 1975), 90; John E. Farquharson, The Plough and the Swastika: The NSDAP and Agriculture in Germany, 1928–45 (London and Beverly Hills, 1976), 26; Larry E. Jones, "Inflation, Revaluation, and the Crisis of Middle-Class Politics: A Study in the Dissolution of the German Party System, 1923–28," Central European History 12 (1979): 146–147; Rudolf Heberle, Landbevölkerung und Nationalsozialismus: Eine soziologische Untersuchung der politischen Willensbildung in Schleswig-Holstein, 1918–1932 (Stuttgart, 1963).

[56] Our findings here are in total agreement with those by Kater, Nazi Party, 27 who established that the "elite were consistently overrepresented in the Party since its very beginnings." Wegner, Politische Soldaten, 223 indicates that 45 to 50 percent of SS-Führer with a rank of Standartenführer or higher came from the upper middle class. Boehnert, "Sociography," puts the percentage of upper middle class occupations for the SS leadership at 33 percent (163–164, table 6.1) and 39.8 percent (206, table 6.3).

class according to our criteria, some 17 to 20 percent of the fathers and roughly one-third of the Führer matched this category. Among the fathers this overall overrepresentation is fairly consistent from one job category to the next, that is, on the average paternal occupations classified as upper middle class occupations were usually five times higher than the corresponding categories were for the general population. As to the SS-Führer themselves, the picture is a little more diverse.

Although in general SS members had twice the representation of upper middle class occupations than their fathers did, there was a good deal of variation in the proportions of individual occupational categories. Whereas those SS recruits who listed themselves as management-level employees made up between .8 and 1.6 percent and the higher civil servants[57] constituted a mere 1.0 to 2.0 percent of all occupations, the so-called entrepreneurial category was void of even a single individual. These relatively low figures are of course balanced by the conspicuously high proportion of recruits who listed themselves as "professionals" and "students."[58] Depending on the SS branch to which an individual belonged, some 12 to 20 percent of all SS leaders claimed to have held or at least trained for professional occupations. Among the professionals, the majority included health-care professionals such as physicians[59] and, to a lesser degree, dentists and a few veterinarians, while the second largest contingent of professionals consisted principally of attorneys. It has been suggested that both doctors and lawyers had solid economic motives for joining the Nazis; the former for the reason that either their earnings were

[57]On the difficulties facing higher civil servants see Childers, "National Socialism and the New Middle Class," 22; Mommsen, *Beamtentum,* 197.

[58]For the attraction that fascist movements and ideas held for intellectual see Linz, "Comparative Study," 40 and Alastair Hamilton, *The Appeal of Fascism: A Study of Intellectuals and Fascism 1919–1945* (New York, 1971).

[59]The manifold activities of the SS offered many employment opportunities for physicians and, for the most part, they carried out legitimate medical functions. Neusüss-Hunkel, *Die SS,* 74. The duties of SS physicians are spelled out in a memorandum dated 21.1.1939 by Brigadeführer Dr. Grawitz, Reichsarzt-SS. In addition to the more obvious tasks that any physician might carry out such as the treatment of injuries, these duties included the selection of recruits, the drawing up of hygiene guidelines for clothing and buildings, dietary counseling, sports medicine, criminal pathology. T–175/17/620621–625.

declining or they feared socialized medicine, and the latter because young attorneys in particular suffered from an overcrowding of their profession.[60]

As to students, their high proportion among SS-Führer comes as no surprise for their attraction to fascist parties in general and their preponderance within the NSDAP in particular have been well established.[61] Since potentially their advanced educational preparation predisposed them for privileged social and economic status, all those SS leaders who represented themselves as students were classified as belonging to the upper middle class. It appears that these young men must have been unwilling to commit themselves to traditional professional careers because virtually all students within our samples had either just finished secondary school, most of them with an Abitur, or had just dropped out of a university before accepting the nontraditional careers of SS leaders in Himmler's Black Order. Within the SS-TV and SS-VT respectively, students constituted 17.4 percent and 16.3 percent of all former occupations within the leadership of the SS. In fact, almost one half of all upper middle class occupations were accounted for by the student category. The only

[60] Kater, *Nazi Party*, 67–68.

[61] Noting the high proportion of high school students and university students within the NSDAP, Kater, *Nazi Party*, 27, 44 speculates that perhaps as much as half of the entire student body may have joined the Nazis by 1930. Linz, "Comparative Study," 67 maintains that students constituted an important segment of all fascist parties. Also germane to this matter are Hans Peter Bleuel and Ernst Klinnert, *Deutsche Studenten auf dem Weg ins Dritte Reich: Ideologien—Programme—Aktionen, 1918–1935* (Gütersloh, 1967); Anselm Faust, *Der Nationalsozialistische Deutsche Studentenbund: Studenten und Nationalsozialismus in der Weimarer Republik* (Düsseldorf, 1973); Jürgen Schwarz, *Studenten in der Weimarer Republik: Die deutsche Studentenschaft in der Zeit von 1918 bis 1923 und ihre Stellung zur Politik* (Berlin, 1971); Michael S. Steinberg, *Sabers and Brownshirts: The German Students' Path to National Socialism, 1918–1935* (Chicago and London, 1977); Wolfgang Zorn, "Student Politics in the Weimar Republic," *Journal of Contemporary History* 5 (1970): 128–143; Michael H. Kater, *Studentenschaft und Rechtsradikalismus in Deutschland, 1918–1933: Eine sozialgeschichtliche Studie zur Bildungskrise in der Weimarer Republik* (Hamburg, 1975). For the period preceding the Great War see Konrad Jarausch, "Liberal Education as Illiberal Socialization: The Case of Students in Imperial Germany," *Journal of Modern History* 50 (1978): 609–630, and by the same author, *Students, Society, and Politics in Imperial Germany: The Rise of Academic Illiberalism* (Princeton, 1982).

exception to this pattern was the membership of the Allgemeine SS where, because the age structure of its membership was more advanced and most of the men had full-time occupations before joining the SS, the proportion of students was relatively insignificant.

EDUCATIONAL ATTAINMENT

It cannot be denied that one of the most precious commodities of the twentieth century has been education. As industrialization progressed, societies demanded higher and higher educational attainment at all levels of employment, thereby increasing the proportion of jobs requiring commensurate levels of education and training. The existing educational system, however, acted as an intermediary between the social standing of father and son, with the predictable outcome that social and economic inequalities among parents led to inequalities in their children's access to formal education. Since the level of education obtained in turn determined to a significant degree subsequent occupations and positions in society, children of "better" families were encouraged to go far beyond the compulsory formal education. Other families realized only too well the mundane values of education, but they were not in a financial position to realize their ambitions and aspirations, and children of the lower orders were forced to leave school much earlier. Advanced education, and in particular university education, remained largely the preserve of the middle and upper middle classes, and the rewards of higher education—top places in government and the private sector of the economy—were consequently limited to the bourgeoisie.[62]

Although literacy was generally quite high in Germany, there, as

[62] In 1928 and 1931, 4 and 3 percent of German students respectively, came from a working-class background. See Fritz Ringer, *Education and Society in Modern Europe* (Bloomington, 1979), 79 and Knight, *The German Executive*, 36. John E. Craig, "Higher Education and Social Mobility in Germany," in Konrad Jarausch, ed., *The Transformation of Higher Learning, 1860–1930: Expansion, Diversification, Social Origins, and Professionalization in Germany, Russia, and the United States* (Stuttgart, 1982), 219–244 argues "that between unification and the Nazi seizure of power the German universities became much more representative . . . although those from the peasantry and the working class may not have gained much during the period considered" (239).

elsewhere, education functioned as a filter and a critical determinant of career opportunity and subsequent social prestige and class standing.[63] Indeed, in contemporary societies "the bias against the uneducated is even greater than the bias against those from the lower socioeconomic classes."[64] Such insights were lost neither on the Nazis nor on Heinrich Himmler. Many followers of National Socialism had suffered, so it seemed, from this trend toward educational exclusivity and proposed to correct it at the first opportunity. The Reichsführer-SS in particular continuously struggled for a "revolution" in elite recruitment, striving against all odds to abolish the social and political dominance of the Abitur or the *Staatsexam*, to free advancement within his elite from academic restraints.[65] The outcome of his efforts are indirectly portrayed in Figure 4.1 and in general corroborate our findings on the occupational makeup of the SS leadership.

SS ideology did not emphasize or particularly value the importance of education,[66] but there is no denying that a large share of the

---

[63] Putnam, *Comparative Study of Elites*, 32. For studies of the increasing demand for education and technical training, the availability of educational opportunities, and the financial, social, and institutional barriers to higher education see Karl M. Bolte, *Sozialer Aufstieg und Abstieg* (Stuttgart, 1959), esp. 117–118, 135; Keller, *Beyond the Ruling Class*, 121; Fritz Ringer, "Higher Education in Germany in the Nineteenth Century," *Journal of Contemporary History* 2 (1967): 123–138. Hartmut Kaelble, "Chancenungleichheit und akademische Ausbildung in Deutschland, 1910–1960," *Geschichte und Gesellschaft* 1 (1975): 129 asserts that with the twentieth century academic education became virtually the only conduit for social upward mobility.

[64] Putnam, *Comparative Study of Elites*, 26.

[65] *Mein Weg zur Waffen-SS*, 4; *Das Schwarze Korps*, 17.2.1938, 11.

[66] The relative nonimportance of formal education was demonstrated by the entrance requirements to the SS cadet schools; acceptance in these Junkerschulen was not dependent on specific educational prerequisites. Stein, *Waffen-SS*, 13, for example, concluded: "The entrance requirements of the SS cadet schools were exacting with respect to racial, physical and political factors, but education and nonpolitical background were discounted." According to Himmler, some 40 percent of the officer candidates accepted before 1939 had only an elementary-school education. "Rede des Reichsführer-SS vor SS-Gruppenführern am 8.11.1937," T–175/90/2612395. See also Paul Hausser, *Waffen SS im Einsatz* (Göttingen, 1953), 13, and Neusüss-Hunkel, *Die SS*, 23–24. By 1939 both professors and students were viewed by National Socialists, including Hitler, with outright contempt. Geoffrey J. Giles, "German Students and Higher Education Policy in the Second World War," *Central European History* 17 (1984): 330–331.

TABLE 4.2
HIGHEST LEVEL OF EDUCATIONAL ATTAINMENT OF THE SS LEADERSHIP IN 1938,
RELATIVE FREQUENCY DISTRIBUTION

	SS Branch		
Educational Level	SS-TV	SS-VT	*Allg. SS*
Primary School	34.7	25.0	37.0
Middle School	8.5	11.6	4.2
Secondary School	22.8	22.1	22.9
Secondary School w. Abitur	13.5	16.4	4.3
University	4.9	8.3	5.3
University w. Degree	12.2	13.7	24.4
Other	3.4	2.9	1.9
Percent Total	100.0	100.0	100.0
Total Number of Cases	386	671	816

SS leadership was rooted in the educated bourgeoisie.[67] As a whole the SS-Führerkorps tended to be much better educated than the German population, with roughly one-third of its membership having either obtained an Abitur or even attended a university.[68] It seems that a university degree, or even an above-average education without a degree, still offered a preferential basis for advancing into the leadership of the SS. The fact that a purposely avowed "open elite" recruited a third of its membership from traditional elite groups of society was not, however, because the educational advantage of an *Abiturient*, or academic, was so highly valued. Rather it was because numerous positions within the SS such as those of physicians who, combined with lawyers, were the largest single academically trained contingent in all SS branches, made certain minimum academic training mandatory.[69]

[67] This is in agreement with the findings of both Wegner, *Politische Soldaten*, 228 and Boehnert, "Sociography," 117–118.

[68] Even though a large number of SS leaders attended a university, a sizable proportion never completed their studies. More precisely, 28.8, 37.8, and 17.8 percent of the SS-TV, SS-VT, and Allg. SS, respectively, never completed their university education.

[69] The major field of study of those who attended a university reinforces the proportion of men whom we could identify as physicians and lawyers. For the three SS branches the breakdown was as follows: SS-TV—67.2% medicine, 10.6% jurispru-

Furthermore, the bimodal distribution of the variable measuring educational attainment also established that an almost equally sizable number of SS Führer had attended only a Volksschule, while another proportion completed only some sort of secondary education without an Abitur. The latter, or any other qualifying school diploma, was not necessary to embark on a Führer career, and neither the SS-VT nor SS-TV had designated officer candidates in the same way the Wehrmacht did.[70] In fact, if the Abitur had been a prerequisite for entry into the SS-Führerkorps, only about one-third of these men would have ended up as leaders of the SS. The result was that university graduates rubbed shoulders with men who had completed as little as eight years of formal education. Despite certain vicissitudes within the various branches of the SS, the pattern brought out by the data is clear and provides a simple and blunt message: in terms of education, the SS leadership was distinguished by diversity. Formal education as an indispensable necessity for social advancement was for all intents and purposes a moot consideration within the SS and, in this respect, National Socialism did bring about a considerable social change.

SOCIAL STRUCTURE: AN ASSESSMENT

The basis of recruitment for the leadership of Heinrich Himmler's order was sufficiently broad to invite the characterization of the SS leadership as an elite that secured recruits—though in varying proportions—from the entire juste milieu of German bourgeois society. A number of scholars and contemporary observers have pointed to a broad base of support for fascism in general and National Socialism in particular. As early as 1923 Clara Zetkin[71] observed that "the carrier of fascism is not a small caste, but broad

---

dence; SS-VT—47.3% medicine, 14.9% jurisprudence; Allg. SS—41.3% medicine, 23.5% jurisprudence. These finding seem to contradict those of Boehnert, "Jurists," 361–374 who identifies lawyers as the single largest academically trained contingent of his "sample."

[70] Wegner, *Politische Soldaten*, 140.

[71] Clara Zetkin, "Der Kampf gegen den Faschismus," cited in Ernst Nolte, ed., *Theorien über den Faschismus* (Cologne and Berlin, 1967), 88

social groups, large masses which reach far into the proletariat." Others have echoed similar sentiments. For example, Wolfgang Sauer[72] has argued that "historical evidence shows that support of Fascism may not be confined to the classical elements of the middle class . . . but may extend to a wide variety of groups." In a similar vein Michael Hurst[73] has suggested that "component sectors of both fascism and national socialism could not be reduced to the lower middle class and the Lumpenproletariat; an assorted variety of social categories took an active part in the fascist movements." Heterogeneity of social structure is also stressed by Eric G. Reiche,[74] who concludes that "Hitler's supporters in the Nürnberg SA came from all classes, except the upper class. Neither predominantly lower middle class nor largely working class in background, the Nürnberg SA appeared indeed to be an organization that appealed to virtually all sectors of the city's male population." As to the membership of the NSDAP, Wolfgang Zapf[75] asserts that people from all occupations could be found in the early NSDAP. Paul Madden[76] suggests that the social composition of the early NSDAP membership "was considerably more heterogeneous than has usually been suggested." Harold J. Gordon, Jr.,[77] likewise concluded that the preputsch Nazi movement as a whole constituted "a heterogeneous mixture of people of all classes and all professions and trades." Heinrich A. Winkler[78] characterized the mass basis of the NSDAP as dominantly middle class. But because of the significant proportion of workers he concluded that the NSDAP was a Volkspartei and not a class party of the bourgeois middle. An even more outspoken position has been taken by Detlef Mühlberger[79] who, after reviewing the quantitative evidence of numerous studies, asserts that "the NSDAP was a genu-

[72] Wolfgang Sauer, "National Socialism: Totalitarianism or Fascism," *American Historical Review* 63 (1967): 410.

[73] Michael Hurst, "What Is Fascism?" *The Historical Journal* 11 (1968): 179.

[74] Reiche, *Development of the SA,* 229.

[75] Zapf, *Wandlungen,* 52.

[76] Madden, "Social Characteristics," 48.

[77] Gordon, *Hitler and the Beer Hall Putsch,* 82.

[78] Winkler, "Extremismus der Mitte," 175–191. See also by the same author, "Mittelstandsbewegung oder Volkspartei," 97–118.

[79] Mühlberger, "The Sociology of the NSDAP," 504.

ine Volkspartei" securing "support from all social classes in German society." On the basis of electoral analysis of fourteen large cities Richard F. Hamilton[80] does not think that the lower middle class provided the mass basis for National Socialism. Thomas Childers[81] described the NSDAP as "a catch-all party of middle class protest" and "party of bourgeois integration" while Jürgen W. Falter[82] argues that, based on the social profile of its voters and members and taking into account geographical variations, the NSDAP was socially the most balanced of all parties. As far as its social structure was concerned, the NSDAP came closest to being the ideal of a *Volks-oder-Integrationspartei*.

SS leaders, as it turned out, come from quite diverse social backgrounds, and the resulting lack of homogeneity in social structure assured that people of dissimilar background and experience—and probably outlook as well—occupied the decision-making posts of the SS. From this heterogeneity in social origins certain conclusions follow. To begin with, the group of people whom we have analyzed hardly conforms to the usual picture we have of lower middle class Germans flocking to the banners of National Socialism. The high proportion of workers on the one hand and the even higher proportion of upper middle class representatives on the other, make it difficult at best to extend and sustain for the leadership of the SS the thesis of lower middle class preponderance repeatedly associated with the NSDAP membership and the Nazi electorate.

Beyond that, the same heterogeneity of the SS's social structure does little to aid and abet the sweeping claims of classical elite theorists that elites are drawn from within narrowly constricted social or economic classes, especially the upper class. Although nobody is methodologically so naive as to accept all National Socialist egalitarian rhetoric as the equivalent of the social-political reality of the Third Reich, our empirical evidence permits the conclusion that with respect to the SS or, more specifically, the leadership of that

---

[80] Richard F. Hamilton, *Who Voted for Hitler?* 420–421.

[81] Childers, "National Socialism and the New Middle Class," 19.

[82] Falter, "Warum die deutschen Arbeiter während des Dritten Reiches zu Hitler standen," 230.

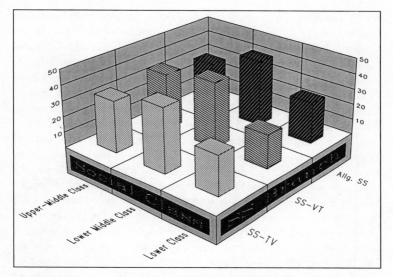

FIGURE 4.1   Relative Frequency Distribution of Class Standing. (For Leaders of the Allgemeine SS, the SS-Verfügungstruppe, and the SS-Totenkopfverbände.)

organization, a case can be made that some of the egalitarian objectives were indeed realized.

Within the confines of Himmler's leadership corps National Socialism broke decisively with the preceding social order.[83] Unless one tries to assess the social policies of Hitler's Germany as reflected in the SS by employing the criterion of an ideal society which has never existed in practice and unless one harbors the unrealistic notion that

[83] In its recruitment the SS displayed a close affinity to a theoretical construct of elite recruitment which has been defined as the Maximum Deferred Achievement Model. Armstrong, *The European Administrative Elite*, 17–18. This model, which is considered the exception rather than the rule of historical development, assumes that individuals required for elite positions are not selected early on in their lives from a small portion of the male cohort that is characterized by certain desirable values and motivations or specific ascriptive attributes. Instead, the "required men are selected by some process which gives all—as far as discernable social characteristics go—equal access" once the male cohort reaches the appropriate age level for elite or, in our case,

leadership groups in a given society should exactly mirror the social makeup of the general population, one must conclude from the diversity of occupational and educational backgrounds that the SS was serious in its efforts to abolish social and educational barriers for its recruits and was indeed more than simply a self-reproducing elite of Besitz und Bildung. The SS-Führerkorps functioned as an instrument of social advancement permitting, and hence attracting, young men from the working and lower middle classes to advance to otherwise unobtainable positions of power and prestige. It went beyond the rhetoric of social mobility and racial hocus-pocus and, on its own terms, was successful in creating a Volksgemeinschaft in microcosm, for which it gained support from a broad section of the population. SS-Führer came close to realizing the ideal of the so-called Volksoffizier, who qualified "on the basis of physical fitness, racial purity, and presumed ideological conviction rather than by virtue of education, social background, and emotional stability."[84] Thus, the fact that especially the younger age groups, who participated neither in World War I nor in the Kampf um die Macht, were offered rapid career opportunities incomparably higher than those in the administration of the state, the Wehrmacht, and the party itself, was one of the most noteworthy features of the SS-Führerkorps.[85]

Potential SS recruits were not simply or solely captivated by a restorative longing for bygone preindustrial utopias or the removal of social and economic inequities, but were stirred by what amounted to a call for the creation of a modern, mobile mass society. The SS extended especially to the proverbial kleine Mann opportunities for social mobility, status, and even prestige, since career fulfillment and advancement were much more likely and rapid under the unconventional conditions of the SS than they were under the Weimar

---

SS-Führer positions. Since no special selection is made among the population, it follows that socialization prior to joining the elite is identical to that of a random sample of the male cohort. The disadvantage of this approach to elite recruitment is that it requires an heavy investment in special socialization. After all, the latter can take place only after entry into the elite.

[84] Stein, Waffen-SS, 291.

[85] Neusüss-Hunkel, Die SS, 22. Bracher, The German Dictatorship, 273 argues that in comparison to Western elites the National Socialist leadership was characterized by extreme youth and lightening careers.

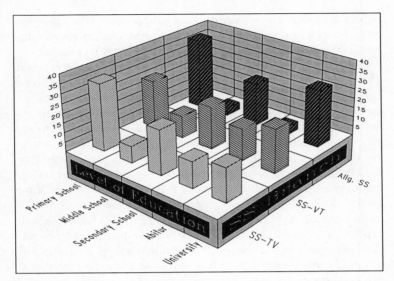

FIGURE 4.2   Relative Frequency Distribution of Highest Level of Educational Achievement. (For Leaders of the Allgemeine SS, the SS-Verfügungstruppe, and the SS-Totenkopfverbände.)

Republic.[86] For many of its recruits the SS may have held an attraction similar to the one held by the German army during the First World War, which "for a brief period of time had been the instrument of upward social mobility that permitted the advancement of young men from the lower middle classes into a station that they would not earlier have dreamed of."[87] It is quite plausible, therefore, that a significant number of SS-Führer enlisted in the SS not so much out of fear of downward mobility but rather out of frustration at the limitations on upward mobility.[88]

At the same time the data also make it explicit that many SS-

[86]Merkl, *Political Violence,* 62–72 indicates that frustrated upward mobility was a salient consideration in prompting commitment to the NSDAP. See also Stein, *Waffen-SS,* 11.

[87]Rogowski, "Gauleiter," 418–419. Höhne, *Order of the Death's Head,* 136.

[88]Rogowski, "Gauleiter," 402 and Jannen, "Social Mobility," 341.

Führer, although representing only one component of the rather incongruous and multifarious membership, had very advanced educational exposure or held relatively high positions in Weimar society before joining Himmler's organization. What possible motives could these men have had for joining the SS? One explanation might be that many of these individuals joined the Black Order in the hope that a career as SS-Führer would preserve in some fashion their existing social status, to provide them, as it were, with a sort of "insurance policy against proletarianization."[89] Members of the conservative upper class may also have been attracted to the SS shortly after the Machtergreifung because they wanted positions of power within the regime to replace those positions they had lost.[90] Others, most notably the large contingent of students, perhaps did not secure their social standing until they assumed a career in the SS and hence paradoxically joined an antibourgeois organization in order to satisfy bourgeois status ambitions.[91] Still others might have enrolled simply because they sincerely believed in what the SS symbolized and stood for.

Leaving aside for the moment the possible motivations for joining, does the high proportion of upper-class SS members negate the conclusion that the SS-Führerkorps was an open elite? The answer is—not necessarily, at least not in the National Socialist sense. The clue to this apparent contradiction lies with the Nazi demand for an open elite, an elite based on achievement and ability. Although the basic determinant of social status in Germany and in the SS was common membership in the national community as expressed in the concept of Volksgemeinschaft, it was also clearly acknowledged that some Germans were superior to other Germans. The so-called Volksgenossen were equal in their subordination to the national community but "would be stratified in terms of income and capital according to their performance within the occupational market-place, but an occupational market-place which must in future be geared to the needs of the community."[92] SS recruitment consequently rested

[89] Hiden and Farquharson, *Explaining Hitler's Germany*, 97.
[90] Neusüss-Hunkel, *Die SS*, 16.
[91] Wegner, *Politische Soldaten*, 237.
[92] Noakes, "Nazism and Revolution," 78.

on the premise of inequality or, as it was called, the *Leistungsgesell-schaft*.[93] Although scornful of traditional social distinctions, neither National Socialism nor the SS was interested in the establishment of a true classless and egalitarian society.[94] One might, indeed, more accurately assert the contrary, to wit: that what they sought was an achievement-oriented society that would remain within the confines of a capitalist order, a society in which men were rewarded and hence able to rise according to their abilities, unhampered by the artificial restraints of class and status barriers of traditional German society.[95] This concept of society was indeed tied to the affirmation—so characteristic of both Himmler and Hitler—of the social Darwinist principle of natural selection through struggle for the fittest and implied a new legitimizing and even brutalizing of the liberal axiom that unrestrained competition promotes performance.[96]

It is tempting to conclude that the picture presented by the SS leadership was the exception, or perhaps even an aberration, with respect to elite recruitment because the regime entertained no serious intentions of implementing similar changes elsewhere. Still, it seems prudent to point out that National Socialism met its defeat in a war it unleashed and consequently did not have the opportunity to implement its full program. As one historian has pointed out, is it possible that the peacetime years served only as "a preparatory phase for a far reaching transformation of Germany to be effected in the wake of Nazi military triumph?"[97] In this case the recruitment practices prevailing in the SS leadership may have played the role of a model of things to come.[98] Moreover, before outrightly dismissing

---

[93] Schoenbaum, *Social Revolution*, 59, 245.

[94] Thus it would seem that both National Socialist and liberal elite theory "called for an elite which would ineluctably function within the parameters of bourgeois society and whose members would be selected in accordance with the basic values of that social order." Struve, *Elites*, 419.

[95] *Dich ruft die SS*, items 8 and 9, p. 24.

[96] Broszat, "Struktur der NS-Massenbewegung," 67; Noakes and Pridham, eds., *Nazism*, 2: 377.

[97] Turner, "Fascism and Modernization," 552–555.

[98] The first, by necessity heterogeneous, Führer generation was to be replaced by a militarily trained and SS-educated second generation of leaders. The war broke out just when this personnel revolution was to begin. Wegner, *Politische Soldaten*, 153.

such a scenario as unrealistic or utopian, one does well to recall that the Nazis were only too willing and indeed successful in realizing equally fantastic goals. What historian would have taken seriously the intent of resettling tens of thousands of Germans in Eastern Europe or the even more absurd and incomprehensible goal of a "final solution"? Yet before the war came to an end the Nazis were planning and effecting the implementation of both.

5

Longitudinal Changes in Recruitment and Vertical Mobility

ON 30 JANUARY 1933, the day President Hindenburg gave in and appointed Adolf Hitler chancellor, the NSDAP became the official state party of Germany. The principal aim of Hitler's movement up to this point—the conquest of governmental power—had been achieved, but subsequent to January and especially after March of the same year this goal was expanded to one stressing the consolidation of power. While the Nazis proceeded with the destruction of the vestiges of Weimar democracy, National Socialism itself became transformed. Beginning in 1933 the SS, like its mother organization the NSDAP, experienced an expansion of its membership. The numerical growth can probably be attributed to the fact that in the aftermath of the seizure of power an increasing number of German citizens were attracted to the SS and its leadership corps in order to advance or "get ahead in life." But this transformation was not limited solely to the swelling of its membership ranks, for the influx of new recruits was associated with organizational growth and a change in the socioeconomic complexion of its personnel, including the SS-Führerkorps.

With the Machtergreifung, the subsequent Gleichschaltung, but especially after the events of 30 June 1934, when the so-called Röhm Putsch was put down with the aid of SS firing squads and the power of the SA was for all intents and purposes broken, the recruitment needs of the SS changed and so accordingly did the type of personnel it attracted and recruited. With the ascendancy of Himmler's order, the SS began to assume a multitude of new and additional responsibilities, all of which required the complex administrative functions

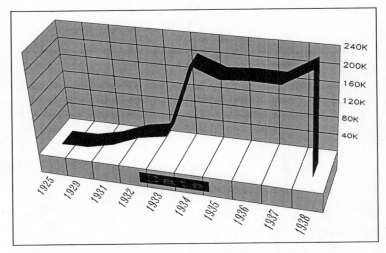

FIGURE 5.1   Membership Growth of the Entire SS, 1925–1938.

so typical of large organizations. The personnel needs of a large-scale organization clearly differ from those of a smaller organization and, while the leadership cadre of the early SS was probably largely dependent on loyal, ideologically oriented idealists and "fighters,"[1] the more mature and bureaucratic SS became more reliant on the educated specialist who possessed administrative and logistical skills.

In view of these observations one would, therefore, expect that the makeup of the SS-Führerkorps changed over time. Moreover, since in a class-stratified society opportunities for education and the development of special talents and skills are class-linked, one would also anticipate that members who joined the organization after 1933 exhibited a higher degree of socioeconomic advantage as measured, for example, by occupational skills and educational attainment than those who joined the SS before the seizure of power. Indeed, such changes in personnel have already been anticipated by studies on both the SA[2] and the SS. With respect to the latter it has been sug-

[1] For a characterization of early SS recruits See Höhne, *Order of the Death's Head*, 53–54.

[2] See, for instance, Reiche, *Development of the SA*, 200, 206.

gested that after 1933 the first to arrive in Himmler's Black Order were aristocrats, to be followed by the sons of the upper middle class, mostly intellectuals, "men of the twentieth century." "They were hard-boiled SS technocrats, the social engineers who provided the *Führer's* dictatorship with the necessary veneer of legality and organization; they were astute realists with no ideology other than power." Another group of newcomers included former officers of the Reichswehr, most of whom joined the precursor of the wartime Waffen-SS, the SS-Verfügungstruppe.[3]

Up to this point our analysis of the social origins of Heinrich Himmler's new aristocracy has been limited to a cross-sectional approach, with the result that our picture of the SS elite is a static one. Because such a view is limited, however, our analysis will be continued with the proper emphasis on temporal and longitudinal factors. Accordingly, to facilitate the detection and delineation of changes in the social structure of SS leaders, we stratified each of our original three samples into two groups. The first group is made up of men who joined the SS before 1933, the old fighters of the Time of Struggle.[4] The second group comprises those who joined the SS after January 1933; many of them were the so-called *Märzgefallenen* or *Märzveilchen*, so dubbed by the veterans of National Socialism because they did not discover their enthusiasms for National Socialism until after the March 1933 elections.

LONGITUDINAL CHANGES IN RECRUITMENT

Significant statistical and substantive longitudinal changes in the makeup of the SS leadership were, somewhat surprisingly, limited principally to variables measuring the educational attainment and occupational structure of SS leaders.[5] This outcome is unexpected

[3] Höhne, *Order of the Death's Head*, 136; the quote is from 135.

[4] Most of these men (90 percent), it has been alleged, were pensioned off by the time of World War II, though a small group of these leaders occupied the decisive posts in the SS up to the end of the Third Reich. See, Höhne *Order of the Death's Head*, 134 and Koehl, *The Black Corps*, 282.

[5] A statistically significant change between those who joined the SS before 1933 and those who enlisted thereafter was detectable in data pertaining to the region of birth. The overall pattern of our data indicates that the early SS recruits tended to

in that no significant change could be observed in the age structure of the SS elite, in spite of the fact that generally "there is a tendency for elites to perpetuate themselves . . . which leads to a progressive aging from a revolutionary young elite to an increasingly aged elite as the revolution is consolidated and the system moves toward greater stability."[6] This general observation has been substantiated with respect to the NSDAP, which has been characterized as an aging party in which "the old, tired cohorts were unwilling to make room for young and eager joiners,"[7] although the same cannot be said of the SS leadership. Within the SS-Verfügungstruppe and the Allgemeine SS the age of those who joined between 1925 and 1933 was identical to those who joined between the seizure of power and the outbreak of the Second World War. Those who ended up as full-time leaders of concentration camp personnel tended to be two to three years younger on the average if they joined the SS after Hitler's appointment as chancellor. Consequently our remarks will be limited to prominent fluctuations in the occupational and educational composition of the SS-Führerkorps.

One can without qualification state that, regardless of the SS branch to which they ultimately became attached as Führer, the men enlisting in the SS during January 1933 and thereafter tended to be much better educated than their counterparts who joined earlier.[8] Some 35.6 percent of the newcomers who ended up directing concentration camp personnel during the 1930s were holders of the

---

originate more frequently from the southern regions of Germany—the birthplace of National Socialism—and correspondingly fewer came from the North. In substantive terms, however, the differences between those two groups were not pronounced, amounting to a 5 to 8 percent difference, depending on the SS branch in question. The proportion of foreign-born men remained the same for each set of subsamples.

[6] Putnam, *Comparative Study of Elites*, 67.

[7] Kater, *Nazi Party*, 145.

[8] Boehnert, "Sociography," 123–124, table 5.2 found that his post-1933 sample was also better educated. Boehnert also claims that of those men joining the SS between February 1933 and June 1934 some 28 percent held a doctorate while a further 21 percent attended a university. Reiche, *Development of the SA*, 206 established that in the ranks of the SA those with a postsecondary education increased after 1933, and those with only elementary school education declined.

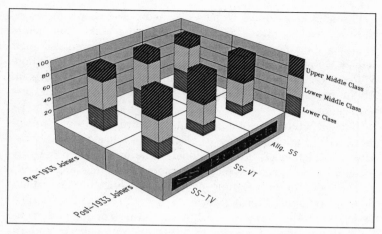

FIGURE 5.2   Cumulative Relative Frequency Distribution of Class Standing according to the Date of Joining the SS. (For Leaders of the Allgemeine SS, the SS-Verfügungstruppe, and the SS-Totenkopfverbände.)

coveted Abitur, and one half of these men even attended a university.[9] Likewise, men who went on to serve in the armed formations of the SS could be stratified educationally on the basis of their time of arrival in Himmler's order. Whereas 23.9 percent of the old fighters were graduated with an Abitur, of which 67.6 percent went on to study at a university, 48.1 percent of the post-1933 joiners completed high school (gymnasium or equivalent) successfully, and of those 53 percent continued their education at institutions of higher learning. However, most striking were the changes that took place within the nucleus of the SS. Of the early recruits to the Allgemeine-SS almost half (46.6 percent) had concluded their schooling at Volksschulen levels and 21.3 percent obtained a secondary school leaving certificate (Abitur). However, of those who came to the SS after January

[9]Of those individuals attending a university, men joining after 1933 were more likely to have completed their collegiate education than their counterparts who joined earlier. This was true for members of all three branches, but the tendency was most pronounced among members of the Allg. SS.

1933 and who remained in the Allgemeine SS to serve mostly as part-time leaders, only 21.7 percent attended a Volksschule before assuming their occupations, while over one-half completed their studies at a gymnasium or similar type of high school. Out of those 52.2 percent late joiners who were fortunate enough to possess an Abitur, more than three-quarters (88.2 percent) pursued a university-level education.

The preponderance of more highly educated men in the ranks of the post-1933 joiners of the *SS-Führerkorps* is reflected in the occupational structure of these individuals. The previously noted very pronounced working-class presence among SS recruits was actually quite dependent on the time of arrival. Among the old fighters roughly one-third (43.4 percent SS-TV, 31.2 percent SS-VT, and 37.6 percent Allg. SS) were identified as having working-class roots. But with the influx of newcomers this complexion changed and the proportion of workers in the ranks of the SS-TV, SS-VT, and Allg. SS was reduced to 17.4 percent, 16.9 percent, and 24.8 percent respectively.[10]

The decline in proletarian backgrounds after 1933 was partly accounted for by a corresponding increase in the proportion of men who evidenced lower middle class origins. Whereas between 44 and 49 percent of the pre-1933 SS recruits originated from that particular stratum of German society, the same can be said for only approximately one-third of the post-1933 joining individuals. Furthermore, among the men with lower middle class backgrounds some subtle but important shifts were discernible. Overall, the proportion of new lower middle class occupations increased at the expense of those representing the old lower middle class. While small businessmen, independent craftsmen, and farmers became fewer and fewer over time and the proportion of white-collar employees either remained stable or declined slightly, the proportion of lower civil servants increased

[10]Boehnert, "Sociography," 166–169 indicates also that worker representation declined in the SS after 1933 while at the same time members of the upper class became more frequent. According to Kater, *Nazi Party*, 160 workers representation in the NSDAP gained strength after the seizure of power and especially after the outbreak of the war. Reiche, *Development of the SA*, 210, on the other hand, established that workers declined from 43 to 33 percent after 1933.

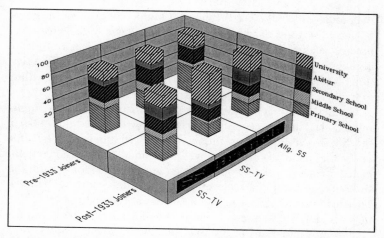

FIGURE 5.3   Cumulative Relative Frequency Distribution of Highest Level of Educational Achievement according to the Date of Joining the SS. (For Leaders of the Allgemeine SS, the SS-Verfügungstruppe, and the SS-Totenkopfverbände.)

dramatically after 1933. To be more precise, the number of lower-level civil servants increased from .7 percent to 3.5 percent in the SS-TV, from 3.6 percent to 5.3 percent in the SS-VT, and from 1.9 percent to 6.3 percent in the Allg. SS. To be sure civil servants remained a small minority among the SS leaders, but it is equally evident that their numbers doubled and even quadruped among those men joining the SS right around the time of the Machtergreifung.

One might speculate that members of the old lower middle class in general felt increasingly less attracted to Himmler's order in the years following the establishment of the Third Reich. With each passing year it must have become obvious to the farmer, the artisan, and the small entrepreneur that pre-1933 rhetoric notwithstanding, the regime was not seriously interested in protecting these people from the growing pains of an industrializing society. Hitler left little doubt that he needed the modern sectors of the economy to realize his far-ranging political aims and, as a result, the old middle class as a whole never felt the threat of proletarianization more than during the peace years of the Nazi regime.[11] On the other side of the equation, civil servants must have felt increasingly comfortable with National Socialism.[12] Whether it was because of plain opportunism or because they felt they could express more openly their pro-Nazi sentiments after 1933, a growing number of civil servants were willing to try their hands at a career in Germany's new elite.

Be that as it may, it was above all else members from the upper middle class and the country's social elite who joined the ranks of the SS in ever-increasing numbers.[13] Indeed, there can be little doubt that members of Germany's upper middle class who contemplated a career in the SS felt an even greater attraction for duty in the ranks of the Reich's newest elite after the victory of National Socialism was no longer in doubt. As has already been established, upper middle class representation in the SS leadership by 1938 hovered around one-third of the total membership. But whereas only 20.2 percent of the SS-TV, 18.2 percent of the SS-VT, and 15.4 percent of the Allg. SS pre-1933 joiners could boast of a high social standing as measured by occupations, some 40 to 50 percent (40.6 SS-TV, 48.9 percent SS-VT, 44.5 percent Allg. SS) of the men coming after 1933 were classified as such. Among Himmler's new elite the proportion of high-level civil servants, academically trained professionals,[14] and former officers[15] of the *Reichswehr* doubled and

[11] Heinrich A. Winkler, "Der entbehrliche Mittelstand. Zur Mittelstandpolitik im Dritten Reich," *Archiv für Sozialgeschichte* 17 (1977): 1–40 has convincingly argued that Hitler, who needed to accommodate the old elites to carry out his expansionist aims, dropped all pretense of protecting the entrepreneurial Mittelstand; the latter was no longer considered important to the regime after the seizure of power. See also by the same author, "From Social Protectionism to National Socialism: The Small Business Movement in Comparative Perspective," *Journal of Modern History* 48 (1976): 1–18.

[12] For the predilection of the new middle class toward National Socialism see Thomas Childers, "National Socialism and the New Middle Class," 19–33.

[13] This trend seems to contradict the one noticeable in the NSDAP. Kater, *Nazi Party*, 160 indicates that members of the social elite responded to National Socialism most enthusiastically in 1932–33. After that point, their quota in the party decreased to such a level that in 1942 their share was equal to that in the general population.

[14] The influx of professionals has been noted by Reiche, *Development of the SA*, 200.

[15] Among the leaders of the Nuremberg SA the proportion of former officers was 15 percent. Reiche, *Development of the SA*, 200.

even quadrupled under the rush of newcomers. Among the membership of the full-time SS formations the influx of high-status men was most clearly marked by the increase of students, whose proportion rose from 10.7 percent to 21.6 percent in the SS-TV and from 8.3 percent to 21.6 percent in the SS-VT. Not surprisingly, the latter formation also experienced the most pronounced growth in the number of ex-officers. The bandwagon effect, and we assume it was operating at full steam, was most remarkable in the Allgemeine SS, whose Führer positions were predominantly staffed by part-time employees. Here the share of academic professionals went from 11.8 percent among the old fighters to 33.2 percent for those who enlisted after 1933.

In fine, all this detailed information points to a relatively narrow recruiting base for the latecomers to the SS. Many, if not most, of these men came from educational and occupational backgrounds whose social status and prestige classified them as members of the upper middle class. In many ways these men fit Robert Koehl's description of SS men as "social engineers." [16] In contrast to them stood the veterans of the movement, whose background was considerably more plebeian, confirming the hypothesis that the class characteristics of the SS elite changed over time—attracting more and more highly trained professionals as the organization became larger and more complex.

SOCIOECONOMIC ADVANTAGE AND ADVANCEMENT

The evidence available from innumerable studies of the social background of political elites strongly supports the generalization that there is a positive correlation between a person's position in a political system and his position in a socially stratified society. That is, political power and leadership positions are monopolized by the socioeconomically privileged. More specifically, it appears that while political leaders are drawn disproportionately from upper-status occupations and privileged family backgrounds, the social backgrounds of administrative elites are at least as exclusive as those

---

[16] Robert Koehl, "Toward an SS Typology: Social Engineers," *American Journal of Economics and Sociology* 18 (1959): 113–126.

of political leaders, and economic subelites are usually drawn from even more privileged backgrounds than are political or administrative elites.[17] In short, most available evidence on elite composition supports a pattern of recruitment that, following Harold Lasswell, is often labeled the "agglutination" model, for it presupposes that many value rankings in society are amalgamated.[18]

Although the so-called agglutination model of elite composition rarely fits reality completely, its main contours seem to be substantiated, at least implicitly, by research on the social basis of National Socialism. For example, in his study on the Nazi party Dietrich Orlow concluded that "the party cadres all but duplicated the status divisions of German middle-class society. The number of university graduates (or at least 'attendants') and the prestige of pre-NSDAP occupations increased significantly in the upper ranks of the party bureaucracy."[19] In a similar vein Bernd Wegner, whose research focused on the Waffen-SS, argues that the upper ranks of the SS-Führerkorps, especially the generals, reflect a high degree of self-recruitment from the upper middle class. In fact, the highest ranking personnel of the Waffen-SS can hardly be distinguished from the officer corps of the German army or other traditional leadership groups in terms of their social origin or educational attainment.[20]

These and similar views were recently reinforced by Michael Kater's impressive statistical study on the social differentiation within the Nazi party. According to Kater, there existed a positive relationship between socioeconomic background and party rank—the higher the party cadre, the greater the degree of social-elite overrepresentation. Thus, the attraction of the Nazi party as a vehicle of social mobility for the young gradually lessened, especially after 1933. Even the SS, "despite its quasi revolutionary appeal served more as an in-status recruitment mechanism, especially for the conventional elite, than as a vehicle of socioeconomic improvement for

[17] Putnam, *Comparative Study of Elites*, 21–24.

[18] Harold D. Lasswell and Daniel Lerner, *World Revolutionary Elites: Studies in Coercive Ideological Movements* (Cambridge, MA, 1965), 9.

[19] Dietrich Orlow, *The History of the Nazi Party, 1919–1933* (Pittsburgh, 1969), 171.

[20] Wegner, *Politische Soldaten*, 236–237.

socially disadvantaged men—at least at the leadership level."[21] In short, the claim of the Nazi leadership to have created a national community, the so-called Volksgemeinschaft, in which talent and not social background determined a man's career and where elites are based on ability and achievement, was never realized. The aim of the following is to determine whether or not the contention that involvement in the Nazi party varied directly with class standing can be extended to the SS. More specifically, we shall examine the relationship, if any, that existed between elite success (highest rank attained) and various social attributes within the context of the most visible elite of the Third Reich, the Führerkorps of Heinrich Himmler's SS.

Who were the men who made it to the top of the SS leadership? Did they perhaps represent an elite of Besitz und Bildung, thus suggesting that prerequisites for the upper and highest levels of the SS leadership were more restrictive than access to the corps in general? Or was it perhaps an open elite of sorts where promotions and advancement were primarily a function of timely arrival or simply reflected an index of Leistung as defined by existing SS leadership?

For the purpose of analysis our original three samples were once again each stratified into two groups: a "Lower Elite" consisting of men who held the rank of SS-Sturmbannführer or lower and an "Upper Elite" that included all those individuals who held a rank of SS-Obersturmbannführer or above.[22] To distinguish between the lower and upper cadres of the SS leadership, we initially made comparisons between the groups on the basis of the distributional characteristics of social-background variables such as level of educational attainment and father's social class. Those who made it to the top echelons of the SS leadership corps, the so-called Upper Elite in our study, possessed these attributes in greater degrees than did the corps as a whole. It therefore seems reasonable to suppose, as did Kater,

[21] Kater, Nazi Party, 196, 239, 229, 235–236.

[22] The definition for the Lower and Upper Elites is based on a Hitler order to the OSAF of November 1931, which divided the SA and SS-Führer ranks into the following three groups: 1) lower = noncommissioned officers, 2) middle = SS-Untersturmführer—SS-Sturmbannführer, 3) upper = SS-Obersturmbannführer—SS-Oberstgruppenführer. This order is cited in Koehl, The Black Corps, 295, n. 43.

that there might be a systematic connection between social background and the level of office acquired.

Next, an attempt was made to gauge the relative importance of the aforementioned two social-background variables in distinguishing between the Lower and Upper Elites of the SS by introducing additional variables such as age, date of joining the SS and NSDAP, and previous military and paramilitary experience. Unfortunately the analysis of bivariate relationships, even when controls are added, does not enable one to identify the relative contribution the variables make in distinguishing among the groups. As the number of variables increases, it becomes exceedingly difficult to interpret the differences between the two groups on each variable singly. Thus the question as to what extent, if any, social background affected advancement within the SS leadership was further pursued with the aid of discriminant analysis, the most appropriate multivariate technique for the analysis of group differences. [23]

Discriminant analysis always begins with the desire to distinguish statistically between two or more groups on the basis of several variables that measure characteristics on which the groups are expected to differ. This is achieved by weighing and linearly combining the discriminating variables in such a fashion as to distinguish statistically between the groups as much as possible. With the criterion or the variable that defines the group being either a dichotomy or multichotomy a crucial aspect of discriminant analysis involves the estimation of discriminant functions that are in the general form

$$D_i = d_{i1}Z_1 + d_{i2}Z_2 + \ldots + d_{ip}Z_p$$

where D_i is the score on the discriminant function i, the d's are discriminant (or weighing) coefficients, and the Z's are the standardized values of the p discriminating variables used in the analysis. Each function represents a unique dimension that can be considered as a defining axis in geometrical space describing the location of one

[23] A good introduction to discriminant analysis is given by Lalitha Sanathana, "Discriminant Analysis" in Daniel J. Amick and Herbert J. Waldberg, *Introducing Multivariate Analysis* (Chicago, 1975) and Spencer Bennett and Daniel Bowers, *An Introduction to Multivariate Technique for Social and Behavioral Sciences* (New York, 1976). A more technical treatment of discriminant analysis can be found in John P. Van de Geer, *Introduction to Multivariate Analysis* (San Francisco, 1971) and Maurice M. Tasuoka, *Multivariate Analysis* (New York, 1971).

group relative to other groups with the proviso that the second or any additional functions are orthogonal or uncorrelated to each other. The maximum number of functions derived is either equal to the number of variables or, if there are more groups than variables, one less than the number of variables.[24] Accordingly, a model was assumed for our study in which the group variable for each SS branch distinguishes between the Lower and Upper Elites of the SS-Führerkorps.[25]

Because age has figured as a relatively important factor in the study of the social base of fascism,[26] the first potential discriminating

[24]The first function is a weighted composite of discriminant scores on the M variables which maximally discriminate between all groups. In the case that it distinguishes well between some groups but not others, a second function is obtained which again is a composite that best separates the groups. Depending on the number of functions derived, each individual in the sample receives a discriminant score and, since the functions are formed in such a fashion as to maximize the separation of groups, individuals within the groups are as much alike as possible on these generated discriminant scores. This in turn is consistent with the fact that the groups themselves are as different as possible on these scores. The general model assumes that the distribution of the variables in the population is multivariate normal with equal variance-covariance matrices within each group. On the robustness of the technique to certain types of nonnormality see Peter Lachenbruch, Cheryl Sneeringer and Lawrence T. Revo, "Robustness of the Linear and Quadratic Discriminant Function to Certain Types of Non-Normality," *Communications in Statistics* 1 (1973): 39–56.

[25]The use of stepwise selection techniques, which enter independent variables into the equation one by one on the basis of some preestablished statistical criteria, were avoided. Instead, we performed an ordinary discriminant analysis where independent or discriminating variables are entered simultaneously in the equation. These latter variables were chosen if, and only if, they could serve as potential discriminators on the basis of theoretical or substantive considerations. Variables that do not have a reasonable expectation of containing information about group differences by themselves should not be included in the analysis. See Carl J. Huberty, "Discriminant Analysis," *Review of Educational Research* 45 (1975): 554. For an evaluation of stepwise selection techniques, variable ranking criteria, subset selection criteria, and optimal subset size see Robert A. Eisenbeis, Gary G. Gilbert, and Robert A. Avery, "Investigating the Relative Importance of Individual Variables and Variable Subsets in Discriminant Analysis," *Communications in Statistics* 2 (1973): 205–219.

[26]A number of scholars have suggested that National Socialism represented a "generational revolt." See for example Loewenberg, "Psychohistorical Origins," 1457–1502; Spitzer, "The Historical Problem of Generations," 1353–1385; Madden, "Generational Aspects of German National Socialism," 445–461; Kater, "Generationskonflikt," 217–243. The role of the war generation within a European wide context is discussed by Wohl, *Generation of 1914*.

variable that was included in the equation was date of birth. Age in turn determines a number of other variables that may or may not have affected the career of an SS-Führer. Two variables, the date of joining the SS and the date of joining the NSDAP, were also chosen for the analysis. (SS and NSDAP membership numbers could also have been used for this purpose.) The reasons for this choice are obvious. All indications are that it was considered prestigious for a follower of National Socialism to have joined the movement before Hitler was appointed chancellor in January of 1933 and there is every reason to believe that the vanguard or *alte Kämpfer* ("Old Fighters") of the movement may have had an advantage when it came to early and quick promotions, regardless of their social background or professional and educational attainment.[27] Not only did age determine how early any given individual might have joined the SS, but it also delineated those who were old enough to have fought during the First World War, especially as officers, and who were attracted to paramilitary formations of the Republic such as the Freikorps. Thus, variables measuring previous paramilitary experience and whether or not a person had been an officer before joining the SS were also submitted for analysis.

The two variables that measured the social standing of SS leaders were the highest educational attainment measured in years of formal education and the social class of fathers.[28] The variable number of

---

[27] Kater, *Nazi Party*, 193–194, 230. The social-political background of the "alten Kämpfer" is the subject of Merkl, *Political Violence*.

[28] "Years of education" summarizes the information on highest educational attainment at the interval level of measurement. Thus, somebody who attended only a Volksschule, for example, received eight years of education, those with an Abitur thirteen years. Two semesters of university education were translated into one year of formal education. Those who were forced to repeat a grade in primary or secondary school were not credited with an additional year of formal education. Although not a major problem, this approach inflates the values for those individuals who spent a long time at a university. The variable measuring father's occupation was an ordinal-type measure. In order to use this information within a multivariate context that requires interval measurement of independent variables, we recoded this variable into a dichotomy. Those whose known occupation had been measured as 1) unskilled worker, 2) skilled worker, or 3) artisan (excluding self-employed artisans) were coded as belonging to the working class and received a score of "1." All other occupations were coded as "zero."

children was included in the analysis because there is some evidence that Himmler took the matter of procreation seriously and gave subordinates without offspring difficulty when it came time for promotions. In fact, there are documented cases where promotions were refused outright because the individuals in question had failed to yield the desired number of children.[29]

In a related matter, it has been argued that a man in the SS could not be promoted to commander unless he turned his back on the church, whether Catholic or Lutheran, and declared himself to be gottgläubig ("God-believing").[30] A variable measuring the frequency of gottgläubigkeit was therefore also included in the equation.

Finally, two other variables which really have nothing to do with social background but had a potential impact on promotions were chosen for the analysis. The first simply measured whether or not an individual had acquired the Reich Sport Badge, and the second indicated if the individual was a recipient of the SS-Ehrendegen (SS Honor Sword). The latter serves as an a priori indicator of those who stood in favor with the Reichsführer-SS himself. The logic behind this is that, except for the graduates of the SS cadet schools who received the sword automatically, the granting of the sword was governed by no formal rule but was dependent exclusively upon the will and pleasure of Heinrich Himmler.[31]

That this list of variables is a miscellaneous assortment is evident, but this was done by design. Not only do we want to see if socioeconomic advantage such as educational attainment can help us distinguish between the Upper and Lower Elites of the SS, but we also

---

[29] It is a well-known fact that Heinrich Himmler had apprehensions regarding the future of the Germanic race and, despite the fact that he was for the most part more concerned with "quality" rather than "quantity," he too intended to take up the fight against the "empty cradle" as part of his battle for the regeneration of Germany. See Herbert F. Ziegler, "The Fight against the Empty Cradle: Nazi Pronatal Policies and the SS-Führerkorps," *Historical Social Research* 38 (1986): 25–40. Evidence gleaned from SS personnel records make it appear that Himmler or his representatives took the matter of procreation seriously when deciding on recommendations for promotion. See the Berlin Document Center SSO files of Graf Gneomer von Hoym, Karl Fichtner, and Konrad Füll.

[30] Höhne, *Order of the Death's Head*, 156, and our discussion in chap. 3.

[31] Höhne, *Order of the Death's Head*, 148, 151.

TABLE 5.1
Summary Statistics of Discriminant Analysis
for Leaders of the SS-Totenkopfverbände

Canonical Correlation	Wilks Lambda	Chi-Squared	D.F.	Significance
0.527	0.723	113.19	11	0.0000

Standardized Canonical Discriminant Function Coefficients

VARIABLE	COEFFICIENT
Date of Joining the SS	0.285
Date of Joining the NSDAP	0.073
SS Honor Sword	−0.120
Reich Sport Badge	−0.024
Paramilitary Experience	0.074
Previously an Officer	−0.589
Date of Birth	0.681
Number of Children	0.078
Gottgläubig	0.101
Years of Formal Education	0.050
Working-Class Origin of Father	−0.017

Group Centroids

Lower Elite — 0.094
Upper Elite — 4.074

Classification Results

ACTUAL GROUP MEMBERSHIP	N of Cases	PREDICTED GROUP MEMBERSHIP	
		Lower Elite	Upper Elite
Lower Elite	390	376 96.4%	14 3.6%
Upper Elite	10	1 10.0%	9 90.0%

Percent of "Grouped" Cases Correctly Classified: 96.25%

TABLE 5.2
Summary Statistics of Discriminant Analysis
for Leaders of the SS-Verfügungstruppe

Canonical Correlation	Wilks Lambda	Chi-Squared	D.F.	Significance
0.593	0.648	251.40	11	0.0000

Standardized Canonical Discriminant Function Coefficients

VARIABLE	COEFFICIENT
Date of Joining the SS	0.261
Date of Joining the NSDAP	0.003
SS Honor Sword	−0.106
Reich Sport Badge	−0.066
Paramilitary Experience	0.033
Previously an Officer	−0.547
Date of Birth	0.777
Number of Children	0.089
Gottgläubig	0.125
Years of Formal Education	−0.249
Working-Class Origin of Father	−0.016

Group Centroids

Lower Elite — 0.204
Upper Elite — −2.650

Classification Results

ACTUAL GROUP MEMBERSHIP		PREDICTED GROUP MEMBERSHIP	
	N of Cases	Lower Elite	Upper Elite
Lower Elite	647	595 92.0%	52 8.0%
Upper Elite	45	10 22.2%	35 77.8%

Percent of "Grouped" Cases Correctly Classified: 91.04%

TABLE 5.3
SUMMARY STATISTICS OF DISCRIMINANT ANALYSIS
FOR LEADERS OF THE ALLGEMEINE SS

Canonical Correlation	Wilks Lambda	Chi-Squared	D.F.	Significance
0.653	0.574	385.54	11	0.0000

Standardized Canonical Discriminant Function Coefficients

VARIABLE	COEFFICIENT
Date of Joining the SS	0.020
Date of Joining the NSDAP	−0.259
SS Honor Sword	0.807
Reich Sport Badge	−0.143
Paramilitary Experience	0.111
Previously an Officer	0.279
Date of Birth	−0.414
Number of Children	−0.010
Gottgläubig	−0.173
Years of Formal Education	−0.035
Working-Class Origin of Father	−0.037

Group Centroids

Lower Elite — −0.369
Upper Elite — 2.007

Classification Results

ACTUAL GROUP MEMBERSHIP	N of Cases	PREDICTED GROUP MEMBERSHIP	
		Lower Elite	Upper Elite
Lower Elite	726	665 91.6%	61 8.4%
Upper Elite	129	38 29.5%	91 70.5%

Percent of "Grouped" Cases Correctly Classified: 88.42%

need to know how important these variables are vis-à-vis those measuring other dimensions. The results of the discriminant analyses for each SS branch are summarized in tables 5.1–5.3.[32]

Beginning with the summary measures for all three tables[33] we note that the eleven variables chosen for the analysis produced a moderately high degree of separation, as is indicated by the canonical correlation coefficients of 0.527, 0.593, and 0.653 for the Totenkopfverbände, Verfügungstruppe, and Allgemeine SS respectively for the first and only discriminant function. These coefficients help in evaluating the importance of the discriminant function by indicating its ability to discriminate between the groups, that is, the lower and upper segments of the SS leadership corps. Moreover, the canonical correlation squared can be interpreted as the proportion of variance in the discriminant function explained by the groups; thus 27.8 percent, 35.2 percent, and 42.6 percent of the difference between the Lower and Upper Elites of the SS-Führerkorps for each SS branch respectively can be attributed to the combined influences of the eleven discriminating variables. The Wilks Lambda that was calculated for individual analysis can be translated into a chi-square statistic, thereby evaluating the statistical significance of the individual discriminant functions. In all three instances the level of significance exceeds .001.

Next, the discriminant function from each analysis was used to compute the discriminant score for each individual in the samples by multiplying each discriminating variable by its corresponding coefficient and adding together these products.[34] As an aid in interpre-

---

[32]This is the summary output of the SPSS "Discriminant" subprogram. See SPSSx: A User's Guide (New York, 1983), 623–646. As is often the case in this type of research some cases in the data file did not have complete information for every variable. In order to process a file that contained cases with incomplete data, missing values were specified for each variable. Because the number of cases for the Upper Elite was relatively small and we did not want to lose any cases that could be used in the discriminant analysis, means were substituted for these missing values.

[33]Helpful comments on the interpretation of discriminant analysis results and potential pitfalls are offered by Donald G. Morrison, "On the Interpretation of Discriminant Analysis," Journal of Marketing 6 (1969): 156–163.

[34]For the purpose of this analysis the scores are in standard form (z-scores). Thus, a single score represents the number of standard deviations a particular case individual is, away from the mean of all cases on the given discriminant function.

tation, the mean discriminant score, or group centroid, for each group on the discriminant function was calculated by averaging the scores for the cases within each group. The mean discriminant function scores for the lower and upper segment of the corps were 0.094 and -4.074 for the Totenkopfverbände, 0.204 and -2.650 for the Verfügungstruppe, and -0.369 and 2.007 for the Allgemeine SS, indicating the most typical location of a score for each elite. In the case of the SS-TV and SS-VT, therefore, individuals with the highest scores were most likely to belong to the Lower Elite, whereas those with the lower discriminant function scores were more likely to belong to the Upper ranks. For the Allg. SS the relationship is an inverse one.

The coefficients used in the computations of the discriminant scores refer to the values of the d's given in the general equation. These coefficients are of great analytical importance by themselves because they not only enable us to determine those variables that are important in discriminating between the ranks of the SS-Führerkorps but also give us some idea about the influence different variables have in deciding to which group an individual is most likely to belong.[35]

With respect to the SS-TV and SS-VT, the variable "date of birth" clearly carried the most weight toward separation of the groups along the discriminant function. The positive coefficient indicates that a high score on this variable contributed to a high score along the discriminant function. In other words, the younger an individual was the more likely he was to be a member of the Lower Elite group. The second largest contribution was made by the variable measuring whether or not the SS-Führer held an officer's rank prior to joining the SS. The negative coefficient here implies that former military officers tended to fall into the group with the lowest discriminant

[35] Generally speaking, a large positive coefficient for a particular variable implies that individuals characterized by high values for this variable are more likely to fall into the group with the highest discriminant score. Conversely, a large negative coefficient implies that individuals with high values for this variable tend to fall into the group with the smallest discriminant score. In order to eliminate spurious effects of units on the magnitude of coefficients, standardized discriminant coefficients were computed by multiplying each raw weight by the standard deviation of the corresponding variable.

score, that is, the Upper Elite. The date for entering the SS figured as the third most discriminating variable for both the SS-TV and SS-VT. The interpretation is analogous to the one associated with the date of birth; the later an individual joined the SS the higher the probability that he was found amongst the Lower Elite. Not unexpectedly, those who possessed the SS Honor Sword tended to congregate in the upper ranks of the SS. Somewhat ironically the men who claimed to be Gottgläubig were more frequently associated with the Lower Elite. With one exception the remaining variables made no significant contribution to the power of the discriminant function. The one exception applies to the SS-Verfügungstruppe, where a moderately high coefficient signifies that Upper-Elite status was more likely to be connected to a high level of education.

As to the leadership of the Allgemeine SS, the results are fairly similar, excepting the fact that the variable that contributed the most to group separation was the one measuring ownership of the SS Honor Sword. The large positive coefficient denotes that the recipients of this honor were most likely to be part of the Upper Elite. As was the case for the SS-TV and SS-VT the age of an individual served as a good predictor of group membership; the older the Führer, the higher the probability that he held a high rank. In a similar fashion we find that the moderately high coefficients associated with the variables "(early) date of entry NSDAP," "former officer," and "paramilitary experience" identified those men who were the least likely to belong to the Lower Elite. The converse held true for those claiming to be "God believers" and, perhaps ironically, those who qualified for the Reich Sport Badge. Formal education and social class as measured by the father's occupation, however, had absolutely no impact on the discriminant function.

Normally, once a set of variables is found that provides satisfactory discrimination for cases with known group membership, techniques are employed that permit the classification of new cases with unknown group membership based on the information provided by the discriminating variables. Yet another use of classification is in testing the adequacy of the derived discriminant functions. For the groups used in our analysis, actual group membership is known because we already knew the rank of each Führer. The purpose of classifying these cases, therefore, is to see how effective the discriminating variables actually are. By classifying the cases used to derive the functions in the first place and comparing predicted group membership with actual group membership, we can empirically measure success in discrimination by observing the proportion of correct classifications. If a large proportion of misclassification occurs, then the variables selected were poor discriminators. Furthermore, the same classification results will also tell us whether the classification errors fall into a certain group or not.[36]

As long as we are working with a 50 percent chance model as we have done here, the interpretation of the classification matrix is relatively simple and straightforward. It is evident that correctly classifying 96.25 percent, 91.04 percent, and 88.42 percent of all Führer for the SS-TV, SS-VT, and Allg. SS, when chance would yield 50 percent, indicates a high degree of success. To determine the probability of obtaining these results by chance alone a final statistic, Cohen's Kappa—the chance-corrected percentage of agreement between the actual and predicted group membership—was computed.[37] Because by chance alone we would expect to classify only 50 percent of the cases correctly, the Kappas calculated for each classification table suggest that knowledge of the scores on the discriminating variables and knowledge of the discriminant functions allow

[36] A sometimes useful yet hazardous feature of classification statistics is that they allow us the use of prior knowledge about the probabilities of group membership as well as information contained in the discriminating variables. Prior knowledge with regard to our samples consists of knowing the group sizes; to the extent that the prior knowledge influences the classification procedure the result would be that cases are more likely to be assigned to the larger group. We have adopted a probability of .50 for a given Führer's belonging to either the Lower or Upper Elite. William W. Cooley and Paul R. Lohnes, *Multivariate Data Analysis* (New York, 1971), 263.

[37] Kappa was defined by J. Cohen, "Weighted Kappa: Nominal Scale Agreement with Provision for Scaled Disagreement or Partial Credit," *Psychological Bulletin* 70 (1968): 213–219 as the sum of the observed proportion of agreement P_o, minus the proportion of agreement expected by chance P_e, divided by one minus the sum of proportion of agreement expected by chance, P_e. Following procedures outlined by Carl F. Wiedemann and Abraham Fenster, "The Use of Chance Corrected Percentage Agreement to Interpret the Results of Discriminant Analysis," *Educational and Psychological Measurements* 38 (1978): 25–39 the marginals of each classification table were converted to proportions as was the agreement diagonal. In addition, the proportion expected in each cell of the agreement diagonal purely by chance was computed by multiplying the row and column proportions associated with each cell of the diagonal.

us to improve prediction about group membership by 92.6 percent, 82.0 percent, and 76.8 percent over and above chance agreement for each SS branch.

The discriminant analysis demonstrated that the hallmark of the men who approached the pinnacle of power in the SS was that they comprised an older membership, a membership that was also characterized by a high proportion of early joiners to the SS, many of whom were former officers who probably had been unable to continue their military careers after 1918. In the course of the analysis it also became apparent that socioeconomic advantages, such as academic or technical skills, and social background did not seem to affect advancement directly or in a decisive way. The Upper Elite of the SS was an open elite with respect to social background, and advancement of its membership was no more dependent on the level of socioeconomic advantage than membership itself was on the much heralded racial criteria.[38] Regardless of the social stratification that existed within the leadership corps of the SS, there is little doubt that it was either modified or entirely suspended by factors that were directly and indirectly linked to age and military leadership abilities. In substantive terms this meant that the older SS leader who had previously been an officer and who received his commission relatively early in his SS career was the most likely to succeed within the SS.

Because older men had the opportunity to join the SS at an earlier stage of its development, they were more likely to have attained the mark of in-group distinction, the status of an "Old Fighter."[39] Aside from the prestige this bestowed, it also permitted these individuals to gain strategic positions more easily and make connections that might prove to be conducive to quick and further advancement. But despite the fact that "even in the SS almost all of the top leadership consisted of veteran party members"[40] who retained the deci-

[38]The promotion guidelines of the Waffen-SS stated the following as decisive factors for promotion: character as a German man, demonstration of worth as Nazi and SS man, and performance as soldier and leader. *Dich ruft die SS*, 24–25.

[39]Kater, *Nazi Party*, 190. Wegner, *Politische Soldaten*, 245 suggests that it was the younger Führer of the Waffen-SS who made up the mass of "Old Fighters," especially those born between 1906 and 1915.

[40]Struve, *Elites*, 445. See also Neusüss-Hunkel, *Die SS*, 16, 22.

sive posts within the SS until the very end of the Third Reich, it also bears emphasizing that they represented only a small minority. The majority of old SS hands simply did not survive the influx of the new joiners who poured into the SS from January and especially after March of 1933 onward.[41] As a result, most of the positions in the SS were filled by younger men who were not alte Kämpfer, or party veterans, and to whom Himmler's organization offered exceptionally rapid advancement.

Because the prewar years witnessed the creation of SS formations that tried to emulate and even surpass the standards of military training prevailing in the Wehrmacht, Heinrich Himmler was in need of personnel who could lead and train the personnel of the SS-Totenkopfverbände and SS-Verfügungstruppe. Consequently, individuals who had been military officers—officers who probably were unable to continue their careers in the Reichswehr—before joining Himmler's Black Order accrued advantages in the quest for promotions. It was not so much the formal educational qualifications[42] that these men possessed, but their military skills—aptitude for command learned from time spent in positions of military authority[43]—that were assets in demand in the SS that were probably rewarded with early commissions and subsequent quick promotions. Menschenführung, "a gift for inspiring and leading men,"[44] was always a quality valued by Himmler and one apparently needed to get to the top of the SS leadership. Under such circumstances the SS attracted ambitious and intelligent individuals, especially those who showed military leadership abilities, who were offered career possibilities generally not available in the Wehrmacht.[45] It would appear that the SS, as the paragon of Nazi purity, provided the foundation for a "test-tube revolution"[46] in elite recruitment and advancement.

[41] Koehl, "The Character of the Nazi SS," 282.

[42] Wegner, Politische Soldaten, 228.

[43] Höhne, Order of the Death's Head, 134.

[44] Sydnor, Soldiers of Destruction, 22 and Kater, Nazi Party, 204–205.

[45] Neusüss-Hunkel, Die SS, 24.

[46] Leonard Krieger, "Nazism: Highway or Byway?" Central European History 11 (March 1978): 15.

Appendix

Comparative Table of Waffen-SS, German Army, and U.S. Army Ranks[1]

WAFFEN SS	GERMAN ARMY	U.S. ARMY
Commissioned		
Reichsführer-SS	Generalfeldmarschall	General of the Army
SS-Oberstgruppenführer[2]	Generaloberst	General
SS-Obergruppenführer	General	Lieutenant General
SS-Gruppenführer	Generalleutnant	Major General
SS-Brigadeführer	Generalmajor	Brigadier General
SS-Oberführer	—	—
SS-Standartenführer	Oberst	Colonel
SS-Obersturmbannführer	Oberstleutnant	Lieutenant Colonel
SS-Sturmbannführer	Major	Major
SS-Hauptsturmführer	Hauptmann	Captain
SS-Obersturmführer	Oberleutnant	1st Lieutenant
SS-Untersturmführer	Leutnant	2nd Lieutenant

[1] Stein, *Waffen-SS*, 295.
[2] This rank was instituted after 1939.

149

Select Bibliography

THIS WORK IS based principally on data relating to the lives of 1,947 SS members who held the rank of SS-Untersturmführer or higher before 1939. Biographical information for these individuals, who had previously been identified by the *Dienstaltersliste der Schutzstaffel der NSDAP, Stand 31.12.1938*, bearbeitet von der Personalkanzlei (Berlin, 1938), was gathered from SS personnel records located at the Berlin Document Center. These records are divided into two collections: (1) the SS Officer Files containing folders of varying completeness for 61,465 SS-Führer and (2) the files of the SS Race and Settlement Main Office, comprising some 238,000 folders pertaining to Führer, Unterführer, and enlisted personnel of the SS. Both collections were used extensively in order to gather biographical information on all members of the SS-Totenkopfverbände, the SS-Verfügungstruppe, and a randomly selected sample of Allgemeine SS members. In the event that certain items could not be located among these records because some entries were illegible or simply missing, an attempt was made to locate the desired information from the SA and NSDAP Masterfiles of the Berlin Document Center.

The kind of material assembled was broad in scope, and much of it was not even utilized for this study. Once collected, the information was coded into numerical equivalents and entered onto magnetic media. More precisely, all data underwent an initial verification by "keypunching" each twice. Next, the data were sorted and checked for improper codes or missing values. As is frequently the case in this type of research some cases in the data file did not have complete information for every variable. In order to process a file that contained cases with incomplete data, missing values were specified for each variable. If a case contained a missing value for any variable, it was designated as deficient and was omitted from subsequent calculations.

These data on the collective biographies of SS-Führer were supplemented by more traditional types of sources. Some of these were derived from various SS publications, which also came from the Berlin Document Center and included among others the following: *Haushaltsplannung der*

Schutzstaffel der NSDAP für das Rechnungsjahr 1938: Lehrplan für die welt-anschauliche Erziehung in der SS und Polizei (Berlin, n.d.); *SS Handblätter für den weltanschaulichen Unterricht: Prüfungsfragen für den Führer* (21.8.1938); *Lehrplan für sechsmonatige Schulung* (Berlin); *Mein Weg zur Waffen-SS* (Berlin, n.d.); Reichsführer-SS, *Dich ruft die SS* (Berlin, 1943); and the *Organisationsbuch der NSDAP*.

The compilation of captured German documents made by the American Historical Association's Committee for the Study of War Records was another source of primary materials. This work benefited in particular from numerous reels of microfilm containing the Records of the Reich Leader SS and Chief of German Police, Washington: National Archives, Microcopy T–175. These sources were complemented by certain materials of the Institute für Zeitgeschichte (*IfZ*) in Munich. More specifically, use was made of SA-related files (FA107), Himmler speeches (F37), and miscellaneous SS-related documents (FA127). The holdings of the Hoover Institute at Stanford University and the U.S. Library of Congress provided access to frequently employed contemporary newspapers, namely, the party newspaper *Völkischer Beobachter* (Berlin edition) and the SS's own paper *Das Schwarze Korps*. Also utilized was the SS serial publication *SS-Leithefte* (1935–1945), procured from the Berlin Document Center. Finally, in order to construct statistical indexes as the basis for a comparison with our own data, regular use was made of the following statistical sources: *Parteistatistik, Stand 1. Januar 1935; Statistik des deutschen Reichs; Statistisches Jahrbuch der Schutzstaffel der NSDAP; Statistische Handbuch von Deutschland, 1928–1945*.

Additional but more easily accessible published primary sources are included in the following select bibliography.

Abel, Theodore. *The Nazi Movement: Why Hitler Came to Power* (New York, 1934).

Ackermann, Josef. *Heinrich Himmler als Ideologe*. Göttingen, 1970.

Alewyn, Richard. "Das Problem der Generation in der Geschichte." *Zeitschrift für deutsche Bildung* 10 (1929): 519–527.

Allen, William Sheridan. "Farewell to Class Analysis in the Rise of Nazism: Comment." *Central European History* 17 (1984): 54–62.

———. *The Nazi Seizure of Power: The Experience of a Single German Town, 1930–1935*. Chicago, 1965.

Amick, Daniel J., and Waldberg, Herbert J. *Introducing Multivariate Analysis*. Chicago, 1975.

Armstrong, John A. *The European Administrative Elite*. Princeton, 1973.

Aron, Raymond. "Social Structure and the Ruling Class." *British Journal of Sociology* 1 (1950): 1–16, 126–143.

Aronson, Shlomo. *Reinhard Heydrich und die Fühgeschichte von Gestapo und Sicherheitsdienst*. Stuttgart, 1971.

Aufmuth, Ulrich. *Die deutsche Wandervogelbewegung unter sozioloischem Aspekt*. Göttingen, 1979.

Banaszkiewicz, Jakub. "German Fascism and People of the Social Fringe." *Polish Western Affairs* 8 (1967): 251–288.

Bartz, Joachim, and More, Dagmar. "Der Weg in die Jugendzwangsarbeit— Massnahmen gegen Jugenarbeitslosigkeit zwischen 1925 und 1935." In Gero Lenhardt, ed., *Der hilflose Sozialstaat: Jugendarbeitslosigkeit und Politik*. Frankfurt, 1979, 28–94.

Beier, Gerhard. "Das Problem der Arbeiteraristokratie im 19. und 20. Jahrhundert: Zur Sozialgeschichte einer umstrittenen Kategorie." In *Herkunft und Mandat: Beiträge zur Führungsproblematik in der Arbeiterbewegung*. Frankfurt/Main and Cologne, 1976, 9–71.

Bénéton, Phillipe. "La génération de 1912–1914: Image, Mythe, et Réalité." *Revue Française de Science Politique* 21 (1971): 981–1009.

Bennecke, Heinrich. *Hitler und die SA*. Munich and Vienna, 1962.

Bennett, Spencer, and Bowers, Daniel. *An Introduction to Multivariate Technique for Social and Behavioral Sciences*. New York, 1976.

Berger, Bennet M. "How Long Is a Generation?" *British Journal of Sociology* 11 (1960): 10–23.

Bessel, Richard. "Living with the Nazis: Some Recent Writing on the Social History of the Third Reich." *European History Quarterly* 14 (1984): 211–220.

Bessel, Richard, and Jamin, Mathilde. "Nazis, Workers, and the Use of Quantitative Evidence." *Social History* 4 (1979): 111–116.

Best, Werner. *Die deutsche Polizei*. Darmstadt, 1941.

———. "Die Schutzstaffel der NSDAP und die deutsche Polizei." *Deutsches Recht* (edition A) 9 (1939): 44–47.

Bihl, W. "Zur Rechtsstellung der Waffen-SS." *Wehrwissenschaftliche Rundschau* 16 (1966): 379–385.

Bleuel, Hans Peter, and Klinnert, Ernst. *Deutsche Studenten auf dem Weg ins Dritte Reich: Ideologien—Programme—Aktionen, 1918–1935*. Gütersloh, 1967.

Blüher, Hans. *Wandervogel: Geschichte einer Bewegung.* 2 vols. Jena, 1912.

Boehnert, Gunnar C. "An Analysis of the Age and Education of the SS-Führerkorps, 1925–1939." *Historical Social Research* 12 (1974): 4–17.

———. "The Jurists in the SS-Führerkorps, 1925–1939." In Gerhard Hirschfeld and Lothar Kettenacker, eds., *Der "Führerstaat": Mythos und Realität, Studien zur Struktur und Politik des Dritten Reiches.* Stuttgart, 1981, 361–374.

———. "A Sociography of the SS Officer Corps, 1925–1939." Ph.D. dissertation, University of London, 1977.

———. "The Third Reich and the Problem of 'Social Revolution': German Officers and the SS." In Volker Berghahn and Martin Kitchen, eds., *Germany in the Age of Total War.* London, 1981, 203–217.

Bolte, Karl Martin. "Die Berufsstruktur im industrialisierten Deutschland: Entwicklung und Probleme." In Karl Martin Bolte, Katrin Aschenbrenner, Reinhard Kreckel, Rainer Schultz-Wild et al., *Beruf und Gesellschaft in Deutschland: Berufsstruktur und Berufsprobleme.* Opladen, 1970, 32–149.

———. *Deutsche Gesellschaft im Wandel.* Opladen, 1966.

———. *Sozialer Aufstieg und Abstieg.* Stuttgart, 1959.

Borinski, Fritz, and Milch, Werner. *Jugendbewegung: The Story of German Youth, 1896–1933.* London, 1945.

Bottomore, Thomas B. *Elites and Society.* London, 1964.

Bracher, Karl D[ietrich]. *The German Dictatorship: The Origins, Structure, and Effects of National Socialism.* New York, 1970.

———. "Tradition und Revolution im Nationalsozialismus." In *Zeitgeschichtliche Kontroversen: Um Faschismus, Totalitarismus, Demokratie.* Munich, 1976, 62–78.

Bracher, Karl Dietrich; Sauer, Wolfgang; and Schultz, Gerhard. *Die nationalsozialistische Machtergreifung: Studien zur Errichtung des totalitären Herrschaftssystem in Deutschland, 1933–34.* Cologne and Opladen, 1960.

Brim, Orville G., Jr. "Personality Development as Role Learning." In Ira Iscoe and Harold W. Stevenson, eds., *Personality and Development in Children.* Austin, 1960, 127–159.

Brim, Orville G., Jr., and Wheeler, Stanton. *Socialization after Childhood: Two Essays.* New York, 1966.

Broszat, Martin. *The Hitler State.* New York, 1981.

————. "National Socialist Concentration Camps, 1933–1945." In Buchheim et al., *Anatomy of the SS State*. New York, 1968, 397–504.

————. "Zur Struktur der NS-Massenbewegung." *Vierteljahrshefte für Zeitgeschichte* 31 (1983): 52–76.

Browder, George C. "Problems and Potentials of the Berlin Document Center." *Central European History* 4 (1972): 362–380.

Buchheim, Hans. "Command and Compliance." In Hans Buchheim et al., *Anatomy of the SS State*. New York, 1968, 303–396.

————. "The SS Instrument of Domination." In Hans Buchheim et al., 127–301. *Anatomy of the SS State*. New York, 1968.

————. "Die Höheren SS-und Polizeiführer." *Vierteljahrshefte für Zeitgeschichte* 11 (1963): 362–391.

————. "Die SS in der Verfassung des Dritten Reiches. " *Vierteljahrshefte für Zeitgeschichte* 3 (1955): 127–157.

Burnham, Walter Dean. "Political Immunization and Political Confessionalism: The United States and Weimar Germany." *Journal of Interdisciplinary History* 3 (1972): 1–30.

Buss, Philip. H., and Mollo, Andrew. *Hitler's Germanic Legions: An Illustrated History of the Western European Legions with the SS, 1941–1943*. London, 1978.

Butterfield, Herbert. *The Discontinuities between the Generations in History*. Cambridge, 1972.

Caplan, Jane. "The Politics of Administration: The Reich Interior Ministry and the German Civil Service." *Historical Journal* 20 (1977): 707–736.

————. "Speaking the Right Language: The Nazi Party and the Civil Service Vote in the Weimar Republic." In Thomas Childers, ed., *The Formation of the Nazi Constituency, 1919–1933*. London, 1986, 182–201.

Childers, Thomas. "National Socialism and the New Middle Class." In Reinhard Mann, ed., *Die Nationalsozialisten: Analysen faschistischer Bewegungen*. Stuttgart, 1980, 19–33.

————. *The Nazi Voter: The Social Foundations of Fascism in Germany, 1919–1933*. Chapel Hill, 1983.

————. "The Social Bases of the National Socialist Vote." *Journal of Contemporary History* 11 (1976): 17–42.

————. "Who, Indeed, Did Vote for Hitler?" *Central European History* 17 (1984): 45–53.

Cochran, W. G. *Sampling Techniques*. New York, 1953.

Cohen, James. "Weighted Kappa: Nominal Scale Agreement with Provision for Scaled Disagreement or Partial Credit." *Psychological Bulletin* 70 (1968): 213–219.

Conway, John S. *The Nazi Persecution of the Churches, 1933–1945*. London and New York, 1968.

Conyer, Sandra J. "Class Consciousness and Consumption: The New Middle Class during the Weimar Republic." *Journal of Social History* 10 (1977): 310–332.

Cooley, William W., and Lohnes, Paul R. *Multivariate Data Analysis*. New York, 1971.

Coxton, Anthony P. M., and Jones, Charles L. *Class and Hierarchy: Social Meanings of Occupations*. London, 1979.

———. *The Images of Occupational Prestige*. London, 1978.

Craig, John E. "Higher Education and Social Mobility in Germany." In Konrad Jarausch, ed., *The Transformation of Higher Learning, 1860–1930: Expansion, Diversification, Social Origins, and Professionalization in Germany, Russia, and the United States*. Stuttgart, 1982, 219–244.

Czudnowski, Moshe M. "Towards a Second Generation of Empirical Elite and Leadership Studies." In *Political Elites and Social Change: Studies of Elite Roles and Attitudes*. 1983, 243–255.

Daheim, Hansjürgen. "Die Vorstellungen vom Mittelstand." *Kölner Zeitschrift für Soziologie und Sozialpsychologie* 12 (1960): 237–277.

Dahl, Robert A. *Modern Political Analysis*. Englewood Cliffs, NJ, 1963.

Dahm, Karl-Wilhelm. "German Protestantism and Politics, 1918–1939." *Journal of Contemporary History* 3 (1968): 29–49.

Dahrendorf, Ralf. "Industrielle Fertigkeiten und soziale Schichtung." *Kölner Zeitschrift für Soziologie und Sozialpsychologie* 8 (1956): 540–568.

———. *Society and Democracy in Germany*. Garden City, 1967.

Dallin, Alexander. *German Rule in Russia, 1941–1945: A Study of Occupation Policies*. London and New York, 1957.

d'Alquen, Günter. *Die SS: Geschichte, Aufgabe, und Organisation der Schutzstaffel der NSDAP*. Munich, 1939.

Darré, Richard Walther. *Das Bauerntum als Lebensquell der nordischen Rasse*. Munich, 1933.

———. *Neuadel aus Blut und Boden*. Munich, 1930.

Diehl, James M. *Paramilitary Politics in Weimar Germany*. Bloomington, 1977.

Diels, Rudolf. *Lucifer ante Portas . . . Es spricht der erste Chef der Gestapo*. Zürich, 1949.

Diephouse, D. J. "The German 'Catastrophe' Revisited: Civil Religion in the Third Reich." *Fides et Historica* 7 (1975): 54–74.

Dingräve, Leopold [Ernst Wilhelm Eschmann]. *Wo steht die junge Generation?* Jena, 1931.

Doblin, Ernest and Pohly, Claire. "The Social Composition of the Nazi Leadership." *American Journal of Sociology* 5 (1945): 42–49.

Douglas, Donald M. "The Parent Cell. Some Computer Notes on the Composition of the First Nazi Party Group in Munich, 1919–1921." *Central European History* 10 (1977): 55–72.

Dreitzel, Hans Peter. *Elitebegriff und Sozialstruktur: Eine soziologische Begriffsanalyse*. Stuttgart, 1962.

Duggan, Thomas J., and Dean, Charles W. "Common Misinterpretations of Significance Levels in Sociological Journals." *American Sociologist* 3 (1968): 45–46.

Dwinger, Edwin Erich. *Wir rufen Deutschland*. Jena, 1932.

Ebeling, Hans. *The German Youth Movement: Its Past and Future*. London, 1945.

Edinger, Lewis J. "Continuity and Change in the Background of German Decision Makers." *Western Political Quarterly* 14 (1961): 17–36.

Edinger, Lewis J., and Searing, Donald D. "Social Background in Elite Analysis: A Methodological Inquiry." *American Political Science Review* 61 (1967): 428–445.

Eisenbeis, Robert A.; Gilbert, Gary G.; and Avery, Robert A. "Investigating the Relative Importance of Individual Variables and Variable Subsets in Discriminant Analysis." *Communications in Statistics* 2 (1973): 205–219.

Eisenstadt, S. N. *From Generation to Generation: Age Groups of Social Structure*. Glencoe, IL, 1956.

Elterlein, Utmann von. "Absage an den Jahrgang 1902?" *Die Tat* 22 (1930–31): 202–206.

Engelhard, Erich. "Die Angestellten." *Kölner Vierteljahrshefte für Soziologie* 10 (1932): 479–520.

Enno, Georg. *Die wirtschaftlichen Unternehmungen der SS*. Stuttgart, 1963.

Etzioni, Amitai. *The Active Society: A Theory of Societal and Political Processes.* London, 1962.

Falter, Jürgen W. "Warum die deutschen Arbeiter während des Dritten Reiches zu Hitler standen: Einige Anmerkungen zu Günther Mais Beitrag über die Unterstützung des nationalsozialistischen Herrschaftssystems durch Arbeiter." *Geschichte und Gesellschaft* 13 (1987): 217–231.

Falter, Jürgen W., and Hänisch, D. "Die Anfälligkeit von Arbeitern gegenüber der NSDAP, 1928–1933." *Archiv für Sozialgeschichte* 26 (1986): 179–216.

Faust, Anselm. *Der Nationalsozialistische Deutsche Studentenbund: Studenten und Nationalsozialismus in der Weimarer Republik, I.* Düsseldorf, 1973.

Fest, Joachim C. *Hitler.* Frankfurt/Main, 1973.

Finch, Robert F., and Campell, Donald T. "Proof? No. Evidence? Yes. The Significance of Significance Tests." *American Sociologist* 4 (1969): 140–143.

Fischer, Conan J. "The Occupational Background of the SA's Rank and File Membership during the Depression Years, 1929 to mid-1934." In Peter D. Stachura, ed., *The Shaping of the Nazi State.* London, 1978, 131–159.

―――. *Stormtroopers: A Social, Economic, and Ideological Analysis, 1925–35.* London, 1983.

Fleischner, Hans-Otto. "Einige Bemerkungen zur besonderen Rolle der SS innerhalb des Systems der faschistischen Organisationen, 1935–1945." *Jenaer Beiträge zur Parteigeschichte* 37/38 (1976): 74–94.

Franz-Willing, Georg. *Die Hitlerbewegung: Der Ursprung, 1919–1922.* Hamburg and Berlin, 1962.

Gasset, José Ortega y. *Man and Crisis.* New York, 1958.

―――. *The Modern Theme.* New York, 1961.

Geiger, Theodor. *Die soziale Schichtung des deutschen Volkes: Soziographischer Versuch auf statistischer Grundlage.* Stuttgart, 1967; 1st printing, 1932.

Gelwick, Robert A. "Personnel Policies and Procedures of the Waffen-SS." Ph.D. dissertation, University of Nebraska, Lincoln, NE, 1971.

Genuneit, Jürgen. "Methodische Probleme der quantitativen Analyse früher NSDAP-Mitgliederlisten." In Reinhard Mann, ed., *Die Nationalsozialisten: Analysen faschistischer Bewegungen.* Stuttgart, 1980, 34–66.

Gerth, Hans. "The Nazi Party: Its Leadership and Composition." *American Journal of Sociology* 45 (1940): 517–541.

Giles, Geoffrey J. "German Students and Higher Education Policy in the Second World War." *Central European History* 17 (1984): 330–354.

Gold, David. "Statistical Tests and Substantive Significance." *American Sociologist* 4 (1969): 42–46.

Goldthorpe, John H., and Hope, Keith. *The Social Gradings of Occupations: A New Approach and Scale.* Oxford, 1974.

Gordon, Harold J., Jr. *Hitler and the Beer Hall Putsch.* Princeton, 1972.

Gossweiler, Kurt. "Faschismus und Arbeiterklasse." In Dietrich Eichholtz and Kurt Gossweiler, eds., *Faschismus—Forschung: Positionen, Probleme, Polemik.* Berlin, 1980, 99–123.

Grill, Johnpeter H[orst]. *The Nazi Movement in Baden, 1920–1945.* Chapel Hill, 1983.

————. "The Nazi Party's Rural Propaganda before 1928." *Central European History* 15 (June 1982): 149–185.

Grünberger, Richard. "Lebensborn: Hitler's Selective Breeding Establishment." *Wiener Library Bulletin* 16 (1962): 52–53.

————. *The 12-Year Reich: A Social History of Nazi Germany, 1933–1945.* New York, 1971.

Gründel, Günther E. *Die Sendung der jungen Generation: Versuch einer umfassenden revolutionären Sinndeutung der Krise.* Munich, 1932.

Günther, A. E. "Der Bürgerhaß der jungen Generation." *Deutsches Volkstum* (1930): 89–95.

Guttsman, W. L. *The German Social Democratic Party, 1875–1933: From Ghetto to Government.* London, 1981.

Hamilton, Alastair. *The Appeal of Fascism: A Study of Intellectuals and Fascism, 1919–1945.* New York, 1971.

Hamilton, Richard F. "Reply to Commentators." *Central European History* 27 (1984): 72–85.

————. *Who Voted for Hitler?* Princeton, 1982.

Hamm, Heinz. *Die wirtschaflichen und sozialen Berufsmerkmale der kaufmännischen Angestellten (im Vergleich mit denjenigen der Arbeiter).* Jena, 1931.

Harcourt, Robert d'. "National Socialism and the Catholic Church in Germany." In Maurice Beaumont, John H.E. Fried, and Edmund Vermeil, eds., *The Third Reich.* New York, 1955, 797–810.

Hardach, Gerd. "Klassen und Schichten in Deutschland, 1848–1970: Probleme einer historischen Strukturanalyse." *Geschichte und Gesellschaft* 3 (1977): 501–524.

Hausser, Paul. *Soldaten wie ander auch: Der Weg der Waffen SS.* Osnarbrück, 1966.

Heiden, Konrad. *Die Geburt des Dritten Reiches: Die Geschichte des Nationalsozialismus bis Herbst 1933.* Zürich, 1934.

———. *Die Geschichte des Nationalsozialismus.* Berlin, 1932.

———. *A History of National Socialism.* London, 1934.

Helmreich, Ernst Christian. *The German Churches under Hitler: Background, Struggle, and Epilogue.* Detroit, 1979.

Hennig, Eike. *Bürgerliche Gesellschaft und Faschismus in Deutschland: Ein Forschungsbericht.* Frankfurt/Main, 1977.

Henry, Clarissa, and Hillel, Marc. *Lebensborn e.V.: Im Name der Rasse.* Vienna and Hamburg, 1975.

Heydrich, Reinhard. *Wandlungen unseres Kampfes.* Berlin, 1936.

Hiden, John, and Farquharson, John. *Explaining Hitler's Germany: Historians and the Third Reich.* London, 1983.

Himmler, Heinrich. *Geheimreden 1933 bis 1945 und andere Ansprachen.* Edited by Bradley F. Smith and Agnes F. Peterson. Berlin, 1974.

———. *Die SS als antibolschewistische Kampforganisation.* Munich, 1937.

Hitler, Adolf. *Mein Kampf.* New York, 1941.

Höhne, Heinz. *The Order of the Death's Head: The Story of Hitler's SS.* New York, 1970.

Huberty, Carl J. "Discriminant Analysis." *Review of Educational Research* 45 (1975): 543–598.

Hughes, John J. "The Reich Concordat 1933: Capitulation or Compromise." *Australian Journal of Politics and History* 20 (1974): 164–175.

Hunt, Alan. "Theory and Politics in the Identification of the Working Class." In Alan Hunt, ed., *Class and Class Structure.* London, 1977, 81–111.

Hunt, James C. "The Bourgeois Middle in German Politics, 1871–1933: Recent Literature." *Central European History* 11 (1978): 83–106.

Hunt, Richard N. *German Social Democracy, 1918–1933.* New Haven, 1964.

Hurst, Michael. "What Is Fascism?" *Historical Journal* 11 (1968): 165–185.

Hüttenberger, Peter. "Nationalsozialistische Polykratie." *Geschichte und Gesellschaft* 2 (1976): 417–442.

Institut für Marxistische Studien und Forschung. *Theorien, Diskussion: Sozialstatistischer Analyse.* Part 1, *Klassenstruktur und Klassentheorie* (Frankfurt/Main, 1973); Part 2, *Klassen und Sozialstruktur der BRD, 1950–1970: Sozialstatistische Analyse,* 2 vols. (Frankfurt/Main, 1974); Part 3, *Die Intelligenz der BRD, 1950–1970* (Frankfurt/Main, 1975).

International Military Tribunal. *Judgement of the International Tribunal for the Trial of German Major War Criminals (with the Dissenting Opinion of the Soviet Member), Nuremberg 30th September and 1st October, 1946.* London, 1946, 79.

Jäckel, Eberhard. *Hitlers Weltanschauung: Entwurf einer Herrschaft.* Tübingen, 1969.

Jaeger, Hans. "Generationen in der Geschichte: Überlegungen zu einer umstrittenen Konzeption." *Geschichte und Gesellschaft* 3 (1977): 429–452.

Jamin, Mathilde. "Zur Kritik an Michael Katers Überlegungen über Quantifizierung und NS-Geschichte." *Geschichte und Gesellschaft* 4 (1978): 536–541.

———. *Zwischen den Klassen: Zur Sozialstruktur der SA-Führerschaft.* Wuppertal, 1984.

Jannen, William J. "National Socialists and Social Mobility." *Journal of Social History* 9 (1975–76): 339–366.

Jarausch, Konrad. "Liberal Education as Illiberal Socialization: The Case of Students in Imperial Germany." *Journal of Modern History* 50 (1978): 609–630.

———. "Occupations and Social Structure in Modern Central Europe: Some Reflections on the Coding of Professions." *Quantum-Information* 11 (1979): 10–19.

———. *Students, Society, and Politics in Imperial Germany: The Rise of Academic Illiberalism.* Princeton, 1982.

Jung, Edgar. *Die Herrschaft der Minderwertigkeiten.* Berlin, 1927; 2d ed., 1929.

Jünger, Ernst, ed. *Krieg und Krieger.* Berlin, 1930.

Kadritzke, Ulf. *Angestellte—Der geduldige Arbeiter: Zur Soziologie und sozialen Bewegung der Angestellten.* Frankfurt/Main and Cologne, 1975.

Kaelble, Hartmut. "Chancenungleichheit und akademische Ausbildung in

Deutschland, 1910–1960." *Geschichte und Gesellschaft* 1 (1975): 121–149.

———. *Historical Research on Social Mobility: Western Europe and the USA in the 19th and 20th Centuries.* New York, 1981.

———. "Long-Term Changes in the Recruitment of the Business Elite: Germany Compared to the U.S., Great Britain, and France since the Industrial Revolution." *Journal of Social History* 13 (1980): 404–423.

———. "Social Mobility in Germany, 1900–1960." *Journal of Modern History* 50 (1978): 439–461.

———. "Social Stratification in Germany in the Nineteenth and Twentieth Centuries: A Survey of Research since 1945." *Journal of Social History* 10 (1976): 144–165.

———. "Sozialer Aufstieg in Deutschland, 1850–1914," *Vierteljahrschrift für Sozial- und Wirtschaftsgeschichte* 60 (1973): 41–71.

Kaelble, Hartmut et al. *Probleme der Modernisierung in Deutschland: Sozialhistorische Studien zum 19. und 20. Jahrhundert.* Opladen, 1978.

Kater, Michael H. *Das "Ahnenerbe" der SS, 1933–1945: Ein Beitrag zur Kulturpolitik des Dritten Reichs.* Stuttgart, 1974.

———. "Ansätze zu einer Soziologie der SA bis zur Röhmkrise." In Ulrich Engelhardt et al., eds., *Soziale Bewegung und politische Verfassung.* Stuttgart, 1976, 798–831.

———. "Die Artamanen—Völkische Jugend in der Weimarer Republik." *Historische Zeitschrift* 213 (1971): 577–638.

———. "Bürgerliche Jugendbewegung und Hitlerjugend in Deutschland von 1926 bis 1939." *Archiv für Sozialgeschichte* 27 (1977): 127–174.

———. "Zum gegenseitigen Verhältnis von SA und SS in der Sozialgeschichte des Nationalsozialismus von 1925 bis 1939." *Vierteljahrschrift für Sozial- und Wirtschaftsgeschichte* 62 (1975): 339–379.

———. "Generationskonflikt als Entwicklungsfaktor in the NS-Bewegung vor 1933." *Geschichte und Gesellschaft* 11 (1985): 217–243.

———. *The Nazi Party: A Social Profile of Members and Leaders, 1919–1945.* Cambridge, MA, 1983.

———. "Quantifizierung und NS-Geschichte: Methodologische Überlegungen über Grenzen und Möglichkeiten einer EDV-Analyse der NSDAP Sozialstruktur von 1925–1945." *Geschichte und Gesellschaft* 3 (1977): 453–484.

———. "Sozialer Wandel in der NSDAP im Zuge der nationalsozialistischen Machergreifung." In Wolfgang Schieder, ed., *Faschismus als soziale Bewegung: Deutschland und Italien im Vergleich.* Hamburg, 1976, 25–67.

————. "Zur Soziographie der frühen NSDAP." *Vierteljahrshefte für Zeitgeschichte* 19 (1971): 124–159.

————. *Studentenschaft und Rechtsradikalismus in Deutschland, 1918–1933: Eine sozialgeschichtliche Studie zur Bildungskrise in der Weimarer Republik.* Hamburg, 1975.

Katz, H. "Arbeiter, Mittelklasse, und die NSDAP." *Internationale wissenschaftliche Korrespondenz zur Geschichte der deutschen Arbeiterbewegung* 10 (1974): 300–304.

Katz, Michael B. "Occupational Classification in History." *Journal of Interdisciplinary History* 3 (1972): 63–88.

Kele, Max H. *Nazis and Workers: National Socialist Appeals to German Labor, 1919–1933.* Chapel Hill, 1972.

Keller, Suzanne. *Beyond the Ruling Class: Strategic Elites in Modern Societies.* New York, 1963.

Kershaw, Ian. *The Nazi Dictatorship: Problems and Perspectives of Interpretation.* London, 1985.

Kersten, Felix. *Totenkopf und Treue—Heinrich Himmler ohne Uniform.* Hamburg, 1952.

Kish, L. "Selection of a Sample." In L. Festinger and D. Katz, eds., *Research Methods in the Social Sciences.* New York, 1953.

Klose, Werner. *Generation im Gleichschritt: Eine Dokumentation.* Oldenburg, 1964.

Knight, Maxwell E. *The German Executive, 1890–1933.* Stanford, 1952.

Koch, Karl W.H. *Das Ehrenbuch der SA.* Düsseldorf, 1934.

Kocka, Jürgen. *Die Angestellten in der deutschen Geschichte, 1850–1980: Vom Privatbeamten zum angestellten Arbeitnehmer.* Göttingen, 1981.

————. "Zur Problematik der deutschen Angestellten, 1914–1933." In Hans Mommsen et al., *Industrielles System und politische Entwicklung in der Weimarer Republik.* Düsseldorf, 1974, 792–811.

Koehl, Robert L. *The Black Corps: The Structure and Struggles of the Nazi SS.* Madison, 1983.

————. "The Character of the Nazi SS." *Journal of Modern History* 34 (1962): 275–283.

————. "Toward an SS Typology: Social Engineers." *American Journal of Economics and Sociology* 18 (1959): 113–126.

Kogon, Egon. *Der SS-Staat: Das System der deutschen Konzentrationslager.* Berlin, 1947.

Kühnl, Reinhard. *Formen bürgerlicher Herrschaft: Liberalismus-Faschismus.* Hamburg, 1971.

Labovitz, Sanford. "Criteria for Selecting a Significance Level: A Note on the Sacredness of .05." *American Sociologist* 3 (1968): 220–222.

Lachenbruch, Peter; Sneeringer, Cheryl; and Revo, Lawrence T. "Robustness of the Linear and Quadratic Discriminant Function to Certain Types of Non-Normality." *Communications in Statistics* 1 (1973): 39–56.

Lane, Barbara Miller. "Nazi Ideology: Some Unfinished Business." *Central European History* 7 (1974): 3–30.

Laqueur, Walter Z. *Young Germany: A History of the German Youth Movement.* London, 1962.

Lasswell, Harold D., and Lerner, Daniel. *World Revolutionary Elites: Studies in Coercive Ideological Movements.* Cambridge, MA, 1965.

Lasswell, Harold D.; Lerner, Daniel; and Rothwell, C. Easton. *The Comparative Study of Elites: An Introduction and Bibliography.* Stanford, 1952.

Lazerwitz, Bernard. "Sampling Theory and Procedures." In Hubert M. Blalock and Ann B. Blalock, eds., *Methodology in Social Research.* New York, 1968.

Lebovics, Hermann. *Social Conservatism and the Middle Classes in Germany.* Princeton, 1969.

Ledeen, Michael A. "Fascism and the Generation Gap," *European Studies Review* 1 (1971): 275–283.

Lepsius, M. Rainer. "Ungleichheit zwischen Menschen und soziale Schichtung," *Kölner Zeitschrift für Soziologie und Sozialpsychologie* 5 (1961): 54–64.

Lerner, Daniel. *The Nazi Elite.* Stanford, 1951.

Linz, Juan J. "Some Notes toward a Comparative Study of Fascism in Sociological Historical Perspective." in Walter Laqueur, ed., *Fascism, A Reader's Guide: Analyses, Interpretations, Bibliography.* Los Angeles, 1976, 3–121.

Lipset, Seymour M[artin]. "'Fascism'—Left, Right, and Center." In his *Political Man.* London, 1960, 131–176.

―――. "History and Sociology: Some Methodological Considerations." In

Seymour Martin Lipset and Richard Hofstadter, eds., *Sociology and History: Methods*. New York and London, 1968, 20–58.

Loewenberg, Peter. "The Psychohistorical Origins of the Nazi Youth Cohort." *American Historical Review* 76 (1971): 1457–1502.

Lozek, Gerhard, and Richter, Rolf. "Zur Auseinandersetzung mit vorherrschenden bürgerlichen Faschismustheorien." In Kurt Gossweiler and Dietrich Eichholz, eds., *Faschismusforschung. Positionen, Probleme, Polemik*. Berlin, 1980, 417–451.

McGrath, William J. "Student Radicalism in Vienna." *Journal of Contemporary History* 2 (1967): 183–201.

Madden, Paul. "Generational Aspects of National Socialism, 1919–1933." *Social Science Quarterly* 63 (1982): 445–461.

———. "Some Social Characteristics of Early Nazi Party Members." *Central European History* 15 (1982): 34–56.

Mai, Gunther. "Worum steht der deutsche Arbeiter zu Hitler? Zur Rolle der Deutschen Arbeitsfront im Herrschaftssystem des Dritten Reiches." *Geschichte und Gesellschaft* 12 (1986): 21–34.

Maier, Charles S. *In Search of Stability: Explorations in Historical Political Economy*. New York, 1987.

Maier, Hedwig. "Die SS und der 20. Juli 1944." *Vierteljahrshefte für Zeitgeschichte* 14 (1966): 299–316.

Mannheim, Karl. "The Problem of Generations." In his *Essays on the Sociology of Knowledge*. London, 1959, 276–322.

Maschke, Erich. *Der Deutsche Ordensstaat*. Hamburg, 1936.

Maser, Werner. *Die Frühgeschichte der NSDAP: Hitlers Weg bis 1924*. Frankfurt/Main and Bonn, 1965.

———. *Der Sturm auf die Republik: Frühgeschichte der NSDAP*. Stuttgart, 1973.

Mason, Timothy W. "Zur Entstehung des Gesetzes zur Ordnung der nationalen Arbeit, vom 20. Januar 1934: Ein Versuch über das Verhältnis 'archaischer' und 'moderner' Momente in der neusten deutschen Geschichte." In Hans Mommsen et al., eds., *Industrielles System und politische Entwicklung in der Weimarer Republik*. Düsseldorf, 1974, 322–351.

Mason, Timothy W. "Labor in the Third Reich, 1933–1939." *Past and Present* 33 (1966): 112–141.

Mason, Timothy. *Sozialpolitik im Dritten Reich: Arbeiterklasse und Volksgemeinschaft*. 2d ed. Opladen, 1978.

Matzerath, Horst, and Volkmann, Heinrich. "Modernisierungstheorie und Nationalsozialismus." In Jürgen Kocka, ed., *Geschichte und Gesellschaft, Sonderheft* 3: *Theorien in der Praxis des Historikers*. Göttingen, 1977, 86–116.

Mau, Hermann. "Die zweite 'Revolution'—Der 30. Juni 1934." *Vierteljahrshefte für Zeitgeschichte* 1 (1953): 119–137.

Mayer, Arno J. "The Lower Middle Class as Historical Problem." *Journal of Modern History* 47 (1975): 409–436.

Mayhew, Leon. "Ascription in Modern Societies." *Sociological Inquiry* 38 (1968): 105–120.

Mayntz, Renate. "Begriff und empirische Erfassung des sozialen Status in der heutigen Soziologie." *Kölner Zeitschrift für Soziologie und Sozialpsychologie* 10 (1958): 58–73.

Meisler, Yoash. "Himmler's Doctrine of Leadership." *Jahrbuch des Instituts für Deutsche Geschichte* 8 (1979): 400–401.

Mendels, Franklin. "Social Mobility and Phases of Industrialization." *Journal of Interdisciplinary History* 7 (1976): 193–216.

Merkl, Peter H. *Political Violence under the Swastika: 581 Early Nazis.* Princeton, 1975.

Milliband, Ralph. *The State in Capitalist Society: An Analysis of the Western European System of Power.* New York, 1969.

Mills, C. Wright. *The Power Elite.* New York, 1956.

Möller, Herbert. "Youth as a Force in the Modern World." *Comparative Studies in Society and History* 10 (1968): 237–260.

Möller, Horst. "Die nationalsozialistische Machtergreifung. Konterrevolution oder Revolution?" *Vierteljahrshefte für Zeitgeschichte* 31 (1983): 52–76.

Mommsen, Hans. *Beamtentum im Dritten Reich: Mit ausgewählten Quellen zur nationalsozialistischen Beamtenpolitik.* Stuttgart, 1966.

——. "National Socialism: Continuity and Change." In Walter Laqueur, ed., *Fascism, A Reader's Guide: Analyses, Interpretations, Bibliography.* Los Angeles, 1976, 179–210.

——. "Die Stellung der Beamtenschaft in Reich, Ländern, und Gemeinden in der Ära Brüning." *Vierteljahrshefte für Zeitgeschichte* 21 (1973): 151–165.

Moore, Harriett, and Kleining, Gerhard. "Das soziale Selbstbild der Gesellschaftsschichten in Deutschland." *Kölner Zeitschrift für Soziologie und Sozialpsychologie* 12 (1960): 86–119.

Morrison, Denton E., and Henkel, Ramon E., eds. *The Significance Test Controversy: A Reader.* Chicago, 1970.

Morrison, Donald G. "On the Interpretation of Discriminant Analysis." *Journal of Marketing* 6 (1969): 156–163.

Mosse, George L. *The Crisis of German Ideology: Intellectual Origins of the Third Reich.* New York, 1971.

———. "The Genesis of Fascism." *Journal of Contemporary History* 1 (1966): 14–65.

Mühlberger, Detlef. "The Sociology of the NSDAP: The Question of Working Class Membership." *Journal of Contemporary History* 15 (1980): 473–511.

Müller, Jakob. *Die Jugendbewegung als deutsche Hauptrichtung neukonservativer Reform.* Zurich, 1971.

Nagle, Jack. *The Descriptive Analysis of Power.* New Haven, 1975.

Nagle, John. *System and Succession: The Social Bases of Political Recruitment.* Austin, 1977.

Neulen, H. W. *Eurofaschismus und der Zweite Weltkrieg: Europas verratene Söhne.* Munich, 1980.

Neusüss-Hunkel, Ermenhild. *Die SS.* Schriftenreihe des Instituts für wissenschaftliche Politik in Marburg/Lahn, No. 2. Hannover, 1956.

Nipperdey, Thomas. "Probleme der Modernisierung in Deutschland." *Saeculum* 30 (1979): 292–303.

Noakes, Jeremy. *The Nazi Party in Lower Saxony, 1921–1933.* Oxford, 1971.

———. "Nazism and Revolution." In Noel O'Sullivan, ed., *Revolutionary Theory and Political Reality.* London, 1983, 73–100.

Noakes, Jeremy, and Pridham, Geoffrey, eds. *Nazism, 1919–1945.* 2 vols. Vol. 2, *State, Economy, and Society, 1933–39: A Documentary Reader.* Exeter, 1984.

Nolte, Ernst. "The Problem of Fascism in Recent Scholarship." In Henry A. Turner, ed., *Reappraisals of Fascism.* New York, 1975, 26–42.

———. *Three Faces of Fascism: Action Francaise, Italian Fascism, National Socialism.* New York, 1966.

Norden, Günther van. "Die Stellung der evangelischen Kirche zum Nationalsozialismus, 1930–1933." In Gotthard Jasper, ed., *Von Weimar zu Hitler, 1930–1933.* Cologne, 1968, 377–402.

Nothaas, Josef. "Sozialer Aufstieg und Abstieg im deutschen Volk." *Kölner Vierteljahrshefte für Soziologie* 9 (1930–31): 61–81.

Nyomarkay, Joseph. *Charisma and Factionalism in the Nazi Party*. Minneapolis, 1967.

Oertzen, Friedrich Wilhelm von. *Die deutschen Freikorps, 1918–1923*. 5th ed. Munich, 1939.

Olehnusen, Irmtraud Götz von. "Die Krise der jungen Generation und der Aufstieg des Nationalsozialismus." *Jahrbuch des Archivs der deutschen Jugendbewegung* 12 (1980): 53–82.

Orlow, Dietrich. "Die Adolf Hitler Schulen." *Vierteljahrshefte für Zeitgeschichte* 13 (1963): 272–284.

———. *The History of the Nazi Party, 1919–1933*. Pittsburgh, 1969.

———. *The History of the Nazi Party, 1933–1945*. Pittsburgh, 1971.

Paetel, Karl O. "The Black Order: A Survey of the Literature on the SS." *Wiener Library Bulletin* 12 (1959): 32–35.

———. *Jugend in der Entscheidung, 1913–1933–1945*. Bad Godesberg, 1963.

———. "The Reign of the Black Order." In Maurice Baumont, ed., *The Third Reich*. New York, 1955.

Pareto, Vilfredo. *The Mind and Society*. Edited by Andrew Bongiorno. 4 vols. New York, 1935.

Payne, Stanley G. *Fascism: Comparison and Definition*. Madison, 1980.

Petzina, Dieter. "Germany and the Great Depression." *Journal of Contemporary History* 4 (1969): 59–74.

Picker, Henry. *Hitler's Table Talks*. London, 1953.

Pierard, Richard V. "Why Did German Protestants Welcome Hitler?" *Fides et Historia* 10 (1978): 8–29.

Pinder, W. *Das Problem der Generation in der Kunstgeschichte Europas*. Berlin, 1926.

Pingel, Falk. *Häftlinge unter SS-Herrschaft: Widerstand, Selbsbehauptung, und Vernichtung im Konzentrationslager*. Hamburg, 1978.

Posisil, Evelyn. "Diskussionsbeitrag: Die Massenbasis des Faschismus." *Jenaer Beitrag für Parteiengeschichte* 31 (1969): 31–40.

Poulantza, Nicos. "The New Petty Bourgeoisie." In Alan Hunt, ed., *Class and Class Structure*. London, 1977, 113–124.

Pridham, Geoffrey. *Hitler's Rise to Power: The Nazi Movement in Bavaria, 1923–1933*. London, 1973.

Project Klassenanalyse. *Materialien zur Klassenstruktur der BRD*. Part 1,

Theoretische Grundlagen und Kritiken (Berlin, 1973); Part 2, *Grundriss der Klassenverhältnisse, 1950–1970* (Berlin, 1974).

Putnam, Robert D. *The Comparative Study of Elites.* Englewood Cliffs, NJ, 1976.

Raabe, Felix. *Die Bündische Jugend: Ein Beitrag zur Geschichte der Weimarer Republik.* Stuttgart, 1961.

Rathke, Arthur. *Wie werde ich Beamter? Ein Wegweiser durch die Vorbildungs-, Ausbildungs-, und Laufbahnvorschriften der Beamtenberufe unter besonderer Berücksichtigung der technischen und der Beamtenlaufbahnen mit Hochschulbildung.* Berlin, 1940.

Rauschning, Hermann. *Gespräche mit Hitler.* Vienna, 1940.

Reiche, Eric G. *The Development of the SA in Nürnberg, 1922–1934.* New York, 1986.

Reitlinger, Gerald. *The Final Solution: The Attempt to Exterminate the Jews of Europe.* 2d ed. London, 1961.

———. *The SS: Alibi of a Nation, 1922–1945.* New York, 1957.

Renouard, Yves. "La notion de génération en histoire." *Revue Historique* 209 (1953): 1–23.

Ringer, Fritz K. "Bildung, Wirtschaft, und Gesellschaft in Deutschland, 1800–1960." *Geschichte und Gesellschaft* 6 (1980): 5–35.

———. *Education and Society in Modern Europe.* Bloomington, 1979.

———. "Higher Education in Germany in the Nineteenth Century." *Journal of Contemporary History* 2 (1967): 123–138.

Rintala, Marvin. "A Generation in Politics: A Definition." *Review of Politics* 25 (1963): 509–522.

———. "Generations in Politics." In A. Esler, ed., *The Youth Revolution: The Conflict of Generations in Modern History.* Lexington, MA, 1974, 15–20.

———. "Generations: Political Generations." In the *International Encyclopedia of the Social Sciences.* 18 vols. New York, 1968, 6: 92–96.

Rogowski, Ronald. "The Gauleiter and the Social Origins of Fascism." *Comparative Studies in Society and History* 19 (1977): 399–430.

Röhl, J.C.G. "Higher Civil Servants in Germany, 1890–1900." *Journal of Contemporary History* 2 (1967): 101–121.

Röhm, Ernst. *Die Geschichte eines Hochverräter.* Munich, 1933.

Ruge, Wolfgang. "Monopolbourgeoisie, faschistische Massenbasis, und NS-Programmatik in Deutschland vor 1933." In Dietrich Eichholtz und

Kurt Gossweiler, eds., *Faschismus—Forschung: Positionen, Probleme, Polemik*. Berlin, 1980, 125–155.

———. *Politik und Beamtentum im Parteistaat: Die Demokratisierung der politischen Beamten in Preussen zwischen 1918 und 1933*. Stuttgart, 1965.

Salvatorelli, Luigi. *Nazionalfascismo*. Turin, 1923.

Sandiford, Peter, ed. *Comparative Education: Studies of the Educational Systems of Six Modern Nations*. London, 1918.

Schauwecker, Franz. *Aufbruch der Nation*. Berlin, 1930.

Schoenbaum, David. *Hitler's Social Revolution: Class and Status in Nazi Germany, 1933–1939*. New York, 1966.

Scholder, Klaus. "Die evangelische Kirche in der Sicht der nationalsozialistischen Führung." *Vierteljahrshefte für Zeitgeschichte* 16 (1968): 15–35.

———. *Die Kirchen und das Dritte Reich: Vorgeschichte und Zeit der Illusionen, 1918–1934*. Frankfurt/Main, 1977.

Scholtz, Harald. *Nationalsozialistische Ausleseschulen: Internatschulen als Herrschaftsmittel des Führerstaates*. Göttingen, 1973.

———. "Die NS–Ordensburgen." *Vierteljahrshefte für Zeitgeschichte* 15 (1967): 269–298.

Schwartz, Mildred A. "Political Support and Group Dominance." In Alan Kornberg and Harold C. Clark, eds., *Political Support in Canada: The Crisis Years*. Durham, NC, 1983.

Schwarz, Jürgen. *Studenten in der Weimarer Republik: Die deutsche Studentenschaft in der Zeit von 1918 bis 1923 und ihre Stellung zur Politik*. Berlin, 1971.

Schweitzer, Arthur. *Big Business in the Third Reich*. Bloomington, 1964.

Searing, Donald D. "The Comparative Study of Elite Socialization." *Comparative Political Studies* 1 (1969): 471–500.

Seidelmann, Karl. "War die Jugendbewegung präfaschistisch?" *Jahrbuch des Archivs der Deutschen Jugendbewegung* 7 (1975): 66–75.

Seligman, Lester G. "Elite Recruitment and Political Development." *Journal of Politics* 26 (1964): 612–626.

———. *Recruiting Political Elites*. New York, 1971.

Skipper, James K.; Guenther, Anthony L.; and Nass, Gilbert. "The Sacredness of .05: A Note concerning the Use of Statistical Levels of Significance." *American Sociologist* 2 (1967): 16–18.

Smith, Bradley F., and Peterson, Agnes F., eds. *Heinrich Himmler Geheim-reden 1933 bis 1945 und andere Ansprachen*. Berlin, Frankfurt/Main, and Vienna, 1974.

Sontheimer, Kurt. "Der Tat-Kreis." *Vierteljahrshefte für Zeitgeschichte* 7 (1959): 229–260.

Speer, Albert. *The Slave State: Heinrich Himmler's Plan for SS Supremacy*. London, 1981.

Spitzer, Allen B. "The Historical Problem of Generations." *American Historical Review* 78 (1973): 1353–1385.

Spranger, Eduard. *Psychologie des Jugendalters*. Leipzig, 1911.

Stachura, Peter D. *The German Youth Movement, 1900–1945: An Interpretative and Documentary History*. New York, 1981.

———. "German Youth, the Youth Movement, and National Socialism in the Weimar Republic." In Peter D. Stachura, ed., *The Nazi Machtergreifung*. London, 1983, 68–84.

———. *Nazi Youth in the Weimar Republic*. Santa Barbara and Oxford, 1975.

———. "Who Were the Nazis? A Socio-Political Analysis of the National Socialist Machtübernahme." *European Studies Review* 11 (1981): 293–324.

Stearns, Peter N. "The Middle Class: Toward a Precise Definition." *Comparative Studies in Society and History* 21 (1979): 377–396.

Stein, George H. *The Waffen-SS: Hitler's Elite Guard at War, 1933–1945*. Ithaca and London, 1966.

Steinberg, Michael S. *Sabers and Brownshirts: The German Students' Path to National Socialism, 1918–1935*. Chicago and London, 1977.

Steiner, Fritz. *Die Armee der Geächteten*. Göttingen, 1963.

Steiner, John M. *Power Politics and Social Change in National Socialist Germany*. Atlantic Highlands, NJ, 1979.

———. "The SS Yesterday and Today: A Socio-Psychological View." In Joel E. Dimsdale, ed., *Survivors, Victims, and Perpetrators: Essays on the Nazi Holocaust*. Washington, 1980, 405–456.

———. "Über das Glaubensbekenntnis der SS." In J. Hutter, R. Meyers, and D. Papenfuss, eds., *Tradition und Neubeginn*. Cologne, 1975, 317–333.

Stock, Phyllis H. "Students versus the University in Pre-War Paris." *French Historical Studies* 7 (1971): 93–110.

Stokes, Lawrence D. "The Social Composition of the Nazi Party in Eutin, 1925–1932." *International Review of Social History* 23 (1978): 1–32.

Strasser, Otto. *Hitler und Ich.* Konstanz, 1948.

Struve, Walter. *Elites against Democracy: Leadership Ideals in Bourgeois Political Thought in Germany, 1890–1933.* Princeton, 1973.

Stuke, Horst. "Bedeutung und Problematik des Klassenbegriffs: Begriffs- und sozialgeschichtliche Überlegungen im Umkreis einer historischen Klassentheorie." In Ulrich Engelhardt et al., eds., *Soziale Bewegung und politische Verfassung: Beiträge zur Geschichte der modernen Welt.* Stuttgart, 1976.

Sydnor, Charles W., Jr. "The History of the SS-Totenkopf Division and the Postwar Mythology of the Waffen-SS." *Central European History* 6 (1973): 339–362.

———. *Soldiers of Destruction: The SS Death's Head Division, 1933–1945.* Princeton, 1977.

Tasuoka, Maurice M. *Multivariate Analysis.* New York, 1971.

Taylor, K. W., and Frideres, James. "Issues versus Controversies: Substantive and Statistical Significance." *American Sociological Review* 37 (1972): 464–472.

Theweleit, Klaus. *Male Fantasies.* Vol. 1, *Women, Floods, Bodies, History.* Minneapolis, 1987.

Thompson, Larry V. "*Lebensborn* and the Eugenics Policy of the Reichsführer-SS." *Central European History* 4 (1971): 54–77.

Turner, Henry A. "Fascism and Modernization." *World Politics* 24 (1972): 547–560.

Tyrell, Albrecht, ed. *Führer befiehl . . . Selbstzeugnisse aus der "Kampfzeit" der NSDAP: Dokumentation und Analyse.* Düsseldorf, 1969.

Überhorst, Horst. *Elite für die Diktatur: Die nationalpolitischen Erziehungsanstalten 1933 bis 1945, Ein Dokumentarbericht.* Düsseldorf, 1969.

Van de Geer, John P. *Introduction to Multivariate Analysis.* San Francisco, 1971.

Volz, Hans. *Daten der Geschichte der N.S.D.A.P.* 9th ed. Berlin and Leipzig, 1939.

Vondung, K. *Magie und Manipulation.* Göttingen, 1971.

von Saldern, Adelheit. "Alter Mittelstand im Dritten Reich: Anmerkungen an einer Kontroverse." *Geschichte und Gesellschaft* 12 (1986): 235–243.

————. *Mittelstand im Dritten Reich: Handwerker-Einzelhändler-Bauern.* 2d ed. Frankfurt/Main, 1985.

Waite, Robert G. *Vanguard of Nazism: The Free Corps Movement in Postwar Germany, 1918–1923.* Cambridge, MA, 1952.

Weber, Eugene. "Revolution? Counterrevolution? What Revolution?" In Walter Laqueur, ed., *Fascism, A Reader's Guide: Analyses, Interpretations, Bibliography.* Berkeley, 1976, 435–467.

Weber, Hermann. "Einleitung." In Ossip K. Flechtheim, *Die KPD in der Weimarer Republik.* Frankfurt/Main, 1969, 5–68.

Wechssler, Eduard. *Die Generation als Jugendreihe und ihr Kampf um die Denkform.* Leipzig, 1930.

Wegner, Bernd. "The 'Aristocracy of National Socialism': The Role of the SS in National Socialist Germany." In H. W. Koch, ed., *Aspects of the Third Reich.* New York, 1985.

————. "Auf dem Wege zur pangermanischen Armee: Dokumente zur Entstehungsgeschichte des III. ('germanischen') SS-Panzerkorps." *Militärgeschichtliche Mitteilungen* 28 (1980): 101–136.

————. "Die Garde des 'Führers' und die 'Feuerwehr' der Ostfront: Zur neuen Literatur über die Waffen-SS." *Militägeschichtliche Mitteilungen* 23 (1978): 210–236.

————. *Hitler's politische Soldaten, Die Waffen-SS 1933–1945. Studien zu Leitbild, Struktur, und Funktion einer nationalsozialistischen Elite.* Paderborn, 1982.

Wehler, Hans-Ulrich. *Modernisierungstheorie und Geschichte.* Göttingen, 1975.

————. "Vorüberlegungen zur historischen Analyse sozialer Ungleichheit." In Hans-Ulrich Wehler, ed., *Klassen in der europäischen Sozialgeschichte.* Göttingen, 1979, 9–32.

Weingartner, James J. *Hitler's Guard: The Story of the Leibstandarte Adolf Hitler, 1933–1945.* London and Amsterdam, 1974.

————. "Law and Justice in the SS: The Case of Konrad Morgan." *Central European History* 16 (September 1983): 276–294.

————. "Sepp Dietrich, Heinrich Himmler, and the Leibstandarte Adolf Hitler, 1933–1938." *Central European History* 1 (1968): 264–284.

Welsh, William A. *Leaders and Elites.* New York, 1979.

Wiedemann, Carl F., and Fenster, Abraham. "The Use of Chance Corrected Percentage Agreement to Interpret the Results of Discriminant

Analysis." *Educational and Psychological Measurements* 38 (1978): 25–39.

Winkler, Heinrich A. "Extremismus der Mitte? Sozialgeschichtliche Aspekte der nationalsozialistischen Machtergreifung." *Vierteljahrshefte für Zeitgeschichte* 20 (1972): 175–191.

———. "From Social Protectionism to National Socialism: The Small Business Movement in Comparative Perspective." *Journal of Modern History* 48 (1976): 1–18.

———. *Mittelstand, Demokratie, und Nationalsozialismus: Die politische Entwicklung von Handwerk und Kleinhandel in der Weimarer Republic.* Cologne, 1972.

———. "Mittelstandsbewegung oder Volkspartei? Zur sozialen Basis der NSDAP." In W. Schiederer, ed., *Faschismus als soziale Bewegung.* Hamburg, 1976, 97–118.

———. "Vom Mythos der Volksgemeinschaft." *Archiv für Sozialgeschichte* 17 (1977): 484–490.

Wippermann, W. *Der Ordenstaat als Ideologie: Das Bild des Deutschen Ordens in der deutschen Geschichtsschreibung und Publizistik.* Berlin, 1979.

Wohl, Robert. *The Generation of 1914.* Cambridge, MA, 1979.

Wright, Jonathon R. "The German Protestant Church and the Nazi Party in the Period of Seizure of Power, 1932–33." *Studies in Church History* 14 (1977): 393–418.

Yamane, Taro. *Elementary Sampling Theory.* Englewood Cliffs, NJ, 1967.

Zapf, Wolfgang. *Wandlungen der deutschen Elite: Ein Zirkulationsmodell deutscher Führungsgruppen, 1916–1961.* Munich, 1965.

Zehrer, Hans. "Absage an den Jahrgang 1902." *Die Tat* 21 (1929–30): 740–748.

———. "Die zweite Welle." *Die Tat* 21 (1929–30): 577–582.

Ziegler, Herbert F. "Elite Recruitment and National Socialism: The SS-Führerkorps, 1925–1939." In Heinrich Best, ed., *Politik und Milieu: Wahl und Elitenforschung im historischen und interkulturellen Vergleich.* St. Katharinen, 1989.

———. "The Fight against the Empty Cradle: Nazi Pronatal Policies and the SS-Führerkorps." *Historical Social Research* 38 (1986): 25–40.

———. "The SS-Führerkorps: An Analysis of Its Demographic and Social Structure, 1925–1939." Ph.D. dissertation, Emory University, 1980.

Ziemer, Gerhard. "Die deutsche Jugendbewegung und der Staat." *Jahrbuch des Archivs der deutschen Jugendbewegung* 5 (1973): 46–48.

Zipfel, Friedrich. *Kirchenkampf in Deutschland, 1933–1945: Religionsverfolgung und Selbstbehauptung der Kirchen in der nationalsozialistischen Zeit.* Berlin, 1965.

Zorn, Wolfgang. "Sozialgeschichte, 1918–1970." In H. Aubin and W. Zorn, eds., *Handbuch der deutschen Wirtschafts-und Sozialgeschichte.* 2 vols. Stuttgart, 1976.

———. "Student Politics in the Weimar Republic." *Journal of Contemporary History* 5 (1970): 128–143.

Index